THE BEST OF
COOKING
IN COLOR
400 Recipes for All Occasions

THE BEST OF
COOKING
IN COLOR

400 Recipes for All Occasions

Edited by Norma MacMillan

BEDFORD PRESS

Contents

Hungarian cabbage soup

Overall timing 2 hours

Freezing Suitable: add flour and sour cream when reheating.

To serve 4

½lb	Onions
1	Garlic clove
3 tbsp	Oil
¾lb	Beef for stew
¾lb	Canned sauerkraut
½ tsp	Fennel seeds
½ tsp	Coarse salt
2 quarts	Beef broth
¼lb	Slab bacon
2	Frankfurters
1 tbsp	Paprika
2 tbsp	Flour
¼ cup	Water
2 tbsp	Sour Cream

Peel and slice onions; peel and crush garlic. Heat 2 tbsp oil in large saucepan. Add onions and garlic and fry over moderate heat till golden. Cut beef into small cubes, add to pan and brown all over.

Add drained canned sauerkraut, fennel seeds and coarse salt to the pan. Cover with the broth (made with 2 bouillon cubes if necessary) and simmer gently for 1 hour or till meat is tender.

Roughly chop the bacon. Fry bacon in a skillet till crisp, then add the sliced frankfurters and paprika. Cook for 5 minutes, then remove and add to the saucepan.

Blend flour with cold water in a bowl till smooth, then stir into the soup mixture and cook for a further 5 minutes. Stir in the sour cream, adjust the seasoning and serve at once with slices of black bread.

Savory dumpling soup

Overall timing 2½ hours

Freezing Suitable: add dumplings after reheating

To serve 6-8

Dumplings

2 cups	Soft bread crumbs
¼ cup	Chopped bacon
¼lb	Calf's liver
¼lb	Ground beef
1	Onion
1	Egg
½ tsp	Dried marjoram
	Salt and pepper

Soup

1 tbsp	Chopped Parsley
1	Onion
¼lb	Carrots
¼lb	Parsnips
5	Stalks of celery
6 tbsp	Butter
2 tbsp	Flour
2 quarts	Chicken broth
2 cups	Chopped cooked chicken

First make dumplings. Soak bread crumbs in 1 cup water for 15 minutes. Fry bacon till crisp. Grind liver. Add beef, squeezed out bread crumbs, chopped onion, drained bacon, egg, marjoram, seasoning and parsley. Shape into small dumplings.

Peel and chop onion, carrots and parsnips; chop celery. Melt butter, add onions and cook for 2-3 minutes. Add carrots, celery and parsnips, cover and cook till tender. Purée vegetables and return to pan. Stir in flour then ⅓ broth. Simmer until thickened. Add remaining broth.

Add chicken to soup with dumplings and simmer for 15 minutes.

Scotch broth

Overall timing 2½ hours

Freezing Not suitable

To serve 4

½ cup	Pearl barley
2lb	Lamb neck for stew
¼ cup	Butter
2	Onions
4	Stalks of celery
1 tbsp	Flour
2½ quarts	Water
1 tsp	Sugar
	Salt and pepper
1lb	Potatoes
4	Carrots
1	Leek

Wash the barley and drain thoroughly. Wipe and trim the lamb and cut into pieces. Melt the butter in a saucepan or flameproof casserole. Add the lamb and fry over a high heat till browned on all sides.

Peel and chop the onions; trim and slice the celery. Add to the meat and fry till transparent. Add the barley and cook for 2 minutes. Sprinkle in the flour and cook, stirring, till flour begins to brown. Gradually add the water and bring to a boil, stirring constantly. Add the sugar, salt and pepper. Cover and simmer for about 1½ hours.

Peel and quarter the potatoes; scrape and slice the carrots. Add to the soup and simmer for a further 30 minutes. Wash and finely chop the leek and add to the soup. Simmer for 3 minutes more. Taste and adjust the seasoning. Serve immediately with toast or whole-wheat biscuits and butter.

Tregaron broth

Overall timing 1 hour

Freezing Not suitable

To serve 6

1 lb	Slab bacon
1 lb	Beef shank
2 tbsp	Butter
1	Large leek
1 lb	Potatoes
½ lb	Carrots
½ lb	Parsnips
1	Small rutabaga
2 quarts	Water
1	Small head white cabbage
⅓ cup	Fine or medium oatmeal
	Salt and pepper

Cut the bacon into 1 inch pieces. Trim the beef and cut into chunks. Melt the butter in a large saucepan and fry the bacon and beef for 5 minutes.

Meanwhile, trim and slice the leek. Peel the potatoes, carrots, parsnips and rutabaga. Cut into chunks. Add vegetables to pan and fry for 5 minutes. Add the water and bring to a boil.

Shred the cabbage and add to the pan with the oatmeal and seasoning. Cover and simmer for 45 minutes. Adjust the seasoning to taste before serving.

Manhattan clam chowder

Overall timing 2 hours

Freezing Suitable

To serve 8

¼ lb	Slab bacon
3	Large Onions
2	Large Tomatoes
2	Leeks
1	Stalk of celery
1	Carrot
2	Potatoes
1 quart	Fish broth
2	Sprigs of parsley
1	Bay leaf
¼ tsp	Grated nutmeg
	Salt and pepper
2 cups	Milk
1 lb	Canned clams
2 tbsp	Butter
2 tbsp	Flour

2 tsp	Worcestershire sauce
¼ tsp	Hot pepper sauce

Dice bacon. Heat a saucepan, add bacon and cook gently. Peel and slice onions and add to pan. Cook till transparent.

Blanch and peel tomatoes. Finely chop leeks and celery. Peel and finely chop carrot and potatoes. Add to pan and cook for 2-3 minutes. Add broth, parsley, bay leaf, nutmeg and seasoning. Cover and simmer for 10 minutes.

Discard parsley and bay leaf. Purée soup in blender, return to rinsed-out pan and add milk and drained clams. Simmer gently for 4 minutes.

Mash butter and flour to a paste. Stir into soup in tiny pieces. Cook for 2-3 minutes until thick. Stir in Worcestershire and pepper sauces and serve.

Fish chowder

Overall timing 1 ½ hours

Freezing Suitable

To serve 4

2lb	Mixed white fish
¼ cup	Diced bacon
1	Large onion
4	Medium-size potatoes
4	Carrots
4	Stalks of celery
1 tbsp	Chopped parsley
16oz	Can of tomatoes
1 quart	Fish broth or water
2 tbsp	Tomato ketchup
2 tbsp	Worcestershire sauce
	Dried thyme
	Salt and pepper

Skin and bone fish and cut into bite-size pieces. Heat a saucepan and fry bacon till crisp. Remove from pan. Peel and chop onion and add to pan. Cook gently till transparent.

Peel and chop potatoes and carrots. Finely chop celery. Add to pan with chopped parsley, tomatoes and their juice, fish broth or water, tomato ketchup, Worcestershire sauce, a pinch of thyme and seasoning. Cover and simmer gently for about 45 minutes.

Add the fish pieces and bacon, cover and cook for a further 15 minutes.

Cantonese fish soup

Overall timing 35 minutes plus marination

Freezing Not suitable

To serve 6

¾lb	White fish fillets
2 tbsp	Soy sauce
2 tsp	Dry sherry
3 tbsp	Oil
2	Medium-size onions
4	Shallots
2	Medium-size carrots
3	Stalks of celery
6 cups	Chicken broth
¼ cup	Long grain rice
	Salt and pepper

Cut across the fillets into thin strips and put into a bowl. Add the soy sauce, sherry and 1 tbsp of the oil. Mix well and leave to marinate in a cool place for 1 hour.

Peel and chop the onions and two of the shallots. Peel and dice the carrots. Trim and chop the celery. Heat remaining oil in a large saucepan, add prepared vegetables, cover and cook gently for 5 minutes. Add the broth and bring to a boil. Stir in rice and salt, bring back to a boil, cover and simmer for 10 minutes.

Add the fish and marinating juices and cook for a further 10 minutes. Taste and adjust seasoning. Pour into soup bowls and garnish with remaining shallots, peeled and finely chopped.

Cock-a-leekie

Overall timing 2¼ hours

Freezing Suitable

To serve 6

2lb	Leeks
2 tbsp	Butter
3lb	Stewing chicken
2 quarts	Chicken broth or water
	Bouquet garni
	Salt and pepper
⅔ cup	Prunes (optional)

Wash, trim and slice leeks. Melt butter in a skillet, add leeks and fry quickly for 5 minutes. Put into a saucepan with the chicken, giblets, broth (made with cubes if necessary) or water, bouquet garni, salt and pepper. Bring to a boil, cover and simmer for 1½ hours.

Pit prunes and add to pan, if using. Cook for 30 minutes longer. Discard bouquet garni.

Remove chicken from pan. Cut the meat into strips, discarding skin and bones. Return meat to pan. Taste and adjust seasoning. Serve with oatcakes.

Pea and ham soup

Overall timing 2¾ hours plus
overnight soaking

Freezing Suitable

To serve 6

1½ cups	Dried whole green peas
2½ quarts	Water
2lb	Ham hock
	Salt and pepper

Put peas in saucepan and cover with the cold water. Leave to soak overnight.

Add the ham hock to the pan and bring to a boil. Skim off any scum. Cover and simmer for 1½-2 hours till the ham and peas are tender.

Remove and drain the ham hock. Discard the skin and bone and cut the meat into small cubes. Reserve one third of the peas. Purée the remaining peas in a blender or by pressing through a sieve. Return the puréed peas and reserved whole peas to the saucepan. Bring to a boil, stirring occasionally.

Add the diced ham, and season to taste. Pour into a warmed tureen and serve with cornbread.

Turkey vegetable soup

Overall timing 1 ¼ hours

Freezing Not suitable

To serve 6

1	Large carrot
1	Large onion
1	Stalk of celery
2	Turkey wings
6 cups	Water
	Salt and pepper
½lb	Waxy potatoes
2	Leeks
4	Thick slices of bread
6 tbsp	Butter

Peel and chop carrot and onion. Trim and chop the celery. Wipe the turkey wings and put into a saucepan with the prepared vegetables, water and seasoning. Bring to a boil, skim off any scum, cover and simmer for 45 minutes.

Peel potatoes and cut into ½ inch cubes. trim and slice leeks.

Lift turkey wings out of pan with a slotted spoon and leave to cool slightly. Add potatoes and leeks to the soup and simmer for 5 minutes till vegetables are tender.

Remove the skin and bones from the turkey wings and cut the meat into strips. Add to the soup and reheat gently.

Meanwhile, remove the crusts from bread and cut into cubes. Melt butter in a skillet, add the bread and fry till golden all over. Drain croûtons on paper towels.

Taste soup and adjust seasoning. Pour into a warmed tureen and sprinkle with croûtons. Serve immediately.

Swiss cream of barley soup

Overall timing 2¾ hours

Freezing Not suitable

To serve 4-6

2	Large onions
3	Cloves
1	Calf's foot
½ cup	Pearl barley
	Bay leaf
2 quarts	Water
	Salt and pepper
¾ lb	Carrots
4	Stalks of celery
2	Small leeks
¼ lb	Bacon slices
1 tbsp	Lard or shortening
2	Egg yolks
½ cup	Light cream
1 tbsp	Chopped chives

Peel one of the onions and spike with cloves. Wash calf's foot, chop in half lengthwise and put into a saucepan with the barley, spiked onion and bay leaf. Add the water and seasoning, then cover and simmer for 2 hours.

Meanwhile, scrape and dice carrots. Peel and chop remaining onion. Trim and slice celery and leeks. Dice bacon. Melt lard or shortening in a large saucepan. Add bacon and vegetables and fry for 10 minutes till golden.

Remove spiked onion and bay leaf from broth and discard. Lift calf's foot out of broth and remove the meat, discarding skin and bones. Add meat to broth with the vegetables. Bring to a boil and simmer for 10 minutes till vegetables are tender.

Put the egg yolks and cream into a tureen and beat together with a fork. Season the soup to taste and gradually stir into tureen. Sprinkle with chives and serve.

Watercress soup

Overall timing 40 minutes

Freezing Suitable: add cream after thawing

To serve 4

1	Large onion
2	Large floury potatoes
2 tbsp	Butter
3	Bunches of watercress
1 quart	Chicken broth
	Salt and pepper
½ cup	Heavy cream

Peel and finely chop onion. Peel and chop or grate potatoes. Melt butter in a saucepan, add onions and potatoes and turn till coated in butter. Cover and cook gently for 10 minutes.

Wash, dry and chop watercress leaves and stalks, reserving some whole leaves. Add to pan with broth and bring to a boil. Cover and simmer for 15 minutes.

Rub soup through sieve or purée in blender. Return to pan, add reserved watercress leaves and reheat. Taste and adjust seasoning. Serve immediately with side dish of whipped cream, or cool, stir in cream and chill well before serving.

Pumpkin soup

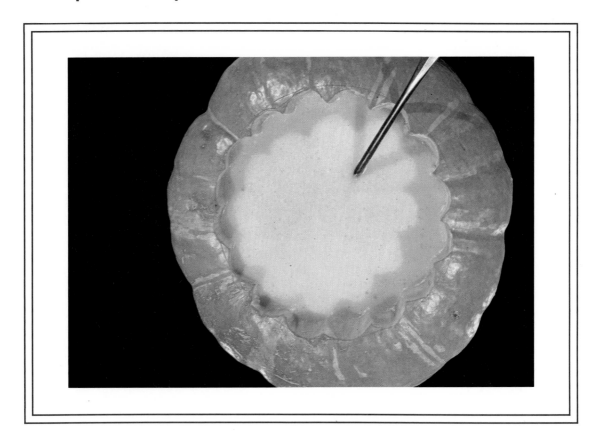

Overall timing 50 minutes

Freezing Not suitable

To serve 6

2lb	Pumpkin or other squash
1 cup	Water
	Salt and pepper
1 quart	Milk
1 tsp	Sugar
¼ tsp	Grated nutmeg
1	Egg yolk
¼ cup	Light cream

Prepare the squash, discarding fibrous center and seeds. Cut the flesh into chunks, put into a saucepan with the water and salt and bring to a boil. Simmer for about 30 minutes till tender, then purée in a blender or food processor. Place purée in saucepan with milk, sugar and nutmeg. Heat through gently till almost boiling, stirring occasionally.

Beat the egg yolk and cream together in a bowl and pour in a little of the hot soup, stirring constantly. Pour back into the pan and stir over a low heat for 3 minutes — do not boil. Taste and adjust seasoning, then serve immediately with toasted rye bread.

Onion soup with wine

Overall timing 45 minutes

Freezing Suitable: pour soup over bread and add cheese after reheating

To serve 4

3	Large onions
¼ cup	Butter
1 tbsp	Flour
½ tsp	Brown sugar
6 cups	Water
8	Slices of French bread
2 tbsp	Dry white wine
	Salt and pepper
½ cup	Grated Gruyère or
	Swiss cheese

Peel and slice onions. melt half the butter in a large saucepan and cook onions till transparent. Sprinkle onions with flour. Cook, stirring, until flour colors. Add sugar, then gradually stir in water. Simmer for 20 minutes.

Preheat the oven to 450°F.

Fry bread in remaining butter. Place bread slices in bottom of individual bowls or ovenproof soup tureen. Add wine and seasoning, then pour soup over bread. Sprinkle cheese into the bowls. Bake for 5-10 minutes to melt the cheese.

Minestrone

Overall timing 2¼ hours

Freezing Not suitable

To serve 8

¼ cup	Chopped bacon
1	Onion
1	Small leek
1 tbsp	Olive oil
1	Garlic clove
1 tbsp	Chopped parsley
2	Sage leaves
3	Carrots
1	Zucchini
2	Large potatoes
3	Stalks of celery
1	Large tomato
¾lb	Savoy cabbage
3	Basil leaves
9 cups	Hot broth
1 tbsp	Tomato paste
	Salt and pepper
16 oz	Can of cannellini beans
¼lb	Elbow macaroni
	Grated Parmesan cheese

Place bacon in saucepan and fry till fat runs.

Peel and finely chop the onion; trim and chop the leek. Add oil to saucepan and heat, then add onion, leek, peeled and crushed garlic, parsley and chopped sage. Cover and sweat for 10 minutes.

Meanwhile, peel the remaining vegetables, as necessary, and chop them. Add prepared vegetables and chopped basil to pan and cook, stirring, for 5 minutes. Gradually add broth, tomato paste, salt and pepper and bring to a boil. Cover tightly and cook gently for 1¼ hours.

Drain the canned beans and add. Add macaroni and cook for 20 minutes more. Serve with Parmesan cheese.

Irish celery soup

Overall timing 35 minutes

freezing Suitable: add cream when reheating

To serve 4

1 lb	Celery
2	Potatoes
2	Onions
¼ cup	Butter
	Salt and pepper
1	Bay leaf
1	Garlic clove
	Grated nutmeg
1 quart	Chicken broth
½ cup	Light cream

Cut off base of celery, then wash and chop stalks and leaves. Peel and finely chop potatoes and onions. Melt butter in saucepan over a low heat. Add celery stalks and leaves, potatoes and onions, cover and cook for 5 minutes, stirring to prevent coloring.

Sprinkle with salt and pepper, add the bay leaf, peeled and crushed garlic, pinch of nutmeg and hot broth (made with 2 cubes if necessary). Cover and simmer for 20 minutes.

Remove bay leaf. Push soup through sieve into a bowl, or liquidize, then return to saucepan and add the cream. Heat through without boiling. Adjust seasoning, then serve with croûtons (diced bread fried in oil till brown).

Gazpacho

Overall timing 20 minutes plus chilling

Freezing Suitable

To serve 6

1¼lb	Tomatoes
½	Cucumber
1	Large onion
1	Sweet green or red pepper
2	Garlic cloves
2 cups	Soft white bread crumbs
3 tbsp	Olive oil
1 tbsp	Wine vinegar
1	Sprig of parsley or mint
	Salt and pepper
5 cups	Water

Blanch, peel and chop the tomatoes. Peel, seed and chop the cucumber. Peel and chop the onion. Seed and chop the pepper; peel and chop the garlic.

Place all the vegetables in a blender with bread crumbs, oil, vinegar, parsley or mint, salt and pepper and 2½ cups of the water. Blend to a purée.

Place purée in a large bowl and stir in the remaining water. Cover and chill for 3 hours.

Before serving, add a few ice cubes. Serve with side dishes of chopped onion, hard-cooked eggs, tomatoes, peppers and croûtons.

Creamy cauliflower soup

Overall timing 35 minutes

Freezing Not suitable

To serve 4

1	Large cauliflower
1	Small onion
	Salt and pepper
¼ cup	Butter
¼ cup	Flour
2 cups	Milk
	Lamb seasoning salt
½ tsp	Dried mixed herbs
¼ tsp	Grated nutmeg
1	Egg yolk
¼ cup	Light cream
	Fresh dill

Trim cauliflower, separate into florets and wash. Peel and finely chop onion. Put cauliflower and onion into pan of boiling salted water, cover and cook for 10 minutes. Drain, saving 2 cups cooking liquid. Mash half cauliflower and onion.

Melt butter in a large saucepan. Stir in flour, then milk and reserved cooking liquid. Add a pinch of lamb seasoning salt, the herbs, nutmeg and pulped and whole cauliflower and onion. Simmer for 7 minutes. Taste and adjust seasoning.

Mix egg yolk and cream in warmed tureen. Pour in soup and serve garnished with dill.

Zucchini and egg soup

Overall timing 30 minutes

Freezing Not suitable

To serve 4

1 lb	Zucchini
2 tbsp	Butter
3 tbsp	Olive oil
1	Garlic clove
1 quart	Boiling water
	Salt and pepper
2	Eggs
10	Basil leaves (optional)
2 tbsp	Chopped parsley
½ cup	Grated mild white cheese
Garnish	
¼ cup	Grated mild white cheese
	Croûtons

Wash zucchini, trim off ends, then dice. Heat the butter, oil and peeled garlic clove in a saucepan or flameproof casserole. Cook over a moderate heat till the garlic turns golden, then discard it.

Add diced zucchini to pan and cook for a few minutes. Add the boiling water and a pinch of salt, cover and cook gently for about 15 minutes.

Break eggs into a warmed soup tureen and add chopped basil, parsley and salt and pepper. Add the cheese. Beat well with a fork.

Gradually add about a quarter of the soup and mix well, then pour in the rest. Garnish with cheese and freshly made croûtons.

Endive soup

Overall timing 25 minutes

Freezing Suitable: add vermouth after reheating

To serve 4

4	Heads of Belgian endive
5 tbsp	Butter
2 tsp	Sugar
1 quart	Chicken broth
2 tsp	Flour
6 tbsp	Dry vermouth
	Salt and pepper

Chop endive. Melt ¼ cup of the butter in a saucepan and fry endive over a gentle heat for about 5 minutes. Tilt pan, add sugar and allow to caramelize. Add broth, cover and simmer for 10 minutes.

Mix remaining butter with the flour to a smooth paste. Stir paste a little at a time into the soup. Return to a boil and simmer for 2-3 minutes.

Add vermouth and seasoning and cook, uncovered, for 1-2 minutes more. Pour into serving bowls and garnish with freshly made, hot croûtons.

Brussels sprout soup

Overall timing 1 ¼ hours

Freezing Suitable: add cream and egg yolk mixture when reheating

To serve 4

1 lb	Brussels sprouts
6 tbsp	Butter
1 quart	Hot beef broth
	Salt
2 tbsp	Flour
	Grated nutmeg
6 tbsp	Light cream
1	Egg yolk

Trim sprouts. Cut a cross in base of each. Melt ¼ cup butter in a saucepan, add sprouts and cook for 3 minutes, stirring continuously. Add broth and salt. Cover and cook for 40 minutes.

Sieve sprouts into a bowl, or liquidize.

Melt remaining butter in a pan. Add flour and cook, stirring, for 3 minutes. Remove pan from heat and gradually add sprout purée. Return to heat and cook for 10 minutes over low heat. Season with salt and pinch of nutmeg.

Mix cream with egg yolk. Off heat, stir cream mixture into soup to thicken.

Avocado soup

Overall timing 15 minutes plus chilling if serving cold

Freezing Suitable: add cream after thawing

To serve 4

1 quart	Chicken broth
2	Ripe avocados
1 tbsp	Lemon juice
1	Egg yolk
3 tbsp	Light cream
	Salt and pepper

Heat chicken broth (made up with 4 cubes if necessary) in a saucepan to boiling point.

Cut open avocados and lift out seeds. If intending to serve soup cold, cut eight very thin slices, sprinkle with lemon juice to prevent discoloration and set aside. Scoop out remaining avocado flesh, place in a bowl and mash well with the egg yolk and cream.

Remove broth from heat. Gradually add the avocado mixture, whisking vigorously. Add salt and pepper to taste. Do not reheat.

Serve hot with fried croûtons. If serving cold, chill the soup for at least 1 hour, then serve garnished with reserved avocado slices.

Pipérade

Overall timing 1 hour

Freezing Not suitable

To serve 4

1 lb	Ripe tomatoes
2	Green peppers
2	Onions
1	Garlic clove
5 tbsp	Oil
	Salt and pepper
¼ tsp	Dried marjoram
	Hot pepper sauce
8	Eggs

Blanch, peel and chop tomatoes. Seed and chop peppers. Peel and slice onions. Peel and crush garlic.

Heat oil in skillet. Add onions and garlic and cook till golden. Add peppers and tomatoes and cook over a high heat for 5 minutes. Season with salt, pepper, marjoram and pepper sauce. Reduce heat, cover and simmer for 30 minutes or until the mixture is reduced to a purée.

Lightly beat eggs in a bowl. Season and pour over vegetable purée. Cook over increased heat, stirring, for 2-3 minutes till creamy. Serve with buttered toast and a green salad.

Baked eggs in potatoes

Overall timing 2 hours

Freezing Not suitable

To serve 4

4x10oz	Potatoes
¼ cup	Butter
	Salt and pepper
½ cup	Grated cheese
4	Small eggs
¼ cup	Heavy cream
2 tsp	Chopped chives

Preheat the oven to 400°.

Scrub and dry the potatoes and push a metal skewer lengthwise through each one. Place on a baking sheet and rub a little of the butter over the skins. Bake for 1-1¼ hours.

Remove from the oven. increase the temperature to 450°F. Cut a slice lengthwise off each potato and scoop out the insides, leaving a shell about ½ inch thick. Mash the scooped-out potato (plus any from the lids) in a bowl with the remaining butter and seasoning. Beat the cheese into potato mixture.

Press the mixture back into the potato shells, leaving a hollow in the center large enough for an egg. Place on baking sheet. Carefully break an egg into each potato. Season and spoon the cream over. Return to the oven and bake for 8-10 minutes till the eggs are lightly set. Sprinkle the chives over and serve hot.

Curried eggs

Overall timing 35 minutes

Freezing Not suitable

To serve 4

6	Eggs
2	Onions
¼ cup	Butter
2 tsp	Curry powder
2½ cups	Chicken broth
1 tsp	Cornstarch
½ cup	Light cream or half-and-half
	Salt and pepper

Place eggs in a saucepan of cold water. Bring to a boil and simmer for 8 minutes, then drain.

Peel and finely chop onions. Melt butter in a skillet, add onions, cover and cook until golden over a low heat (about 15 minutes).

Sprinkle with curry powder and cook for 2 minutes, stirring. Pour in the broth and simmer for 10 minutes. Mix cornstarch and cream or half-and-half together well, then stir into curry mixture with seasoning. Heat gently but do not boil.

Shell eggs and cut in half lengthwise. Remove yolks with a spoon and mash yolks and a little of the curry mixture together with a fork. Spoon back into egg whites. Place eggs in curry sauce and heat through without boiling. Serve with rice or hot buttered toast.

Egg and pea scamble

Overall timing 50 minutes

Freezing Not suitable

To serve 2-4

2lb	Fresh peas
1	Onion
2oz	Bacon slices
2 tbsp	Butter
	Salt and pepper
4	Eggs
1 cup	Soft bread crumbs
½ cup	Grated cheese

Shell peas. Peel and thinly slice the onion; dice the bacon. Melt the butter in a saucepan and gently fry the onion and bacon till transparent.

Add the peas and salt and enough water to half cover them. Bring to a boil, then cover and simmer for 15-20 minutes till the peas are tender and most of the liquid has evaporated.

Lightly beat the eggs in a bowl with the bread crumbs, cheese and pepper. Pour over the peas and cook, stirring gently, till the eggs are lightly set. Serve immediately.

Eggs florentine

Overall timing 45 minutes

Freezing Not suitable

To serve 4

2lb	Bulk spinach
¼ cup	Butter
	Salt
¼ tsp	Grated nutmeg
3 tbsp	Flour
2 cups	Milk
¾ cup	Grated cheese
	Cayenne
½ tsp	Prepared mustard
8	Hard-cooked eggs
2 tbsp	Soft white bread crumbs

Preheat the oven to 425°.

Wash spinach well in several changes of water. Remove any coarse stalks. Put into saucepan with only the water that still clings to the spinach after washing. Cook for 5-10 minutes till tender. Stir in 1 tbsp of the butter and season with salt and grated nutmeg, then spread over the bottom of a greased ovenproof dish.

Melt remaining butter in a pan. Stir in the flour and cook for 1 minute. Gradually add the milk, bring to a boil, stirring, and cook for 2 minutes.

Reserve 2 tbsp of cheese for the topping and stir the rest into the sauce with a pinch each of salt and cayenne and the mustard.

Shell eggs and arrange on top of spinach. Pour sauce over eggs. Mix reserved grated cheese and bread crumbs and sprinkle over the top. Bake for 10 minutes till cheese is bubbly and golden. Serve immediately.

Eggs in a nest

Overall timing 50 minutes

Freezing Not suitable

To serve 4

2lb	Potatoes
	Salt and pepper
1 cup	Milk
6 tbsp	Butter
8	Eggs
2 tbsp	Dried bread crumbs
	Grated nutmeg
	Parsley

Peel the potatoes. Put into a pan of salted water, bring to a boil and cook for 25 minutes. Drain.

Preheat the oven to 425°. Grease ovenproof dish.

Add milk to the potatoes and return to low heat. Mash the potatoes and beat in 4 tbsp of the butter until smooth and creamy. Season to taste.

Spread creamed potatoes in ovenproof dish. Using the back of a spoon, hollow out eight "nests" for the eggs. Break an egg into each of the "nests." Sprinkle with bread crumbs, dot with remaining butter and season with salt, pepper and nutmeg.

Bake for 8-9 minutes or until the eggs are lightly set. Garnish with parsley.

Eggs in mushroom sauce

Overall timing 30 minutes

Freezing Not suitable

To serve 6

¾lb	Mushrooms
6	Large eggs
1 tbsp	Oil
1	Garlic clove
16oz	Can of tomatoes
2 tsp	Chopped parsley
	Salt and pepper
¼ cup	Butter
1 cup	Grated cheese
1 tbsp	Flour

Wipe, trim and thickly slice the mushrooms. Hard-cook the eggs for 10 minutes.

Meanwhile, heat the oil in a skillet. Add peeled garlic and fry till golden. Discard garlic. Add the mushrooms and fry over a high heat for 3-4 minutes. Sieve canned tomatoes and their juice and add to the pan with the parsley, salt and pepper. Cook for about 10 minutes.

Cool the eggs quickly by running cold water over them. Cut eggs in half lengthwise. Scoop out yolks and place in a bowl.

Soften the butter. Add to the egg yolks with the cheese, flour and seasoning. Mix well with a fork. Shape the mixture into 12 balls about 1 inch in diameter, using floured hands. Place one ball in each egg half.

Add egg halves to pan and spoon a little sauce over them. Cover and cook for a further 5 minutes. Divide between warmed serving dishes. Serve immediately with crusty bread.

Flamenco eggs

Overall timing 45 minutes

Freezing Not suitable

To serve 4-6

1	Onion
¼lb	Canadian bacon
2 tbsp	Oil
8oz	Can of tomatoes
2	Potatoes
1	Small sweet red pepper
2oz	Green beans
2 tbsp	Frozen peas
2 tbsp	Canned asparagus tips
6oz	Chorizo or other
	spicy sausage
3 tbsp	Dry sherry
	Salt and pepper
6	Eggs

Peel and finely chop onion. Dice bacon. Heat oil in a saucepan or flameproof casserole. Add onion and bacon and cook till golden. Add tomatoes, mashing them into the onion/bacon mixture till well combined.

Peel potatoes and cut into small dice. Wash, seed and chop pepper. Wash beans. Top and tail them and remove any strings. Cut into short lengths. Add potatoes, pepper, beans and peas to pan and cook for 10 minutes.

Add asparagus tips, sliced sausage and sherry. Season and cook for a further 5 minutes.

Break eggs carefully on top of the mixture. Cover and cook for 5 minutes more or until the eggs are lightly set.

Tomatoes and eggs American style

Overall timing 20 minutes

Freezing Not suitable

To serve 4-6

½lb	Bacon slices
6	Large tomatoes
1 cup	Milk
	Salt and pepper
6	Eggs

Preheat the broiler. Cook the bacon till crisp and golden. Remove and keep hot.

Wipe the tomatoes and cut in half. Place the tomatoes cut sides down on the broiler pan and brush with a little fat from the bacon. Broil about 3 inches below heat for 3-4 minutes.

Meanwhile, pour the milk into a skillet, add a pinch of salt and heat till simmering. Break an egg onto a saucer, then slide it into the milk. Repeat with remaining eggs. Cover and poach for 3 minutes.

Turn the tomatoes over, brush with bacon fat and broil for 2 more minutes. Arrange stalk halves cut sides up in a warmed serving dish and season. Lift the eggs out of the milk with a slotted spoon and drain on paper towels. Place one on each tomato half and cover with the remaining halves. Arrange the bacon around the tomatoes and serve immediately with plenty of hot buttered toast.

Italian shredded omelette

Overall timing 35 minutes

Freezing Not suitable

To serve 4

1	Small onion
1	Garlic clove
1	Stalk of celery
1	Carrot
2oz	Bacon slices
1 tbsp	Oil
16oz	Can of tomatoes
	Salt and pepper
9	Eggs
1 tsp	Chopped fresh mint
3 tbsp	Chopped parsley
¼ cup	Butter

Peel and finely chop the onion. Peel and crush the garlic. Trim and chop the celery. Scrape and thinly slice the carrot. Finely chop the bacon.

Heat the oil in a saucepan, add the bacon and vegetables and fry gently for 5 minutes. Add the tomatoes and juice, garlic and seasoning, bring to a boil and simmer for 20 minutes, stirring to break up the tomatoes.

Meanwhile, lightly beat the eggs in a bowl with the mint, parsley and seasoning. Melt one-third of the butter in a skillet. Add one-third of the egg mixture and cook over a moderate heat, drawing the liquid into the center as the mixture begins to set. When set, slide the omelette onto a board. Make two more omelettes in the same way.

Roll the omelettes loosely and cut into strips about ½ inch wide. Add to the tomato sauce and heat through for 3 minutes. Season to taste and pour into a warmed serving dish.

Shrimp omelette in béchamel sauce

Overall timing 40 minutes

Freezing Not suitable

To serve 2

1	Small onion
1	Small carrot
1	Stalk of celery
1 cup	Milk
1	Bay leaf
5 tbsp	Butter
2 tbsp	Flour
6 oz	Shelled shrimp
2 tbsp	Light cream
	Salt and pepper
6	Eggs
2 tsp	Chopped parsley

Peel and roughly chop the onion and carrot. Trim and chop the celery. Put the milk into a saucepan with the bay leaf and prepared vegetables, cover and bring to a boil. Remove from heat and leave to infuse for 10 minutes.

Melt ¼ cup of the butter in a saucepan, add the flour and cook for 1 minute. Gradually add the strained milk and bring to a boil, stirring constantly. Cook, stirring, for 2 minutes. Reduce heat, stir in shrimp, cream and seasoning. Heat without boiling.

Lightly beat the eggs in a bowl with a pinch of salt. Melt remaining butter in a skillet, pour in the eggs and cook until set.

Spoon half the shrimp sauce into the centre of the omelette and fold two sides over. Turn out of pan, placing join side down on warmed serving dish. Pour the remaining sauce around. Make a cut along the top of the omelette to expose the filling, sprinkle the parsley over and serve immediately with a tossed green salad.

Omelette forestière

Overall timing 25 minutes

Freezing Not suitable

To serve 2

¼lb	Thick bacon slices
¼lb	Button mushrooms
2	Small potatoes
2 tbsp	Butter
4-6	Eggs
1 tbsp	hopped parsley
	Salt and pepper

Cut bacon into thin strips. Thinly slice mushrooms. Peel and thinly slice potatoes. Melt the butter in a skillet, add potatoes and bacon and fry till tender and golden all over. Add mushrooms and cook for 5 minutes more.

Meanwhile, lightly beat the eggs in a bowl with parsley and seasoning. Pour over the ingredients in the skillet. Cook for a few minutes, lifting the edges to ensure the underneath is evenly cooked. Fold over and slide onto warmed serving plate. Serve immediately.

Anchovy brochettes

Overall timing 30 minutes

Freezing Not suitable

To serve 2

4	Large slices of white bread
¼ lb	Mozzarella or Gouda cheese
6 tbsp	Butter
	Salt and pepper
8	Anchovy fillets
¼ cup	Milk

Preheat the oven to 400°.

Cut bread and cheese into small squares. Thread alternately onto four skewers. Arrange in an ovenproof dish so that each end of the skewer is supported by the rim.

Melt half of the butter and brush generously over the brochettes. Season with salt and pepper. Bake for about 15-20 nutes, basting occasionally with butter in dish. The brochettes should be golden brown.

Meanwhile, melt remaining butter in a saucepan. Mash anchovies and add tobutter. Gradually add milk and mix well together over gentle heat. Bring to boiling point.

Pour hot anchovy sauce over brochettes and serve immediately.

Welsh rarebit

Overall timing 30 minutes

Freezing Not suitable

To serve 4

8	Slices of bread
6 tbsp	Butter
¾ lb	Cheddar cheese
½ tsp	Ground mace
	Pinch of powdered mustard
5 tbsp	Beer
	Pepper

Preheat the oven to 400°.

Toast the bread, and butter the slices while still hot. Place on baking sheet.

Cut the cheese into small cubes and put in a saucepan with mace, mustard and beer. Cook over a low heat, stirring with a wooden spoon, until cheese melts and is thick and creamy. Spread mixture over toast. Sprinkle generously with pepper and bake for 10 minutes. Serve immediately.

Cheese quiche

Overall timing 1 ½ hours

Freezing Suitable: reheat in 425° oven for 10-15 minutes

To serve 4-6

½ cup + 2 tbsp	Butter
¾ cup	Water
	Salt and pepper
2 cups	Self-rising flour
2	Medium-size onions
1 tbsp	Flour
½ cup	Milk
3	Eggs
¼ tsp	Grated nutmeg
	Cayenne
1 cup	Grated Cheddar cheese
1 cup	Grated Gruyère cheese

Melt ½ cup of the butter. Cool slightly, then stir in 3 tbsp of the water and salt. Sift self-rising flour into a bowl. Slowly add butter mixture and mix until smooth. Chill for 30 minutes.

Preheat the oven to 350°.

Peel and chop onions. Melt remaining butter in a saucepan and fry onions for 10 minutes until soft. Cool.

Mix 1 tbsp flour and a little of the milk in a bowl, then add the rest of the milk and the remaining water. Separate the eggs. Mix the yolks into the flour and milk mixture. Season with salt, pepper, nutmeg and a pinch of cayenne. Beat egg whites till stiff, then fold into yolk mixture.

Roll out dough and use to line a greased 9 inch quiche or flan pan. Spread onions over bottom of pastry case then sprinkle both sorts of cheese on top. Cover with egg and milk mixture.

Bake for 15 minutes. Reduce heat to 325° and bake for a further 45 minutes. Serve hot.

Cheese soufflé

Overall timing 45 minutes

Freezing Not suitable

To serve 4-6

6 tbsp	Butter
4	Eggs
½ cup	Cornstarch
2½ cups	Milk
	Salt and pepper
	Paprika
	Grated nutmeg
1 cup	Grated Gruyère,
	Parmesan or sharp
	Cheddar cheese

Preheat the oven to 400°.

Grease a 7 inch diameter soufflé dish with 2 tbsp of the butter, and tie with paper collar if liked. Separate the eggs.

Melt the remaining butter in a saucepan, stir in cornstarch and cook for 1 minute. Gradually add the milk, and bring to the boil, stirring all the time until the sauce thickens. Season with salt and pepper and a pinch of both paprika and grated nutmeg. Take pan off heat and allow mixture to cool slightly.

Stir the cheese into sauce. Add egg yolks one at a time to the sauce, beating well.

In a large bowl, beat egg whites till they hold stiff peaks, then carefully fold into the sauce with a metal spoon.

Pour soufflé mixture into prepared dish. Bake for about 25 minutes or until risen and golden. Remove from oven and serve immediately with a crisp green salad, dressed with herb vinaigrette.

Croque monsieur

Overall timing 20 minutes

Freezing Not suitable

To serve 4

8	Slices of bread
	Butter
8	Slices of Gruyère
	or Cheddar cheese
4	Slices of cooked
	ham
	Extra grated cheese
	(optional)

Preheat the broiler.

Butter four slices of bread. Place a slice of cheese on each of the unbuttered slices of bread. Cover with the ham, then top with the rest of the sliced cheese. Place the buttered bread on top, buttered sides up.

Broil the sandwiches, buttered sides up, until golden brown. Turn and spread the other sides with butter. Continue broiling until golden. Sprinkle with a little extra grated cheese, if liked, and broil until the cheese has melted.

Variation

For a Croque Milady, add sliced tomato to the sandwich and top with fried eggs.

Gnocchi

Overall timing 50 minutes plus cooling

Freezing Suitable: bake from frozen, allowing 1 hour

To serve 4

1 quart	Milk
1 cup	Coarse semolina
	Salt and pepper
	Grated nutmeg
1½ cups	Grated Parmesan cheese
1	Egg yolk
2 tbsp	Milk

Heat milk just to boiling in a saucepan, then sprinkle on semolina. Season with salt, pepper and nutmeg. Cook gently, stirring, for 4-5 minutes till mixture becomes solid. Remove pan from heat and beat in 1 cup of the cheese. Pour into a greased jelly roll pan. Leave in a cool place (not the refrigerator) for 45 minutes to 1 hour till cold.

Preheat the oven to 400°.

Cut the cooled mixture into about 20 rounds, 2½ inches in diameter. Arrange the rounds, overlapping them, in a greased round ovenproof dish. Beat egg yolk and milk and pour over. Sprinkle with the rest of the cheese and bake for 30 minutes till golden brown. Serve immediately.

Gougère

Overall timing 1 ½ hours

Freezing Not suitable

To serve 6

1 cup	Water
½ tsp	Salt
½ cup	Butter
⅔ cup	Flour
4	Eggs
½lb	Gruyère cheese

Preheat oven to 400°.

Put water and salt into a saucepan with 6 tbsp of the butter, chopped. Bring to a boil, stirring to melt the butter. Remove from heat and quickly add the flour all at once, stirring well. Return pan to heat and beat till the paste is smooth and leaves the sides of the pan cleanly. Remove from heat and allow to cool slightly.

Add three of the eggs, one at a time, beating well between additions. Grate 1¼ cups of the cheese and stir into the paste.

With a large spoon, make a ring of the paste on a greased baking sheet. Beat the remaining egg and brush over paste. Dice remaining cheese and place on top of the paste with tiny pieces of the remaining butter.

Bake for 20 minutes, then lower heat to 375°, and bake for a further 20-25 minutes. Serve hot.

Deep-fried Mozzarella sandwiches

Overall timing 20 minutes

Freezing Not suitable

To serve 4

8	Slices of bread
4	Slices of
	Mozzarella cheese
	Flour
1	Egg
	Oil for deep frying

Remove the crusts from the bread. Make four sandwiches with the cheese and coat lightly and evenly with flour. Beat the egg in a shallow dish. Dip in the sandwiches so the sides and edges are all coated.

Heat oil in a deep-fryer to 360°. Deep fry the sandwiches until they are golden brown. Drain on paper towels and serve hot, with salad.

Italian deep-fried cheese

Overall timing 1 ¼ hours plus chilling

Freezing Not suitable

To serve 2

½	Onion
2 tbsp	Butter
¼ cup	Long grain rice
½ cup	Chicken broth
1 tsp	Grated Parmesan cheese
	Pinch of grated nutmeg
	Salt and pepper
1 oz	Lean cooked ham
1 ½ oz	Mozzarella cheese
1	Egg
½ cup	Fine soft bread crumbs
	Oil for deep frying

Peel and finely chop onion. Melt butter in a saucepan and fry onion till transparent.

Add rice and stir over a low heat for 2 minutes. Stir in broth, cover and bring to a boil. Simmer gently for 15-20 minutes till rice is tender. Remove from heat and stir in Parmesan, nutmeg and seasoning. Leave to cool completely.

Meanwhile chop ham finely. Cut Mozzarella into four sticks about 1 ½ inches long and ½ inch thick. Break egg onto a plate and beat lightly with a fork. Spread bread crumbs on another plate.

Beat a little egg and the ham into rice. Put 2 tbsp rice mixture in palm of one hand. Place a cheese stick on top and cover with more rice. Pat into a cylinder shape about 2 ½ inches long and 1 inch thick. Brush beaten egg over croquette, then coat with bread crumbs. Shape and coat three more croquettes. Chill for 1 hour.

Heat oil in a deep fryer to 360°. Fry the croquettes for 5-6 minutes till golden. Drain on paper towels and serve hot.

Broiled cod with bacon

Overall timing 25 minutes

Freezing Not suitable

To serve 2

2	Large cod fillets
2 tbsp	Oil
	Salt and pepper
2oz	Thin bacon slices
2 tbsp	Butter
1 tbsp	Lemon juice
	Sprigs of parsley
	Lemon wedges

Preheat the broiler.

Brush the cod fillets with oil and season with salt and pepper. Place under the broiler and cook for about 15 minutes, turning fillets over halfway through cooking time.

Meanwhile, broil or fry bacon. Drain on paper towels. Melt the butter in a small saucepan, taking care not to color it. Arrange the fish and bacon on warmed serving plates. Pour the butter over and sprinkle with lemon juice. Garnish with parsley sprigs and lemon wedges. Serve with boiled potatoes tossed in butter and sprinkled with chopped parsley, and a crisp lettuce salad.

Cod croquettes

Overall timing 45 minutes

Freezing Suitable: bake cooked croquettes from frozen in 375° oven for 30 minutes

To serve 4-6

1 lb	Cooked cod fillets
2 cups	Mashed potatoes
	Salt and pepper
	Grated nutmeg
1	Egg
	Dried bread crumbs
	Oil for deep frying
	Lettuce leaves
1	Lemon

Finely grind cod, or blend in a food processor until coarse-fine then mix with potatoes in a large bowl. Season well with salt, pepper and a pinch of nutmeg. Make small round or oval shapes of the mixture.

Lightly beat egg in a bowl. Dip croquettes in egg, then bread crumbs.

Heat oil in deep-fryer to 360°. Add croquettes and fry for about 5 minutes till golden. Remove croquettes and drain on paper towels. Pile them up on a bed of lettuce with pieces of lemon between. Serve with tomato sauce.

Halibut with spicy sauce

Overall timing 1 hour

Freezing Not suitable

To serve 4

4	Onions
4-6	Garlic cloves
1 lb	Tomatoes
1	Lemon
¼ cup	Oil
¼ tsp	Cayenne
4	Halibut steaks
	Salt
	Chopped parsley

Peel and slice onions. Peel and crush garlic. Blanch, peel and chop tomatoes. Cut four thin slices from lemon and squeeze juice from remainder.

Heat oil in a saucepan. Add onions, garlic and tomatoes and cook gently for about 25 minutes.

Add cayenne and mix in well. Place fish steaks on top of mixture in pan. Sprinkle with salt and lemon juice, cover with lid and cook for a further 15 minutes, turning the fish steaks once.

Arrange fish steaks on a bed of boiled rice on warmed serving dish. Spoon tomato mixture on top and garnish with lemon slices and chopped parsley.

Fish and chips

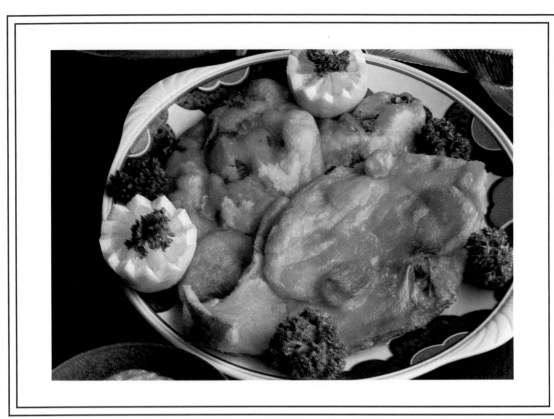

Overall timing 35 minutes plus
30 minutes soaking

Freezing Not suitable

To serve 4

2lb	Waxy potatoes
2	Whole flounder,
	halved and boned
	Salt and pepper
¼ cup	Flour
	Oil for frying
	Lemon wedges
	Sprigs of parsley
Coating batter	
2 cups	Flour
½ tsp	Salt
2	Eggs
2 tbsp	Oil
6 tbsp	Cold water

Peel the potatoes and cut into chips (french fries). Soak in cold water for 30 minutes.

Wipe the fish. Season the flour and lightly coat the fish.

To make the batter, sift flour and salt into a bowl. Separate eggs. Add yolks, oil and water to flour and beat till smooth.

Heat oil in a deep-fryer to 360°. Drain the chips and dry well. Fry, in batches, for 4-5 minutes till tender but not brown. Remove and drain on paper towels.

Reduce the temperature of the oil to 340°. Beat the egg whites till stiff but not dry and fold into the batter. Coat the fish with batter.

Fry the fish, one at a time if necessary, for 2-3 minutes each side till crisp and golden. Drain on paper towels and keep hot, uncovered.

Increase the temperature of the oil to 360° again, put the chips in the basket and fry till crisp and golden. Drain on paper towels and pile into a warmed serving dish.

Garnish fish with lemon wedges and sprigs of parsley. Serve immediately.

Fried flounder

Overall timing 30 minutes

Freezing Not suitable

To serve 6

6 tbsp	Unsalted butter
2 tbsp	Chopped parsley
1 tbsp	Lemon juice
	Salt and pepper
3 tbsp	Flour
3	Whole flounder, halved and boned
2	Eggs
1⅓ cups	Dried bread crumbs
	Oil for frying
	Lemon slices
	Sprigs of parsley

Mash the butter with the chopped parsley and lemon juice. Shape into a roll and chill.

Season the flour and lightly coat the fish. Beat the eggs in a shallow dish. Spread the bread crumbs on a plate. Dip the fish into the egg so that it covers both sides. Dip into the crumbs, pressing them on lightly till evenly coated.

Heat the oil in a large skillet and add two or three of the coated fillets, skin side up. Fry gently for 3-5 minutes, then turn the fish carefully and cook for a further 3-5 minutes till the fish is tender and the coating crisp. Lift out of the pan with a spatula and drain on paper towels. Arrange on a warmed serving platter and keep hot while the rest of the fish is cooked.

Garnish with slices of parsley butter, lemon slices and sprigs of parsley. Serve with sauté potatoes.

Grilled herrings with parsley butter

Overall timing 20 minutes

Freezing Not suitable

To serve 4

½ cup	Unsalted butter
2 tbsp	Chopped parsley
1 tbsp	Lemon juice
4	Cleaned whole fresh herrings
1 tbsp	Oil
	Salt and pepper
1	Lemon
	Sprigs of parsley

Mash butter with chopped parsley and lemon juice. Form into a roll, wrap in wax paper and chill till ready to use.

Preheat a charcoal grill.

Brush herrings with oil and season. Place on grill and cook for 7 minutes on each side.

Arrange herrings on serving plate. Garnish with lemon, pats of chilled butter and parsley sprigs.

Skate with capers

Overall timing 25 minutes

Freezing Not suitable

To serve 2

2 x ½ lb	Pieces of skate
	Salt and pepper
1 ½ tsp	Vinegar
3 tbsp	Butter
1 tbsp	Capers
1 tbsp	Chopped parsley
1 ½ tbsp	Lemon juice
2 tbsp	Light cream

Put the skate into a saucepan. Cover with cold water and add a little salt and a few drops of vinegar. Bring to a boil, then remove from the heat, cover and leave to stand for 10 minutes.

Drain and dry the skate; remove the skin. Place on a warmed serving dish and keep hot.

Melt the butter in a small saucepan and stir in remaining vinegar, the capers, parsley, lemon juice, cream and seasoning. Cook for 2-3 minutes, without boiling, till heated through. Pour over the skate. Serve with boiled or steamed potatoes and a tossed green salad.

Poached kippers

Overall timing 20 minutes

Freezing Not suitable

To serve 4

8	Kipper fillets
6 tbsp	Butter
2 tsp	Lemon juice
½ tsp	Pepper
	Sprigs of parsley
	Lemon wedges

Place kipper fillets in a large saucepan with the skins facing up. Cover with cold water and slowly bring to a boil.

As soon as the water boils, remove from heat, drain well and place on a warmed serving dish with the skin side down. Garnish with parsley.

Melt the butter and stir in the lemon juice and pepper. Pour over kippers at the table and serve with boiled new potatoes and lemon wedges.

Marinated kipper fillets

Overall timing 15 minutes plus marination

Freezing Not suitable

To serve 6

1	Carrot
2	Onions
1 lb	Kipper fillets
	Sprigs of thyme
4-5	Bay leaves
4-5	Cloves
½ cup	Oil
¼ cup	Wine vinegar or
	lemon juice

Peel and slice the carrot and onions. Place kipper fillets in a glass or pottery bowl, layered with slices of carrot, onion rings, sprigs of fresh thyme, bay leaves and cloves. Pour oil and wine vinegar or lemon juice over and leave for 24 hours in a cool place.

Serve with potato and onion salad, or bread.

Scrowled smelts

Overall timing 30 minutes plus salting

Freezing Not suitable

To serve 4

1 lb	Fresh smelts
	Salt
2	Sprigs of rosemary
¼ cup	Butter
	Lemon wedges

Cover the smelts with salt and leave overnight.

The next day, rinse off the salt. Cut off the heads and tails, then slit each fish along the belly and remove the insides, including the backbone. Do this under cold running water. Dry the fish with paper towels.

Preheat a charcoal grill.

Strip the rosemary leaves from the sprig. Melt the butter. Arrange the fish on the grill and sprinkle with the butter and rosemary. Grill until cooked, turning once. Serve with lemon wedges.

Mackerel in mushroom sauce

Overall timing 40 minutes

Freezing Not suitable

To serve 4

½lb	Button mushrooms
2	Onions
1	Garlic clove
¾lb	Tomatoes
5 tbsp	Oil
	Salt and pepper
2 tbsp	White wine vinegar
2lb	Mackerel fillets
2 tbsp	Flour

Slice mushrooms. Peel and finely chop onions. Peel and crush garlic. Wash tomatoes and cut into ½ inch thick slices.

Heat 2 tbsp of the oil in a saucepan. Add onions, mushrooms and garlic and fry for 10 minutes, stirring frequently. Season. Stir in the vinegar and boil rapidly till it evaporates.

Coat fillets with seasoned flour. Heat the remaining oil in a large skillet, add the fillets and fry for 5 minutes on each side. Drain, arrange on a warmed serving dish and keep hot.

Add tomato slices to skillet and fry for 2 minutes. Spoon mushroom mixture over fillets. Season tomatoes and arrange on top. Serve immediately with minted peas.

Porgy with mushrooms

Overall timing 1 hour

Freezing Not suitable

To serve 2

2 lb	Porgy or other whole fish
¼ lb	Button mushrooms
1	Small onion
	Salt and pepper
½ cup	Water
1 tsp	Chopped parsley
	Pinch of dried thyme
2 tbsp	Butter
1	Lemon

Preheat the oven to 400°.

Clean fish, but don't remove head. Trim tail and fins, and wash well. Dry on paper towels.

Thinly slice button mushrooms. Peel and finely chop onion. Cover bottom of ovenproof dish with most of mushrooms and onion and place the fish on top. Season with salt and pepper, and pour in the water. Sprinkle fish with parsley, thyme and remaining mushrooms and onion.

Melt butter and pour over fish. Cover dish with foil or a lid and bake for 40 minutes, basting frequently with juices in dish. Turn fish over halfway through cooking time and remove foil for last 10 minutes. The fish is cooked when the flesh becomes opaque.

Garnish with lemon and serve with boiled new potatoes.

Barbecued haddock

Overall timing 20 minutes plus marination

Freezing Not suitable

To serve 2

1½ tbsp	Oil
1½ tsp	Lemon juice
1 tbsp	Brown sugar
¼ tsp	Chili powder
½ tsp	Worcestershire sauce
1 tsp	Tomato paste
1 lb	Smoked haddock (finnan haddie)

Mix together oil, lemon juice, sugar, chili powder, Worcestershire sauce and tomato paste in a shallow dish. Add the haddock, cover and marinate in the refrigerator for 1 hour, turning fish once or twice.

Preheat a charcoal grill.

Remove fish from marinade and place on a large piece of foil on the grill or in a fish grilling basket. grill for 5-7 minutes on each side, brushing with marinade from time to time.

Trout with almonds

Overall timing 20 minutes

Freezing Not suitable

To serve 2

2	Trout, cleaned
¼ cup	Flour
¼ cup	Butter
2 tbsp	Chopped parsley
½ cup	Flaked almonds
	Salt and pepper
2	Lemon slices

Dredge trout with flour. Melt butter in skillet. Add trout and cook gently on one side for 5 minutes.

Turn trout over with a spatula. Add half the parsley, the almonds and seasoning. Cook for a further 7-8 minutes till fish is tender and almonds are golden brown (turn them as they cook).

Place fish on warmed serving plates and spoon over almonds. Ganish with lemon slices and remaining chopped parsley. Serve with boiled potatoes and a mixed salad.

Salmon cakes

Overall timing 25 minutes

Freezing Suitable: fry straight from frozen

To serve 4

1 lb	Boiled potatoes
2 tbsp	Milk
2 tbsp	Butter
7½ oz	Can of salmon
2	Lemons
	Salt and pepper
2	Eggs
2 tbsp	Flour
¼ cup	Dried bread crumbs
½ cup	Oil
	Lettuce leaves

Mash the boiled potatoes with the milk and butter. Drain canned salmon and discard skin and bones. Mash flesh and add to potatoes.

Squeeze juice from one of the lemons. Add to salmon with seasoning to taste. Mix well and bind with one of the eggs.

Lightly beat remaining egg. Spread flour and dried bread crumbs on separate plates. Divide salmon mixture into eight and shape into flat patties. Dip first in flour, then egg, then coat lightly with dried bread crumbs.

Heat oil in skillet. Add patties and fry for 5 minutes on each side until crisp and golden. Remove from pan with a slotted spoon and arrange on serving plate. Serve immediately, garnished with lettuce leaves and the remaining lemon, cut into wedges.

Indonesian fish curry

Overall timing 40 minutes

Freezing Not suitable

To serve 4

1½lb	Cod fillets
	Salt and pepper
2 tbsp	Flour
1	Onion
1	Large tart apple
1 tbsp	Lemon juice
¼ cup	Butter
2 tbsp	Oil
2 tbsp	Curry powder
2½ cups	Fish broth
2 tbsp	Golden raisins
2 tbsp	Cornstarch
½ cup	Split almonds

Cut fish into pieces, sprinkle with salt and coat with the flour. Peel and slice onion. Peel, core and slice apple and sprinkle with the lemon juice.

Heat the butter and oil in a flameproof casserole. Add curry powder and onion and fry for 5 minutes. Add fish and cook for a few minutes on all sides. Add apple slices and cook for 3 minutes.

Pour broth into casserole and add raisins. Blend cornstarch with a little broth or water and stir in. Bring to a boil and simmer for 10-15 minutes.

Add almonds and cook for a further 2 minutes. Taste and adjust seasoning and serve.

Cheesy fish croquettes

Overall timing 40 minutes

Freezing Suitable: reheat from frozen in 375° oven for 30 minutes

To serve 2

½lb	White fish fillets
1 cup	Milk
1	Small onion
¼ cup	Butter
¼ cup	Flour
1	Hard-cooked egg
1 tbsp	Grated Parmesan cheese
	Salt and pepper
	Oil for frying

Place the fish fillets in a large skillet with the milk. Cover and cook over a moderate heat for about 10 minutes till fish is tender. Lift fish out of milk. Discard skin and any bones, then mash flesh. Reserve fish and milk.

Peel and finely chop the onion. Melt the butter in clean skillet and fry onion till transparent. Add the flour and cook for 2 minutes, stirring. Gradually stir in the reserved milk and bring to a boil.

Remove pan from the heat and add the reserved fish. Shell and finely chop the hard-cooked egg and add to the sauce with the Parmesan and seasoning. Spread the mixture thickly onto a plate, cover and chill till firm.

Divide the mixture into four and shape on a well floured board into round patties about ½ inch thick.

Heat oil in deep-fryer to 340° and fry the croquettes for 5 minutes till crisp and golden. Drain on paper towels and serve hot.

Shrimp ravigote

Overall timing 20 minutes plus marination

Freezing Not suitable

To serve 2

1 tbsp	Sour cream
¼ cup	Thick mayonnaise
1 tbsp	Lemon juice
1 tbsp	White wine vinegar
½ tsp	Prepared mustard
	Salt and pepper
1	Stalk of celery
½	Sweet red pepper
½	Green pepper
½lb	Large shelled shrimp
1 tsp	Chopped herbs
½	Head Bibb or Boston lettuce
1	Hard-cooked egg

To make marinade, mix the sour cream and mayonnaise in a bowl. Gradually add the lemon juice and vinegar, a few drops at a time, stirring constantly. Stir in the mustard and season to taste.

Trim the celery and cut into thin strips. Seed and thinly slice the peppers. Place the prepared vegetables in a bowl and add the chopped shrimp and herbs. Pour the marinade over, toss lightly and leave to marinate for 30 minutes.

Wash and dry the lettuce and line serving dish with the leaves. Spoon the shrimp salad into the center.

Shell the egg, cut in half and remove yolk. Slice the white; press yolk through a sieve. Use to garnish the salad.

Shrimp magenta

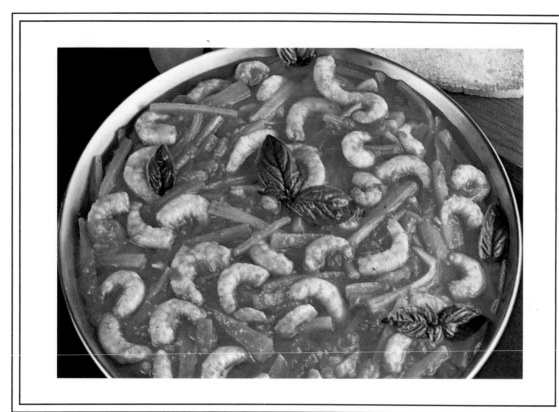

Overall timing 40 minutes

Freezing Not suitable

To serve 2

2	Stalks of celery
1	Large carrot
1	Small leek
2 tbsp	Olive oil
½lb	Shrimp
¾ cup	Dry white wine
8oz	Can of tomatoes
	Salt and pepper
3	Fresh basil leaves
2 tbsp	Butter

Trim the celery and cut into thin sticks. Peel the carrot and cut into sticks. Trim and thinly slice the leek.

Heat the oil in a saucepan, add the prepared vegetables, cover and cook over a low heat for 10 minutes to release the flavors without browning vegetables.

Shell the shrimp and add to the pan with the white wine and tomatoes and juice. Season, cover and cook over a low heat for 10 minutes, shaking pan occasionally.

Add the whole basil leaves and butter, adjust the seasoning and serve hot with boiled rice.

Baked cod with rosemary

Overall timing 45 minutes

Freezing Not suitable

To serve 4-6

2½lb	Tail piece of cod
¼ cup	Oil
8	Anchovy fillets
	Fresh rosemary
4	Basil leaves
	(optional)
2 tbsp	Dried bread crumbs
	Salt and pepper

Ask your fish man to remove bones from cod, leaving two halves attached at one side. Scale fish, using a descaler or the blunt side of a knife.

Preheat the oven to 350°.

Heat half the oil in a flameproof casserole, add the chopped anchovies and heat through. Mash anchovies well, then transfer to a bowl. Put a little of the mashed anchovy mixture inside the fish, together with a few sprigs of fresh rosemary and the basil leaves, if using.

Place fish in the casserole and pour the remaining anchovy mixture and oil over. Add a little more rosemary and sprinkle with bread crumbs, salt and pepper. Bake for about 30 minutes till the fish is cooked and the top is golden. Serve with boiled potatoes and a green vegetable or salad.

Hake au gratin

Overall timing 30 minutes

Freezing Not suitable

To serve 4

1	Small onion
2 tbsp	Chopped parsley
1¾ lb	Hake steaks
	Salt and pepper
	Grated nutmeg
2 tbsp	Lemon juice
2 tbsp	Butter
1 cup	Grated cheese
1 cup	Soft bread crumbs

Preheat oven to 375°.

Peel and chop onion and place in a shallow ovenproof dish with half the parsley and the fish steaks. Season with salt and pepper and a pinch of nutmeg. Sprinkle the lemon juice over the fish and dot with butter. Mix the cheese with the bread crumbs and remaining parsley. Sprinkle over the fish. Bake for about 20 minutes.

Remove from oven and baste with liquid in dish. Bake for another 10 minutes until topping is golden. Serve immediately with baked potatoes.

Haddock creole

Overall timing 1 hour

Freezing Not suitable

To serve 4

1	Onion
1	Garlic clove
1	Sweet red pepper
1	Green pepper
2 tbsp	Butter
2 tbsp	Oil
16oz	Can of tomatoes
	Salt and pepper
2lb	Haddock fillets
3 tbsp	Lemon juice
	Chopped parsley

Preheat the oven to 375°.

Peel and chop onion and garlic. Seed and slice peppers. Heat the butter and oil in a pan. Add onion, garlic and peppers and fry gently for 10 minutes.

Add tomatoes and mash with a wooden spoon to break them up. Season with salt and pepper. Bring to a boil and simmer gently for 10 minutes.

Place half tomato mixture in ovenproof dish, add haddock and season with salt and pepper. Sprinkle with lemon juice and cover with remaining tomato mixture.

Cover with lid or foil and bake for about 25 minutes. Sprinkle with chopped parsley and serve with plain boiled rice.

Roast pork with stuffing balls

Overall timing 2¼ hours

Freezing Not suitable

To serve 6

2½lb	Rolled boneless pork loin roast
	Oil
	Salt
Stuffing balls	
1	Onion
¼ cup	Butter
2 cups	Soft bread crumbs
2 tsp	Dried sage
	Salt and pepper
2	Eggs
2 tbsp	Lard

Preheat the oven to 450°.

Score the skin on the roast, then rub it well with oil and sprinkle with salt. Place in a roasting pan and roast for 20 minutes. Reduce the temperature to 375° and continue roasting for 1½ hours.

Meanwhile make the stuffing balls. Peel and chop the onion. Melt the butter in a skillet and fry the onion till golden. Tip the onion into a bowl and add the bread crumbs, sage and seasoning. Bind with the eggs, then shape into small balls.

About 45 minutes before the pork has finished cooking, melt the lard in an ovenproof dish in the oven. Arrange the stuffing balls in the dish and place on a shelf below the pork. Turn once during the cooking.

Transfer the pork to a warm serving platter and surround with the stuffing balls.

Roast pork with oranges

Overall timing 2¼ hours

Freezing Not suitable

To serve 6-8

3lb	Rolled boneless pork blade Boston roast
2 tbsp	Butter
	Salt and pepper
5	Oranges
2 tbsp	Lemon juice
½ cup	Hot water
6	Sugar cubes
1 tbsp	Wine vinegar
2 tsp	Arrowroot

Preheat the oven to 450°.

Place pork in a roasting pan. Spread butter over lean parts and rub salt and pepper into fat. Roast for 20 minutes.

Meanwhile, squeeze juice from two oranges. Peel remaining oranges. Cut two into slices and one into sections.

Remove pork from pan and keep warm. Pour off any fat from pan and add orange and lemon juices and water. Stir well, scraping any sediment from bottom of pan. Reduce oven temperature to 400°.

Replace meat in pan and roast for a further 1½ hours, basting occasionally.

Meanwhile, put sugar cubes into a saucepan with 1 tbsp water. Stir till dissolved, then boil rapidly, without stirring, till golden. Remove from heat and stir in vinegar. Return to heat and stir till caramel dissolves.

Place pork on a warmed serving platter. Stir cooking liquid from pan into caramel. Blend arrowroot with 2 tbsp water and add to caramel. Bring to a boil, stirring. Add the sliced and sectioned oranges. Heat through for 1-2 minutes.

Cut pork into thick slices and arrange the pieces of orange around. Serve the sauce separately in a warmed sauceboat.

Cowboy's pork and beans

Overall timing 50 minutes

Freezing Not suitable

To serve 6

1½lb	Slab bacon
1	Large onion
2 tbsp	Oil
2	Garlic cloves
¼ tsp	Chili powder
2 tbsp	Molasses
1 tbsp	Vinegar
½ tsp	Powdered mustard
2 tbsp	Tomato ketchup
1 cup	Chicken broth
	Salt and pepper
2x16oz	Cans of Navy or other white beans

Preheat the oven to 425°. Cut the bacon into ½ inch pieces, discarding any bones. Place in roasting pan with no extra fat. Cook in the oven for about 20 minutes till crisp and golden.

Meanwhile, peel and finely chop the onion. Heat the oil in a flameproof casserole and fry the onion till transparent. Peel and crush the garlic and add to the pan with the chili powder. Fry, stirring, for 2 minutes.

Stir in the molasses, vinegar, mustard, ketchup and chicken broth. Bring to a boil, season and simmer for 5 minutes.

Drain and rinse the canned beans and add to the sauce.

Remove the bacon from the oven and reduce the temperature to 350°. Add the bacon pieces to the beans with 1 tbsp of the fat from the pan. Put the casserole in the oven and cook for about 15 minutes, stirring once till liquid is reduced by half. Taste and adjust the seasoning, then serve immediately with a tomato and onion salad and crusty bread.

Country pork with parsnips

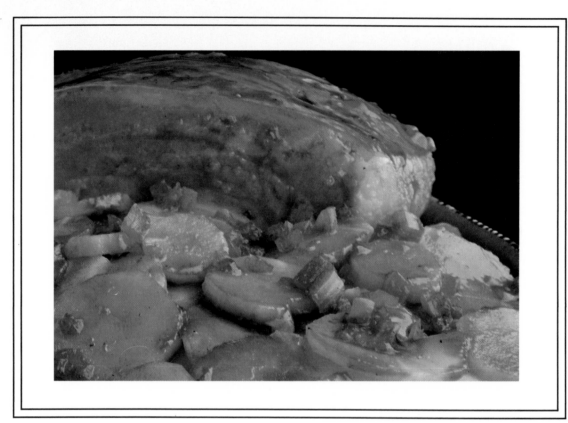

Overall timing 2¼ hours

Freezing Not suitable

To serve 4-6

¼ cup	Butter
2½lb	Boneless pork picnic
	shoulder roast
2	Onions
2lb	Parsnips
1 cup	Broth
	Bouquet garni
1 tbsp	Flour
¾ cup	Dry white wine
	Salt and pepper

Preheat the oven to 400°.

Melt the butter in a roasting pan, place the pork in it and roast for 1 hour.

Meanwhile, peel and chop the onions. Peel and slice the parsnips.

Remove the roasting pan from the oven and arrange the onions and parsnips around the pork. Pour in the broth, add the bouquet garni and return to the oven. Roast for a further 45 minutes, basting the parsnips occasionally.

Discard the bouquet garni. Place the pork on a warmed serving platter and arrange the parsnips around it. Keep hot.

Pour all but 2 tbsp of the juices from the roasting pan into a pitcher. Sprinkle the flour into the pan and cook for 1 minute, stirring. Gradually add the reserved cooking juices and the wine and bring to a boil, stirring constantly. Taste and adjust seasoning and spoon over the parsnips.

Meatballs and spinach

Overall timing 45 minutes

Freezing Not suitable

To serve 4

1 lb	Ground pork
1 tbsp	Chopped chives
1	Egg
2 tbsp	Soy sauce
¼ cup	Oil
2 tbsp	Dry sherry
½ cup	Water
2 lb	Bulk spinach
1 tsp	Cornstarch
	Salt and pepper

Pound ground pork with chives, egg and half the soy sauce till mixture binds together. Shape into eight balls.

Heat half the oil in a skillet, add the meatballs and fry over a medium heat for 10 minutes, turning till browned. Add the remaining soy sauce, the sherry and water, bring to a boil, cover and simmer for 15 minutes.

Meanwhile, shred the spinach. Heat the remaining oil in another skillet, add the spinach and stir-fry over a high heat for 3 minutes.

Blend the cornstarch with 1 tbsp cold water and add to the meatballs. Bring to a boil, stirring till thickened. Season to taste.

Arrange the spinach on a warmed serving dish and place the meatballs on top. Spoon the sauce over the meatballs and serve with a side dish of soy sauce.

Iowa skillet chops

Overall timing 1 hour

Freezing Suitable

To serve 4

4	Pork loin chops
	Salt and pepper
3 tbsp	Oil
2 lb	Can of tomatoes
1 tbsp	Tomato paste
1 tbsp	Worcestershire sauce
1	Onion
11½ oz	Can of whole kernel corn
1 tbsp	Arrowroot (optional)
	Sprigs of parsley

Sprinkle chops with salt and pepper. Heat oil in a skillet and cook chops in two batches for 2 minutes on each side. When all chops are cooked, return first batch to pan. Remove from heat.

Purée the tomatoes with juice, tomato paste and Worcestershire sauce in a blender, then pour over chops. Finely chop the onion and add with the drained corn (use some of the corn water if the mixture is too thick). Bring back to a boil and add salt and pepper.

Cover the pan and cook over moderate heat for 25 minutes. Remove lid to reduce sauce a little and cook for a further 10 minutes. Thicken with arrowroot, if you like, blended with a little hot water, and cook till clear. Garnish with parsley and serve straight from the pan.

Barbecued pork chops

Overall timing 20 minutes plus
marination

Freezing Not suitable

To serve 4

4	Pork chops
Marinade	
1	Large onion
2 tbsp	Lemon juice or vinegar
2 tbsp	Oil
½ tsp	Powdered mustard
2 tsp	Worcestershire sauce
½ tsp	Salt
½ tsp	Freshly ground black pepper
1 tsp	Sugar
½ tsp	Paprika

Place pork chops in bowl. Peel and grate the onion and place in a pitcher. Add rest of marinade ingredients and mix well, then pour over chops. Leave to marinate for 1 hour in a cool place, turning chops at least twice.

Preheat a charcoal grill or the broiler.

Cook the chops on the grill (or under a broiler), occasionally brushing them with the reserved marinade. Serve with mixed salad, dressed with vinaigrette flavored with fresh dill or other herb of choice.

Chinese spareribs

Overall timing 45 minutes

Freezing Not suitable

To serve 4

1½lb	Pork country style spareribs
2 tbsp	Oil
1 tbsp	Hoisin sauce
1 tbsp	Soy sauce
Sauce	
½ inch	Piece of ginger root
1	Green pepper
2	Garlic cloves
2 tbsp	Oil
1 tbsp	Soy sauce
2 tbsp	Dry sherry
2 tbsp	Tomato paste
2 tbsp	Vinegar
2 tbsp	Sugar
1 tbsp	Cornstarch
¼ cup	Pineapple juice
3 tbsp	Water

Separate the pork into ribs. Cook in boiling water for 15 minutes, then drain and dry on paper towels.

Heat oil in skillet. Add ribs and stir in hoisin and soy sauces. Cook gently for 20 minutes.

Meanwhile, prepare sauce. Shred ginger. Seed pepper and cut into thin strips. Peel and crush garlic. Heat oil in a saucepan, add garlic, ginger and pepper and stir-fry for 2 minutes. Remove from heat and stir in soy sauce, sherry, tomato paste, vinegar and sugar. Blend cornstarch with fruit juice and water and add to the pan. Bring to a boil and cook for 2 minutes, stirring constantly.

Place ribs in a warmed serving dish. Pour sauce over and serve immediately with boiled rice.

Orange pork rolls

Overall timing 1 hour

Freezing Not suitable

To serve 6

6x4oz	Slices of lean pork
1	Onion
6 tbsp	Butter
2 cups	Soft bread crumbs
2 tbsp	Chopped parsley
1 tsp	Dried mixed herbs
	Salt and pepper
1	Large orange
1	Egg
2 tbsp	Flour
½ cup	Hard cider
½ cup	Chicken broth

Preheat the oven to 375°.

Place slices of pork between damp wax paper and beat till very thin. Peel and finely chop onion. Melt 2 tbsp of the butter in a skillet and fry onion till golden. Add bread crumbs, parsley, herbs and seasoning. Cook for 2 minutes, then remove from the heat.

Grate orange rind into stuffing, add egg and mix well. Divide stuffing between pork slices. Roll them up carefully, turning sides in to cover stuffing, and secure with wooden toothpicks.

Arrange rolls in roasting pan and dot with remaining butter. Squeeze orange and pour juice over. Cook in the oven for about 35 minutes, basting occasionally, till pork is tender.

Place pork rolls on a warmed serving dish and keep hot. Sprinkle flour into roasting pan and stir over heat for 1 minute. Gradually add cider and broth and bring to a boil, stirring. Season to taste, pour into a sauceboat and serve with the pork rolls.

Sweet and sour pork

Overall timing 40 minutes plus marination

Freezing Suitable

To serve 4

1 lb	Lean boneless pork
2 tbsp	Dry sherry
	Salt and pepper
1	Egg
3 tbsp	Flour
3 tbsp	Oil
2	Carrots
2	Onions
1	Large cucumber
1	Garlic clove
¼ cup	Tomato ketchup
2 tsp	Soy sauce
2 tbsp	Vinegar
1 tbsp	Brown sugar
1 tbsp	Cornstarch
1¼ cups	Water

Cut meat into ½ inch cubes. Put into a bowl with sherry and seasoning and marinate for 30 minutes.

Lightly beat egg. Dip pork cubes in egg, then coat with flour. Heat oil in a large skillet. Fry pork for 8 minutes till golden brown on all sides. Remove from pan.

Peel and chop carrots, onions and cucumber. Peel and crush garlic. Add all to skillet and stir-fry for 5 minutes over fairly high heat. Reduce heat to moderate. Add ketchup, soy sauce, vinegar, sugar, cornstarch dissolved in water and reserved marinade to the pan. Bring to a boil and cook for 3 minutes, stirring.

Return pork to pan and cook for 3 minutes more till heated through. Serve with plain boiled rice and side dishes of tomato wedges, chunks of cucumber and a little shredded coconut for sprinkling over the finished dish.

Roast pork with turnips

Overall timing 2¼ hours

Freezing Not suitable

To serve 6

2½lb	Rolled boneless pork loin roast
1	Garlic clove
¼ cup	Butter
	Salt and pepper
2lb	Small white turnips
2 tsp	Sugar
2 cups	Light broth
1 tbsp	Flour
1 tbsp	Chopped parsley

Preheat the oven to 425°.

Peel the garlic clove, cut in half and rub all over the pork. Place the pork in a roasting pan and spread the butter over. Sprinkle with salt and pepper and roast for 20 minutes. Reduce the temperature to 375° and cook for a further 40 minutes.

Meanwhile, peel and halve or quarter the turnips according to size. Put into a saucepan, cover with cold salted water and bring to a boil. Drain, then dry on paper towels.

Arrange the turnips around the pork. Sprinkle with the sugar and add the broth. Cover with foil and roast for 30 minutes. Remove the foil, turn the turnips over and cook for a further 15 minutes. Test pork for doneness and cook a little longer if necessary.

Place the pork on a warmed serving platter and carve into thick slices. Arrange the turnips on the dish and keep hot.

Pour off liquid from pan and reserve. Sprinkle the flour into the pan and cook, stirring, for 1 minute. Gradually add the reserved liquid and bring to a boil, stirring constantly. Adjust seasoning. Sprinkle the parsley over the turnips and serve.

Polish-style pork with sauerkraut

Overall timing 1 hour

Freezing Not suitable

To serve 6

3 tbsp	Oil
6	Pork loin chops
1	Large onion
1	Garlic clove
	Salt and pepper
2lb	Sauerkraut
1	Bay leaf
1 cup	Chicken broth
1	Large apple
1 tsp	Cumin seeds

Heat the oil in a flameproof casserole and fry the chops till browned on both sides. Remove from the pan and reserve.

Peel and finely chop the onion; peel and crush the garlic. Add both to the casserole and fry till transparent. Season, and add the drained sauerkraut and bay leaf. Arrange the chops on top. Pour the broth over, bring to a boil and simmer for 15 minutes.

Meanwhile, peel, core and dice the apple. Add to the pan with cumin seeds and stir well, then simmer for a further 15 minutes till the chops are tender.

Taste and adjust the seasoning. Discard the bay leaf. Serve with creamed potatoes, buttered carrots and thin slices of wholewheat bread.

Pork and sausage stew

Overall timing 1¾ hours

Freezing Not suitable

To serve 6

1½lb	Onions
¼ cup	Lard
6	Thin cut pork loin chops
1lb	Coarse pork sausage links
2 tbsp	Flour
2 cups	Chicken broth
3 tbsp	Tomato paste
	Salt and pepper

Peel and thinly slice the onions. Heat the lard in a flameproof casserole, add the onions and fry gently for 10 minutes till pale golden.

Meanwhile, wipe the chops and remove the bones and any excess fat. Twist the sausages in half.

Sprinkle flour over the onions and cook for 1 minute. Gradually add the broth and bring to a boil, stirring. Stir in the tomato paste.

Add the chops and sausages. Bring to a boil, cover and simmer for 1¼ hours, or cook in the oven preheated to 350°, for 1¼ hours.

Adjust the seasoning to taste, then serve immediately with buttered pasta and a green salad.

Kidney-stuffed roast pork

Overall timing 3½ hours

Freezing Not suitable

To serve 6-8

1	Veal kidney
4lb	Boned loin of pork
	Sprig of thyme
	Salt and pepper
¾ cup	Butter
1½lb	Cooked potatoes
3 tbsp	Oil
1lb	Button mushrooms
1 tbsp	Chopped parsley

Preheat the oven to 375°.

Prepare kidney. Spread out the pork loin and put kidney in the center with thyme and seasoning. Roll meat tightly around kidney and tie at regular intervals with string. Place meat in roasting pan with ¼ cup of the butter. Roast for 3 hours, basting occasionally.

Meanwhile, slice cooked potatoes. Melt ¼ cup of the butter with the oil in a skillet, add the potatoes and fry until golden.

Halve mushrooms. Melt remaining butter in another skillet and cook the mushrooms for 5 minutes, shaking the pan from time to time.

Place meat on warmed serving platter. Surround with drained potatoes and mushrooms and garnish with chopped parsley. Serve with gravy made from roasting juices.

Pork brochettes

Overall timing 30 minutes

Freezing Not suitable

To serve 4

1 lb	Lean boneless pork
¼ lb	Thick bacon slices
2	Pork kidneys
12	Bay leaves
	Oil
	Salt and pepper

Cut pork into 1 inch cubes. Cut bacon into strips. Wash and dry kidneys. Cut them open, remove the fat and cut each into four.

Preheat charcoal grill or broiler.

Arrange bay leaves, pork cubes, bacon and kidney pieces on skewers. Brush with a little oil and season liberally.

Grill or broil for about 20 minutes, turning skewers occasionally. Serve with boiled rice and peas or a mixed salad with vinaigrette dressing.

Russian pork chop casserole

Overall timing 30 minutes

Freezing Not suitable

To serve 4

1 lb	Potatoes
2 tbsp	Oil
4	Pork rib chops
	Salt and pepper
3 tbsp	Water
¼ lb	Button mushrooms
1 tsp	Garlic salt
½ cup	Sour cream
2 tbsp	Chopped parsley

Peel potatoes and cut them into very small, thin pieces. Melt the oil in a flameproof casserole and fry the potatoes for 5 minutes. Remove from pan with slotted spoon.

Season chops with salt and pepper. Add to casserole and cook for 1 minute on each side.

Drain off excess fat. Add water, cover and cook for 10 minutes.

Slice mushrooms. Add to casserole with fried potatoes and garlic salt and cook for a further 10 minutes. Stir in sour cream and 1 tbsp of the chopped parsley. Heat through. Sprinkle with remaining parsley just before serving.

Scandinavian pork

Overall timing 2½ hours plus soaking

Freezing Not suitable

To serve 6-8

½lb	Plump prunes
1	Large tart apple
2 tbsp	Lemon juice
3lb	Boneless pork blade
	Boston roast
	Salt and pepper
1 tbsp	Oil
1 cup	Broth
1 tbsp	Flour
	Sprig of parsley

Soak prunes in 1 cup hot water for 1 hour.

Preheat oven to 375°.

Drain prunes, reserving soaking water, and remove pits. Peel, core and slice apple. Toss in lemon juice to prevent browning and add to prunes.

Season pork. Place apple and prunes along the center, then roll up lengthwise and tie into a neat shape with fine string. Place in a roasting pan and rub oil into skin. Sprinkle with salt and roast for 45 minutes.

Pour prune soaking water and broth over pork. Reduce the temperature to 350° and roast for a further 1¼ hours.

Place meat on a warmed serving dish discard the string and keep hot. Drain pan juices into a small saucepan and skim off any fat. Blend flour to a smooth paste with ¼ cup cold water. Add to meat juices and bring to a boil, stirring constantly. Simmer for 4-5 minutes. Carve pork into thick slices and garnish with sprigs of parsley. Serve with gravy.

Pork with bananas and peanuts

Overall timing 1¾ hours

Freezing Not suitable

To serve 4

¾lb	Onions
2	Garlic cloves
¼ cup	Oil
2lb	Boneless pork
½ cup	Rice
16oz	Can of tomatoes
1	Chicken bouillon cube
¼ tsp	Paprika
¼ tsp	Ground cinnamon
½lb	Potatoes
2	Bananas
½ cup	Salted peanuts
	Salt

Peel and chop onions. Peel and crush garlic. Heat 2 tbsp of the oil in saucepan.

Add onions and garlic and fry until browned.

Cut pork into cubes and add to pan with rice. Cook till rice has absorbed oil, stirring frequently to prevent sticking. Add a little water if necessary to prevent burning. Remove from heat.

Pour juice from canned tomatoes into measuring cup.

Crumble in bouillon cube and add enough boiling water to give 2 cups. Chop tomatoes and add to pan with bouillon mixture, paprika and cinnamon. Cover and simmer gently for 20 minutes.

Meanwhile, peel and cube potatoes. Heat remaining oil in a skillet and fry potatoes over a low heat for about 10 minutes. Add them to the pan. Peel and slice bananas and stir into the stew with the peanuts. Cook for 10 minutes. Taste and add salt if necessary.

Beef pot roast

Overall timing 3 hours plus marination

Freezing Suitable: reheat in sauce in 400° oven for 1 hour

To serve 8-10

4lb	Beef pot roast
	Salt and pepper
6oz	Pork fat with rind
1	Large onion
3	Carrots
3	Stalks of celery
1	Garlic clove
	Sprigs of parsley
2	Bay leaves
	Sprigs of thyme
1 cup	Red or white wine
2 tbsp	Butter
2 tbsp	Oil
1	Pig's foot
½ cup	Water
1 tbsp	Tomato paste

Season the beef. Slice the pork fat. Wrap the fat around the beef and secure with string.

Peel and chop the onion and carrots. Trim and chop the celery. Peel and crush the garlic. Tie the parsley, bay leaves and thyme together with string (or use a bouquet garni).

Put the beef in a bowl and add the prepared vegetables, herbs, wine and seasoning. Marinate overnight.

The next day, drain the beef, reserving the marinade. Pat the beef dry with paper towels.

Melt the butter with the oil in a flameproof casserole and brown the beef on all sides.

Split the pig's foot and add to the casserole with the marinade, water and tomato paste.

Bring to a boil, then cover and simmer for 2½ hours.

Transfer the beef to a warmed serving platter and keep hot. Strain the cooking liquid discarding the foot and vegetables, and return to the casserole. Boil the liquid till reduced, then pour into sauceboat. Serve beef with sauce, and carrots and button onions.

Corned beef

Overall timing 3½ hours plus 2 weeks salting

Freezing Not suitable

To serve 8-10

2lb	Coarse salt
½ cup	Sugar
1 tbsp	Saltpeter
1oz	Pickling spice
4	Bay leaves
1	Sprig of thyme
5lb	Brisket of beef
3	Large onions
5	Cloves
1	Stalk of celery
1 tsp	Black peppercorns
1lb	Medium-size carrots
2	Medium-size white turnips
1lb	Leeks

Put salt, sugar and saltpeter into a large saucepan with pickling spices tied in cheesecloth. Add bay leaves, thyme and 4½ quarts water and heat gently, stirring, till sugar and salt have dissolved. Bring to a boil, then pour into bowl and cool.

Add meat to bowl, making sure that salt solution covers it. Cover with clean dish-towel and leave to soak in cold place for up to 2 weeks. Turn meat occasionally.

To cook, remove from brine and wash under cold running water. Put into a large saucepan with one onion, peeled and spiked with cloves. Chop celery and add to pan with peppercorns. Cover with cold water and bring to a boil slowly. Skim, reduce heat, cover and simmer for 2½ hours.

Meanwhile, peel and chop carrots and turnips. Peel remaining onions and slice thickly. Chop leeks. Add vegetables to pan, bring back to a boil and simmer for 30 minutes. Use strained cooking liquid to make a sauce.

Beef and bean casserole

Overall timing 3 hours plus soaking

Freezing Suitable: reheat from frozen in 325° oven.

To serve 4-6

1 cup	Dried navy beans
2	Onions
2 tbsp	Oil
1 lb	Beef for stew
¼ tsp	Chili powder
1 tsp	Curry powder
2 tbsp	Flour
1 cup	Beef broth
16 oz	Can of tomatoes
2 tbsp	Tomato paste
2 tsp	Sugar
	Salt and pepper
1	Large tart apple
⅓ cup	Golden raisins

Put beans in a large saucepan and cover with cold water. Bring to a boil. Boil for 2 minutes, them remove from the heat, cover and leave to soak for 2 hours.

Preheat the oven to 325°.

Peel and chop onions. Heat oil in a flameproof casserole and fry onions for 3 minutes. Cut beef into chunks. Add to pan and fry quickly till brown. Stir in the chili and curry powder and flour. Fry for 2 minutes.

Gradually add broth and bring to a boil, stirring. Add the tomatoes with their juice and tomato paste. Drain beans and add to casserole with the sugar and seasoning. Cover and cook in the oven for 2 hours.

Peel, core and chop apple. Stir into casserole with raisins and cook for a further 30 minutes. Taste and adjust seasoning. Serve with crusty bread.

Beef and split pea stew

Overall timing 2 hours plus soaking

Freezing Not suitable

To serve 6

1½ cups	Split peas
1	Onion
1½ lb	Beef for stew
2 tbsp	Butter
2 tbsp	Oil
2	Large carrots
	Bouquet garni
¼ tsp	Grated nutmeg
3½ cups	Beef broth
	Salt and pepper
½ lb	Potatoes
½ lb	Fresh bulk spinach

Wash and pick over the split peas and put into a saucepan of cold water. Bring to a boil and boil for 2 minutes. Remove from the heat, cover and leave to soak for 2 hours.

Peel and chop the onion. Cut the meat into bite-sized pieces. Heat the butter and oil in a flameproof casserole and fry the onion and meat till lightly browned.

Drain the split peas and add to the meat.

Scrape the carrots, slice thinly and add to the pan with the bouquet garni, grated nutmeg and broth. Add seasoning and bring to a boil. Reduce the heat, cover and simmer for 1 hour.

Peel and dice the potatoes. Chop the spinach and add both to the meat. Cook for a further 30 minutes. Taste and adjust the seasoning. Serve with creamed potatoes and a green vegetable, or boiled rice, or with crusty bread for a lighter meal.

Beef and vegetable stew

Overall timing 2 hours

Freezing Suitable: simmer for
30 minutes only; add vegetables after
reheating in 350° oven for 45 minutes.

To serve 6-8

2lb	Beef for stew
	Salt and pepper
¼ cup	Flour
1lb	Onions
3 tbsp	Oil
3 cups	Beef broth
2 tbsp	Tomato paste
	Bay leaf
1lb	Carrots
1lb	Potatoes
1lb	Parsnips
½lb (2 cups)	Frozen peas

Wipe and trim the meat and cut into 1½ inch cubes. Season the flour and toss pieces of meat in it till evenly coated. Peel and slice the onions.

Heat the oil in a heavy-based saucepan and fry the onions till transparent. Add the meat and fry till browned all over, then add any remaining flour. Gradually add the broth and bring to a boil, stirring constantly. Add the tomato paste, bay leaf and seasoning, cover and simmer for 1 hour.

Scrape the carrots and peel the potatoes and parsnips. Cut all into chunks and add to the meat. Cover and simmer for a further 30 minutes. Taste and adjust seasoning.

Stir in the peas and simmer for 10 minutes, then serve.

Beef carbonnade

Overall timing 2-2½ hours

Freezing Suitable

To serve 4

2¼lb	Beef for stew
6 tbsp	Butter
½lb	Onions
1 tbsp	Flour
1 tbsp	Brown sugar
1 tbsp	Wine vinegar
2¼ cups	Dark beer
	Salt and pepper
1	Bouquet garni

Trim off any fat, then cut meat into large thin slices. Melt ¼ cup of the butter in a flameproof casserole. Add the meat and brown over a high heat. Remove beef from pan and put aside.

Peel and finely chop onions. Add onions to pan with remaining butter. Reduce heat, cover and cook for 10 minutes without burning.

Sprinkle flour into pan with the brown sugar and stir with a wooden spoon. Add vinegar, then the beer and stir till thick.

Replace beef in pan, season with salt and pepper and add bouquet garni. Cover and simmer for about 1½-2 hours over a low heat or cook in the oven at 350°. Discard bouquet garni before serving with mashed potatoes and chicory salad.

Boeuf en croûte

Overall timing 1 ½ hours plus cooling and chilling

Freezing Not suitable

To serve 6

1 lb	Frozen puff pastry
3 lb	Fillet of beef
1	Garlic clove
2 tbsp	Softened butter
	Salt and pepper
1 tsp	Dried thyme
½ cup	Smooth liver pâté
1	Egg

Thaw pastry. Preheat the oven to 425°.

Trim meat of all fat, then tie into a neat shape with fine string. Make tiny slits in meat with tip of a sharp knife and insert slivers of peeled garlic. Spread butter over beef, season and sprinkle with half the thyme. Place in roasting pan and roast for 10 minutes. Take meat out of pan, place on a wire rack and leave to cool completely.

Remove string from meat. Roll out dough to a large rectangle just over twice the size of the meat. Place meat on one half of dough rectangle and brush dough edges with water.

Spread pâté over top of meat and sprinkle with remaining thyme. Fold dough over to enclose meat and seal edges. Trim around three sides and, if liked, make a hole in the top. Make a funnel from foil and place in hole if liked.

Place on dampened baking sheet.

Cut decorative shapes out of dough trimmings, dip them into beaten egg and arrange on dough. Glaze all over with egg and chill for 1 hour.

Preheat oven to 425°. Bake for 35 minutes till pastry is well risen and golden. Place on a warmed serving platter, garnish with watercress and serve, cut into thick slices.

Chile con carne

Overall timing 3¼ hours plus
overnight soaking

Freezing Suitable

To serve 4-6

1 cup	Dried brown or
	red beans
1 quart	Water
2lb	Beef for stew
1	Onion
1 tbsp	Pork drippings or
	olive oil
2 tbsp	Butter
	Salt and pepper
1 tsp	Chili powder
1 tbsp	Sweet paprika
8oz	Canned tomatoes
2 tsp	Cornstarch
	(optional)

Soak beans in water overnight. The next day,
place water and beans in saucepan, cover and
cook gently for 1½ hours.

Cut the beef into 1 inch cubes.

Peel and chop onion. Heat the drippings or
oil and butter in a skillet. Add the beef. Cook
till brown, then add the onion and cook till
transparent.

Mix the meat and onion in with the cooked
beans and season with salt, pepper, chili
powder and paprika. Cover and cook gently
for 1 hour.

Add the drained tomatoes, cover and cook
for 30 minutes more. Adjust seasoning. If you
wish to thicken the sauce, blend the
cornstarch with a little water and add it to the
mixture.

Cook for a few minutes, then serve from
the cooking pot with plain boiled rice or
wholewheat bread and a crisp green salad.

Corned beef hash

Overall timing 1 hour

Freezing Not suitable

To serve 4

2	Medium-size onions
6 tbsp	Oil or
	drippings
1	Stalk of celery
1	Large carrot
1 lb	Corned beef
	Salt and pepper
½ tsp	Powdered mustard
1 lb	Potatoes
2½ cups	Beef broth

Peel and thinly slice onions. Heat oil or drippings in saucepan. Add the onions and cook gently till transparent.

Finely chop celery. Peel and grate or dice carrot. Cut corned beef into 1 inch cubes. Add all of these to onions and cook for a few minutes, then season with salt, pepper and mustard (add more if a stronger taste is preferred). Cook gently for 5 minutes.

Meanwhile, peel potatoes and cut into chunks. Add to pan with boiling broth and cook for 20 minutes. Serve in warm bowls topped with fried or poached eggs, and with lots of fresh bread to mop up the juices.

Corned beef patties

Overall timing 30 minutes

Freezing Suitable: Cook from frozen

To serve 4

1 cup	Soft bread crumbs
3 tbsp	Warm milk
1 lb	Corned beef
2	Eggs
2 tbsp	Grated Parmesan
	cheese
	Grated rind of ½
	lemon
	Flour
¼ cup	Butter
1 tbsp	Oil
	Lemon wedges
	Sprigs of parsley

Soak ¼ cup bread crumbs in the milk. Cut off any excess fat from the edge of the corned beef and discard. Mash beef in a bowl with a fork, then add squeezed-out bread crumbs, 1 egg, the cheese and lemon rind. Mix well.

With well floured hands, make patties from the mixture, then coat with flour. Lightly beat remaining egg. Using two forks, dip the patties first into beaten egg, then into remaining bread crumbs.

Heat butter and oil in a large skillet.

Add the patties and cook over a moderate heat till brown on both sides. Remove from pan and drain on paper towels. Garnish with lemon wedges and parsley.

Steamed steak and kidney pudding

Overall timing 5¾ hours

Freezing Suitable: steam from frozen for 2½-3 hours

To serve 6

1½lb	Chuck steak
½lb	Beef kidney
1	Large onion
	Salt and pepper
3 tbsp	Flour
3 cups	Self-rising flour
¾ cup	Shredded suet
1¼ cups	Cold beef broth

Cut the meat into 1½ inch cubes. Trim the kidney, removing any core, and cut into 1 inch cubes. Peel and thinly slice the onion. Season flour and use to coat the steak, kidney and onion.

Sift the self-rising flour and 1½ tsp salt into a bowl and stir in the suet and enough cold water to mix to a soft but not sticky dough. Knead lightly till smooth.

Roll out on a floured surface to a round, big enough to line a 2 quart pudding basin or steaming mold (about 14 inches in diameter).

Cut out one-quarter of the dough round and reserve. Lift the large piece and place it in the basin, curving it so it fits neatly, and sealing the edges together. Place the meat mixture in the basin and add the cold broth to come half-way up the meat.

Roll out the reserved dough to a round slightly larger than the top of the basin. Brush the top edge of the dough lining with water and cover with the dough lid. Seal the edges well.

Cover with greased, pleated parchment paper and pleated foil, or a pudding cloth and secure with string. Steam for 5 hours, replenishing with boiling water as required.

Texan stew

Overall timing 2¼ hours

Freezing Suitable

To serve 4

1½ lb	Chuck steak
2 tbsp	Butter
1 tbsp	Oil
2½ cups	Beef broth
2	Green peppers
4	Tomatoes
11½ oz	Can of whole kernel corn
10 oz	Can of peas and carrots
	Salt and pepper
2 tsp	Cornstarch

Chop meat into 1 inch cubes. Heat butter and oil in saucepan, add meat and cook for 10 minutes till brown all over. Pour in broth and cook, covered, for 1½ hours over a gentle heat.

Wash, seed and cut green peppers into strips. Blanch, peel and chop tomatoes. Drain corn and peas and carrots. Add vegetables to meat and season well with salt and pepper.

Cook, covered, for 15 minutes over a moderate heat.

Blend cornstarch with a little water in a cup.

Stir into saucepan, then bring to a boil again, stirring until thickened. Serve stew in warmed bowls.

Beef and horseradish loaf

Overall timing 1 hour

Freezing Suitable: Reheat in 375° oven for 30 minutes.

To serve 4

½ cup	Strong beef broth
2 cups	Soft bread crumbs
1 lb	Ground beef
1	Large onion
1 tbsp	Grated horseradish
3	Eggs
2 tbsp	Cream sherry
	Salt and pepper

Preheat the oven to 350°.

Put the broth in a saucepan and bring to a boil. Sprinkle in the bread crumbs and stir till the crumbs have absorbed all the broth.

Put ground beef into a bowl with the bread crumb mixture. Peel and finely chop onion and add to meat with the grated horseradish, eggs, sherry and seasoning. Mix well with a wooden spoon until all ingredients are well blended.

Grease ovenproof dish and press in the mixture. Smooth the top and bake for 45 minutes. Serve hot with boiled potatoes and buttered carrots.

Beef with onions

Overall timing 1 1/2 hours

Freezing Suitable

To serve 4

1 1/2 lb	Chuck steak
3/4 lb	Onions
2 tbsp	Butter
1 tbsp	Oil
1 tbsp	Flour
1 1/4 cups	Beef broth
1	Garlic clove
1/2 tsp	Ground cumin
	Pinch of dried marjoram
2 tbsp	Wine vinegar
	Salt and pepper

Cut meat across the grain into thin finger-length strips. Peel onions, slice crosswise and separate rings. Heat the butter and oil in skillet. Add the onion rings and cook, covered, over a low heat till transparent. Turn them over frequently so that they cook evenly but do not brown. Remove from pan.

Increase heat, put strips of meat into pan and brown them. Return onion rings. Sprinkle with flour and stir. When flour begins to color, stir in broth, peeled and crushed garlic, cumin, marjoram, wine vinegar and seasoning. Cover and simmer for 1 hour. Serve with potatoes or rice and a crisp mixed salad.

Goulash

Overall timing 2¼ hours

Freezing Suitable

To serve 6

2lb	Beef for stew
¼ cup	Pork drippings
½lb	Onions
2	Garlic cloves
1 tbsp	Flour
1	Beef bouillon cube
2½ cups	Boiling water
	Salt and pepper
½ tsp	Dried marjoram
½ tsp	Caraway seeds
	Brown sugar
½ tsp	Paprika
½lb	Potatoes
2	Green peppers
5	Tomatoes
½ cup	Red wine
½ cup	Sour cream
	(optional)

Cube beef. Heat drippings in a large kettle.

Add beef and fry till meat is brown on all sides. Peel and chop onions and garlic. Add to meat and cook till transparent.

Sprinkle in flour and stir into mixture.

Mix bouillon cube into boiling water and pour over meat. Season with salt, pepper, marjoram, caraway seeds, a pinch of sugar and paprika. Cover tightly and cook gently for 1¼ hours.

Peel and roughly chop the potatoes. Seed and slice peppers. Blanch, peel and chop tomatoes. Add all to pan, cover and cook for a further 25 minutes.

Add wine and check seasoning. Bring to simmering point and stir in sour cream, if using, or serve it separately.

Spicy meatballs

Overall timing 30 minutes

Freezing Not suitable

To serve 4-6

1	Small onion
1	Garlic clove
1½lb	Lean ground beef
1	Egg
½ cup	Soft white
	bread crumbs
	Salt and pepper
½ tsp	Ground allspice
	Oil for frying

Peel and finely chop the onion; peel and crush the garlic. Put with rest of ingredients (except for the oil) into a bowl and mix well together.

Shape mixture into walnut-sized balls.

Fry the meatballs in shallow oil for about 15 minutes, turning once. Arrange on a warmed serving plate and serve with rice or pasta, and a tomato sauce or gravy.

Beef and carrot fry-up

Overall timing 45 minutes

Freezing Suitable

To serve 4

1 lb	Carrots
2	Leeks
¼ cup	Butter
1 cup	White wine or
	beef broth
	Salt and pepper
1 lb	Ground beef
½ tsp	Worcestershire
	sauce

Scrape carrots and chop into 1 inch pieces. Trim, wash and cut leeks into ½ inch slices. Melt half the butter in a skillet or saucepan and fry chopped carrots for 3 minutes. Pour in white wine or broth, cover and cook over a low heat for 20 minutes.

Add the leeks, season with salt and pepper and cook for a further 15 minutes, or until tender.

Meanwhile, put beef in bowl and mix in salt and pepper with a fork. Roughly shape mince into 1 inch pieces. Melt remaining butter in another skillet and fry meat for about 15 minutes until lightly browned and no longer pink in the middle. Stir from time to time.

Reduce any excess liquid in vegetable pan by boiling rapidly for a minute or two. Add meat and sprinkle with Worcestershire sauce.

Serve from the pan, with creamy mashed potatoes and a green vegetable.

Hamburgers

Overall timing 20 minutes

Freezing Suitable: cook after thawing

To serve 4

1 lb	Finely ground beef
2	Onions
	Salt and pepper
3 tbsp	Oil
4	Hamburger buns
¼ cup	Butter
1 tbsp	Dijon-style mustard

Put the beef into a large bowl. Peel and finely chop one of the onions and add to the beef with plenty of seasoning. Mix. Divide into four portions and shape each into a thick burger.

Preheat a skillet or griddle and brush lightly with 1 tbsp oil. Fry the burgers for about 5 minutes, then turn carefully cook for a further 3-5 minutes.

While the hamburgers are cooking peel and slice the second onion into rings. Heat the remaining oil in another skillet and cook the onion till golden.

Meanwhile, halve and lightly toast the rolls, then spread cut sides with the butter mixed with the mustard.

Place a hamburger in each roll and top with fried onions. Serve immediately.

New Zealand roast lamb

Overall timing 3-3½ hours

Freezing Not suitable

To serve 4-6

4lb	French-style leg of lamb
2 tbsp	Oil
	Fresh rosemary or dried rosemary
	Salt and pepper
¾ cup	Water
2lb	Potatoes

Preheat oven to 350°.

Place lamb in roasting pan, then rub the oil into the skin. Either make small slits in the meat and insert fresh rosemary leaves, or sprinkle surface with dried rosemary leaves, then season well. Add water to the pan and roast for 3-3½ hours — the meat should almost be falling off the bone.

Meanwhile, peel, halve, parboil and dry the potatoes. Add them to the roasting pan 1½ hours before end of cooking time and turn them till coated in fat. Turn again once during roasting.

Beanpot with lamb

Overall timing 2 hours 50 minutes plus overnight soaking

Freezing Not suitable

To serve 4

1 cup	Dried navy beans
½ tsp	Salt
2 tbsp	Drippings
1 lb	Lamb blade chops
1	Onion
¼ cup	Tomato paste
½ tsp	Ground cumin
1	Bay leaf
½ tsp	Dried rosemary
½ tsp	Garlic salt
	Brown sugar
½ tsp	Vinegar
1 tbsp	Chopped chives

Soak beans in 1½ quarts water overnight. Next day, transfer beans and water to a saucepan and cook for 1 hour. Add salt.

Melt drippings in a flameproof casserole and brown chops well on all sides. Peel and chop onion and add to casserole. Cook till transparent. Add beans and water, tomato paste, cumin, bay leaf, rosemary and garlic salt. Cover and cook for 1 hour.

Uncover and cook for a further 20 minutes till meat is tender.

Just before serving, stir in a pinch of sugar and the vinegar and sprinkle with chopped chives.

Minted lamb meatballs

Overall timing 30 minutes

Freezing Suitable: fry after thawing

To serve 4

1¼lb	Ground lamb
4	Garlic cloves
2 tbsp	Chopped fresh mint
1	Egg
	Salt and pepper
1 tsp	Ground coriander
	Flour
2 tbsp	Oil
	Mint or coriander leaves

Place the lamb in a bowl with the peeled and finely chopped garlic, chopped mint, egg, salt, pepper and coriander and mix with a wooden spoon till well combined. Make little balls of the mixture, flouring your hands so it doesn't stick, and roll the balls in the flour to coat.

Heat oil in a skillet, add meatballs and cook over a moderate heat for 8-10 minutes on each side till well browned. Drain on paper towels, then garnish with mint or coriander leaves and serve with rice.

Lamb curry

Overall timing 1 ½ hours

Freezing Suitable

To serve 2

1 lb	Boneless lamb
1	Onion
2 tbsp	Butter
1 tbsp	Oil
1 tsp	Curry powder
	Salt and pepper
1 ½ tbsp	Flour
1 cup	Broth
½ tsp	Tomato paste
	Bouquet garni
1	Tomato
½	Green pepper
2 oz	Button mushrooms
6 oz	New potatoes

Cut meat into cubes. Peel and chop onion.

Heat butter and oil in a skillet and fry onion till transparent.

Add curry powder and cook, stirring, for 2 minutes. Add meat and cook till golden on all sides. Season with salt and pepper, sprinkle with flour and stir over a high heat for a few minutes.

Reduce heat and stir in broth and tomato paste. Add bouquet garni and bring to a boil, stirring. Cover and cook gently for 40 minutes, stirring occasionally.

Chop tomato; seed and slice pepper; halve or slice larger mushrooms. Scrub potatoes but don't peel; cut into chunks.

Add prepared vegetables to pan and cook for a further 20 minutes. Discard bouquet garni before serving with plain boiled rice.

Stuffed shoulder of lamb

Overall timing 2 hours

Freezing Not suitable

To serve 6

2	Onions
6 tbsp	Butter
¾ lb	Bulk sausage meat
2 tbsp	Chopped parsley
	Salt and pepper
2½ lb	Boneless shoulder of lamb
1 cup	Dry white wine
1 cup	Broth
	Bouquet garni
2½ lb	New potatoes
2	Tomatoes

Peel and chop onions. Melt 2 tbsp of butter in a skillet, add onions and fry until golden.

Add to the sausage meat with the parsley and seasoning.

Spread the lamb out, skin side down, on a board and season. Shape stuffing mixture into a large ball and place on lamb. Fold meat around stuffing to make a ball and tie firmly with string.

Melt 2 tbsp of butter in a flameproof casserole and brown meat all over. Add wine, broth, bouquet garni, salt and pepper. Cover and cook slowly for 1 hour.

Meanwhile, scrape potatoes. Melt remaining butter in a skillet, add potatoes and fry until golden brown. Arrange around the meat and cook uncovered for 20 minutes.

Blanch and peel tomatoes. Add to casserole and cook for 10 minutes more.

Remove bouquet garni. Place meat on warmed serving platter and remove string. Arrange potatoes and tomatoes around. Keep hot.

Transfer cooking liquid to a saucepan.

Thicken with 1 tbsp each of butter and flour mashed together. Serve this gravy separately.

Moussaka

Overall timing 2¼ hours

Freezing Suitable: bake from frozen in 375° oven for 1½ hours; add cheese sauce and bake 30 minutes more

To serve 6

1 lb	Onions
4	Garlic cloves
½ cup	Oil
1 tbsp	Chopped parsley
2 lb	Ground lamb
4	Tomatoes
2 tbsp	Tomato paste
	Salt and pepper
½ cup	Broth
1 cup	Soft bread crumbs
2 lb	Eggplants
¼ cup	Flour
2	Egg yolks
2 cups	Thick white sauce
1 cup	Grated sharp cheese

Peel and chop onions; peel and crush garlic.

Heat 1 tbsp oil in saucepan and fry onions, parsley, garlic and lamb till browned.

Peel and quarter tomatoes and add to pan with tomato paste, seasoning and broth.

Cover and simmer for 45 minutes. Remove from heat and stir in bread crumbs.

Preheat oven to 350°.

Thinly slice eggplants. Dust lightly with flour. Heat remaining oil in skillet and brown eggplants. Drain on paper towels.

Arrange two-thirds of eggplants to cover bottom and sides of greased casserole. Add meat mixture, then top with remaining eggplants. Stir beaten egg yolks into sauce with half cheese. Pour sauce over eggplants. Cover with rest of grated cheese.

Put casserole in a roasting pan containing a little water. Bake for 1 hour.

Lamb kabobs with prunes

Overall timing 50 minutes

Freezing Not suitable

To serve 4

12	Prunes
¾ cup	Red wine
1 lb	Boneless lamb cut from the leg
3 tbsp	Oil
	Salt and pepper
½ tsp	Dried thyme
2	Firm tomatoes
1	Medium-size onion
3	Thick slices of bacon

Put the prunes into a saucepan, add the red wine and bring to a boil. Remove from the heat and leave to soak for 30 minutes.

Cut lamb into 12 large cubes. Place in bowl with oil, seasoning and thyme. Cover and leave for 30 minutes.

Meanwhile, quarter the tomatoes. Peel the onion and cut through the root into eight wedges. Cut each bacon slice into four. Preheat a charcoal grill or the broiler.

Drain the prunes, reserving the wine. Make a slit in each prune and remove the pit.

Thread the lamb, prunes, tomatoes, bacon and onion onto four skewers. Brush the kabobs with the lamb marinade and the wine from the prunes, then sprinkle with salt and pepper.

Cook for about 15 minutes, turning occasionally, till the lamb is tender. Arrange on a warmed serving dish and serve with boiled rice.

Braised lamb with green beans

Overall timing 1¾ hours

Freezing Suitable: cook for only 1 hour; reheat from frozen in 400° oven for 1½ hours.

To serve 4

1½lb	Green beans
2 tbsp	Oil
2lb	Lamb arm chops
2	Large onions
16oz	Can of tomatoes
	Salt and pepper
¼ tsp	Allspice
¼ tsp	Grated nutmeg
2	Sweet red peppers

Preheat oven to 350°.

Wash, trim beans and, if necessary, remove strings. Cut into 2 inch lengths.

Spread over the bottom of large ovenproof dish.

Heat oil in a large skillet. Trim lamb, removing excess fat. Fry in oil until brown on all sides. Drain and arrange on top of beans in casserole.

Peel onions and cut into wedges. Fry in oil until golden. With a spoon, break up tomatoes in their juice. Add to onions with salt, pepper, allspice and nutmeg, stir well and cook for 5 minutes.

Seed and slice peppers and add to casserole with tomato mixture. Cover tightly and cook in oven for 1½ hours. Serve with boiled rice.

Navarin

Overall timing 1¾ hours

Freezing Not suitable

To serve 6

¼ cup	Butter
2½lb	Lamb neck slices
4	Small onions
1 tbsp	Flour
2 cups	Broth
3 tbsp	Tomato paste
	Bouquet garni
	Salt and pepper
1lb	Carrots
1lb	White turnips
1lb	Potatoes
2 cups	Frozen peas
1 tbsp	Chopped parsley

Melt butter in flameproof casserole, add lamb and brown on all sides. Peel and quarter the onions. Add to casserole and fry gently for 5 minutes.

Sprinkle flour over and cook, stirring, for 2 minutes. Gradually stir in the broth, then add tomato paste, bouquet garni and seasoning and bring to a boil. Cover and simmer gently for 45 minutes.

Scrape and chop carrots. Peel turnips and cut into cubes. Add to casserole and cook for 15 minutes.

Meanwhile, peel potatoes and cut into chunks. Add to casserole and cook, covered, for 20 minutes. Add peas and cook for a further 10 minutes. Remove bouquet garni and adjust seasoning. Garnish with parsley and serve hot.

Dolma kara

Overall timing 1¾ hours

Freezing Not suitable

To serve 6

2 tbsp	Oil
2	Onions
1 lb	Boneless lamb
½ cup	Canned chickpeas
1¼ cups	Broth
	Salt and pepper
2 tbsp	Tomato paste
½ lb	Ground cooked lamb
⅓ cup	Cooked rice
1	Egg
1 tsp	Lemon juice
2 tbsp	Chopped parsley
	Ground cinnamon
1 lb	Zucchini

Heat oil in a saucepan. Peel and chop one of the onions and fry till tender. Cut the raw lamb into small pieces and add to the pan. Cook for 5-10 minutes.

Add the drained chickpeas, broth, salt, pepper and tomato paste. Cover and simmer for 30 minutes.

Preheat the oven to 375°.

Mix the cooked lamb with the cooked rice, remaining onion, peeled and finely chopped, egg, lemon juice, half the parsley, seasoning and a pinch of cinnamon.

Trim zucchini, then cut them in half lengthwise. Scoop out the seeds with a teaspoon. Blanch zucchini in boiling salted water for 5 minutes. Drain, then stuff the zucchini with the rice and lamb mixture.

Put the lamb and chickpea stew in an ovenproof dish and place stuffed zucchini on top. Cover with foil and bake for 40 minutes.

Serve hot sprinkled with remaining parsley.

Lamb with lima beans and potatoes

Overall timing 1½ hours

Freezing Not suitable

To serve 6

4	Tomatoes
¼lb	Bacon slices
2	Onions
2	Garlic cloves
2 tbsp	Oil
6	Lamb blade chops
1¼ cups	Broth
1 tbsp	Lemon juice
½ tsp	Dried thyme
	Salt and pepper
1½lb	Shelled fresh lima beans
1½lb	Potatoes

Blanch, peel and chop tomatoes. Chop bacon. Peel and slice onions. Peel and crush garlic. Heat oil in a flameproof casserole and fry onion and garlic till transparent. Add the chops and bacon and brown on all sides. Pour off excess fat from pan.

Add tomatoes, broth, lemon juice, thyme and seasoning. Cover and simmer for 30 minutes.

Blanch beans in boiling water for 5 minutes, then drain. Peel and slice the potatoes. Add potatoes to casserole and cook for 10 minutes. Add beans and cook for a further 15 minutes. Serve immediately.

Sweet sour lamb riblets

Overall timing 1¼ hours plus overnight marination

Freezing Not suitable

To serve 4

1	Onion
2	Garlic cloves
2 tbsp	Honey
1 tbsp	Oil
¼ cup	Soy sauce
½ cup	Dry sherry
1 tsp	Ground ginger
¼ cup	Sugar
1 tsp	Ground allspice
2½lb	Breast of lamb riblets

Peel and slice onion. Peel and crush garlic. Put into a bowl with honey, oil, soy sauce, sherry, ginger, sugar and allspice. Add the breast riblets, cover and marinate overnight in the refrigerator, turning occasionally.

The next day, preheat the oven to 375°.

Put the meat into a roasting pan and spoon the marinade over. Bake for 1 hour, basting frequently with the marinade. Serve with plain boiled rice.

Shepherd's pie

Overall timing 1 hour

Freezing Not suitable

To serve 4

2lb	Potatoes
	Salt and pepper
1	Large onion
3 tbsp	Oil
1	Garlic clove
1 lb	Ground cooked lamb
¼ cup	Butter
½ cup	Milk
¾ cup	Grated cheese

Peel and halve potatoes. Cook in boiling salted water for 25-30 minutes.

Peel and finely chop onion. Heat oil in a skillet, add onion and cook for about 10 minutes. Peel and crush garlic. Add garlic and meat to pan and cook for about 5 minutes, stirring.

Preheat the oven to 425°.

Drain potatoes and mash with half the butter and the milk. Season to taste. Cover bottom of overproof dish with half of the mashed potato, cover with the meat, then spread or pipe the remaining potato on top.

Sprinkle cheese over potato, dot with remaining butter and bake for about 15 minutes till the top is browned. Serve with green salad.

Greek lamb stew with spinach

Overall timing 1 ½ hours

Freezing Not suitable

To serve 6

2lb	Boneless shoulder of lamb
1	Large onion
2 tbsp	Oil
2 tbsp	Butter
1lb	Ripe tomatoes
2 tbsp	Tomato paste
	Dried oregano
	Salt and pepper
2½ cups	Hot water or broth
1¼lb	Fresh bulk spinach

Cut the lamb into bite-size pieces. Peel and thinly slice the onion. Heat the oil and butter in a flameproof casserole, add the lamb and onion and fry over a moderate heat for about 10 minutes till browned, stirring occasionally.

Blanch, peel and chop the tomatoes. Add to the pan with the tomato paste, a pinch of oregano, seasoning and water or broth. Mix well and bring to a boil. Cover and simmer for 1½ hours till the lamb is tender.

Wash spinach and shred finely. Add to the pan, stir, cover and cook for a further 10 minutes. Taste and adjust the seasoning. Pour into a warmed dish and serve.

Lamb with potatoes and onions

Overall timing 2½ hours

Freezing Not suitable

To serve 8

4½lb	Leg of lamb, french-style
½ cup	Butter
	Salt and pepper
1lb	Onions
2lb	Potatoes
2 cups	Broth
	Sprigs of rosemary
	Bouquet garni

Preheat the oven to 350°.

Place the meat in roasting pan, spread with half the butter and season. Roast for 1¼ hours.

Peel and slice the onions. Peel and quarter potatoes. Melt remaining butter in skillet, add onions and potatoes and fry till golden brown. Add broth, rosemary, bouquet garni and seasoning and cook for 5 minutes, stirring occasionally.

Arrange potato mixture around meat and roast for a further 45 minutes till meat is tender.

Remove bouquet garni. Place lamb on warmed serving dish and surround with potato mixture. Serve with green vegetables.

Stuffed breast of lamb

Overall timing 2½ hours

Freezing Not suitable

To serve 8

Stuffing	
3	Lamb kidneys
½lb	Slab bacon
½lb	Bulk sausage meat
½ tsp	ground allspice
3 tbsp	Chopped parsley
1 tsp	Dried marjoram
1	Egg
	Salt and pepper
1 or 2	Boneless breasts of lamb
2lb	Potatoes
1½lb	Small carrots
4	White turnips
2	Stalks of celery
4	Leeks
1	Onion
4	Cloves
¼ cup	Butter
2½ cups	Broth
	Bouquet garni

Preheat the oven to 325°.

Prepare and finely chop kidneys. chop bacon. Mix all stuffing ingredients.

Cut a deep pocket in lamb and fill with stuffing. Sew up opening. If using two breasts, place together with skin side out and sew around sides.

Peel potatoes and carrots. Peel and halve turnips. Chop celery and leeks. Peel onion and spike with cloves. Melt butter in flameproof casserole, add meat and brown all over. Remove. Add vegetables and fry for 2 minutes. Return meat and add broth, bouquet garni and salt. Cover and cook in oven for 2 hours.

Slice meat. Arrange vegetables around meat, discarding onion. Boil broth till reduced by half. Strain over vegetables.

Lamb chops with garlic and anchovy

Overall timing 40 minutes

Freezing Not suitable

To serve 4

2lb	Lamb rib chops
2	Garlic cloves
5 tbsp	Oil
	Salt and pepper
	Sprigs of rosemary
2	Anchovy fillets
3 tbsp	White wine vinegar

Trim chops of all fat. Peel and crush one garlic clove. Heat the oil in a large skillet. Add the garlic and chops. Fry quickly on both sides till golden, then season, reduce heat and cook for a further 10-15 minutes.

Put a few pieces of fresh rosemary, the remaining garlic clove, peeled, and the anchovies in a mortar. Pound with a pestle, gradually mixing in the vinegar. Add garlic mixture to pan and cook till the liquid reduces by half.

Arrange chops on warmed serving dish and spoon cooking juices over. Garnish with remaining rosemary sprigs.

Paprika lamb stew

Overall timing 2 hours

Freezing Suitable

To serve 6

2	Green peppers
2	Onions
1	Garlic clove
4	Slices bacon
2lb	Boneless shoulder of lamb
16oz	Can of tomatoes
2 tbsp	Tomato paste
1 tsp	Paprika
1 tsp	Sugar
2½ cups	Broth
	Salt and pepper
½ cup	Sour cream

Seed the peppers and cut into strips. Peel and finely chop the onions. Peel and crush the garlic. Dice the bacon. Heat a flameproof casserole, add the onions, garlic and bacon and fry over a high heat till golden.

Cut the meat into cubes and add to casserole. Brown on all sides. Stir in peppers, tomatoes and their juice, tomato paste, paprika, sugar, broth and seasoning. Cover and cook gently for 1½ hours till meat is tender.

Taste and adjust seasoning and serve with boiled potatoes and sour cream for everyone to spoon on top of the stew.

Roast lamb with garlic

Overall timing 2 hours

Freezing Not suitable

To serve 6

2-3	Garlic cloves
3½lb	Leg of lamb
2 tbsp	Butter or drippings
	Salt and pepper

Preheat the oven to 350°.

Peel the garlic cloves and cut each into thin slivers. Place lamb in roasting pan with the thickest fat uppermost. Using a sharp, thin bladed knife, make incisions about 1 inch deep in the meat. Insert a sliver of garlic into each incision, pressing it down so it is level with the surface of the meat.

Spread the softened butter or drippings over the lamb and season well. Roast for 1¾ hours or until the juices run clear when a skewer is inserted into the thickest part of the meat.

Transfer meat to warmed serving plate and make the gravy in the usual way. Serve with green beans and tomatoes.

Liver and onions

Overall timing 20 minutes

Freezing Not suitable

To serve 6

1½lb	Onions
6	Slices of calf's or
	lambs' liver
	Salt and pepper
3 tbsp	Flour
6 tbsp	Butter
2 tbsp	Chopped parsley
	(optional)

Peel and slice onions. Trim and wipe liver. Season the flour and use to coat the liver.

Melt the butter in a large skillet. Add the onions and fry till golden. Add liver slices and fry for 3-4 minutes on each side. Stir in parsley if using.

Transfer to a warmed serving dish and top with fried onions. Spoon pan juices over. Serve with boiled potatoes and parsleyed baby carrots.

Brains Milan-style

Overall timing 15 minutes plus
soaking and cooling

Freezing Not suitable

To serve 4

4	Lambs' brains
2 tsp	Vinegar
	Salt and pepper
	Bouquet garni
¼ cup	Flour
1	Egg
¼ cup	Soft bread crumbs
¼ cup	Butter
	Sage leaves
	Lemon wedges

Put the brains in a bowl of cold water with
1 tsp of the vinegar. Soak for 15 minutes.

Drain the brains. Holding them under
running water, carefully pull away
membranes and blood vessels. Put the brains
into a saucepan and cover with cold water.
Add the remaining vinegar, salt and bouquet
garni. Bring to a boil, then remove from the
heat. Leave to cool in the liquid.

Drain the brains and dry on paper towels.
Break into small pieces and coat with the
flour. Beat the egg. Dip the brains into the
egg, then coat with the bread crumbs.

Melt the butter in a skillet till foaming. Add
the brains and cook for 5 minutes till brown on
all sides. Garnish with sage leaves and serve
with lemon wedges.

Sweetbread kabobs

Overall timing 35 minutes plus marination

Freezing Not suitable

To serve 4

1 lb	Prepared lambs' sweetbreads
4	Thick bacon slices
6 tbsp	Oil
1 tbsp	Lemon juice
	Salt and pepper
½	Lemon
	Sprigs of parsley

Cut the sweetbreads in half. Cut the bacon into 1 inch pieces. Thread the sweetbreads and bacon alternately onto four greased skewers.

Mix the oil, lemon juice and seasoning in a shallow dish. Add the kabobs, turning them to coat with the marinade. Leave in a cool place for 1 hour.

Preheat the broiler. Place each kabob on a piece of foil, shaping the foil into a dish so it will hold the marinade, and pour the marinade over. Arrange the kabobs on the broiler pan and broil for 15-20 minutes, turning frequently in the marinade, till the sweetbreads are tender.

Arrange the kabobs on a warmed serving dish and pour the marinade over. Garnish with the lemon and parsley and serve immediately with crusty bread.

Piquant kidneys

Overall timing 30 minutes

Freezing Not suitable

To serve 2

½ lb	Lamb kidneys
2	Bacon slices
1	Onion
½ lb	Long macaroni
	Salt and pepper
2 tbsp	Butter
1½ tsp	Flour
1¼ cups	Beef broth
1½ tsp	Tomato paste
¼ tsp	Dried sage

Prepare and thinly slice kidneys. Dice bacon. Peel and chop onion. Cook macaroni in boiling salted water for 15 minutes till tender.

Meanwhile, melt butter in skillet and fry kidneys for 3 minutes, stirring from time to time. Remove from pan.

Add bacon and onion to pan and fry gently till golden. Sprinkle flour over and cook, stirring, for 2 minutes. Add broth, tomato paste, sage and seasoning. Bring to a boil, stirring, then return kidneys to pan, reduce heat and simmer for 15 minutes.

Drain macaroni and arrange in warmed serving dish. Spoon kidneys and sauce over and serve hot with crisp lettuce and cucumber salad.

Ham roasted in stout

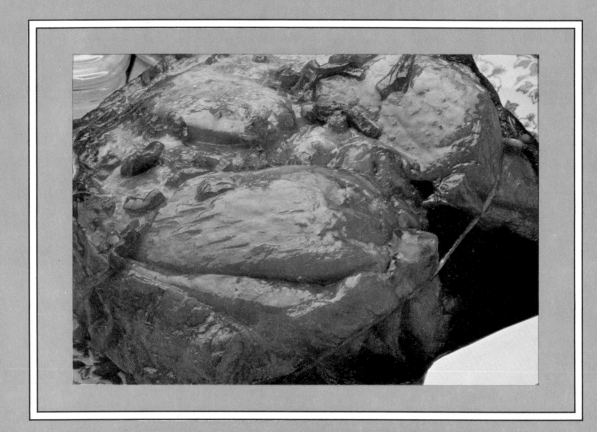

Overall timing 2½ hours plus cooling

Freezing Suitable; slice meat and cover with sauce; reheat from frozen in moderate oven.

To serve 6

3lb	Ham
2	Onions
1¼ cups	Stout or other dark beer
2 tbsp	Butter
2 tbsp	Flour
¼ tsp	Crushed caraway seed
	Pepper

Preheat the oven to 400°.

Place ham in an ovenproof dish. Peel and chop onions. Cover ham with onion. Pour stout over. Roast for 2 hours, turning meat once during cooking.

Remove meat from dish and place on warmed serving dish. Keep hot. Skim fat from surface of cooking liquid. Place liquid in measuring cup and make up to 1¼ cups with water if necessary.

Melt butter in saucepan. Stir in flour and allow to brown lightly. Gradually add cooking liquid and simmer, stirring, till thickened. Season with crushed caraway seed and black pepper. Cook for 5 minutes, then pour over the roast and serve.

Bacon and cabbage casserole

Overall timing 1 ¼ hours

Freezing Not suitable

To serve 4

1	Medium-size head white cabbage
2	Onions
2 tbsp	Lard
½ lb	Canadian bacon
1 lb	Ground beef
1 tsp	Caraway seeds
½ cup	Beef broth
	Salt and pepper
¼ cup	Butter
½ lb	Bacon slices

Preheat the oven to 375°.

Discard any marked outer leaves of the cabbage. Save two or three good ones. Cut the remaining cabbage in half. Remove the core, then shred the cabbage. Put with reserved leaves into a saucepan of cold water. Bring to a boil and drain. Set aside.

Peel and chop the onions. Melt the lard in a large saucepan, add the onions and cook gently for 3-4 minutes. Chop Canadian bacon. Add to the saucepan. Cook for 2-3 minutes. Add the ground beef and cook, stirring, until brown. Add the caraway seeds, broth and seasoning. Simmer for 10 minutes.

Melt the butter in a small saucepan. Put half of the shredded cabbage in the bottom of an ovenproof dish and pour the melted butter over. Spread the beef mixture evenly over the cabbage. Cover with remaining shredded cabbage and top with whole leaves. Arrange the bacon slices over the top of the cabbage. Bake for 45 minutes.

Sausage surprise

Overall timing 35 minutes

Freezing Not suitable

To serve 4-6

2lb	Potatoes
	Salt and pepper
1lb	Pork link sausages
1¼ cups	Milk
¼ cup	Butter
1½ cups	Grated cheese
½ tsp	Grated nutmeg

Preheat the broiler. Peel the potatoes and cut into quarters. Cook in boiling salted water for about 10 minutes till tender.

Meanwhile, broil the sausages for about 15 minutes, turning occasionally till well browned.

Drain the potatoes in a colander. Add the milk to the pan and bring just to a boil. Return the potatoes to the pan with the butter and mash till smooth.

Beat 1 cup of the cheese into the potatoes with nutmeg and seasoning. Spread the mixture in a flameproof dish and push the sausages diagonally into the potato so that the tops are just showing.

Sprinkle the remaining cheese over and broil for about 5 minutes till golden.

Savory smoked pork mold

Overall timing 2½ hours plus setting

Freezing Not suitable

To serve 8-10

2lb	Smoked pork shoulder or arm picnic
1	Onion
1	Clove
1	Stalk of celery
2	Garlic cloves
	Bouquet garni
	Salt and pepper
5 tbsp	Chopped parsley
1 tbsp	White wine vinegar
2 tsp	Unflavored gelatin
1 tsp	Dried tarragon
1 tsp	Dried chervil
2	Egg whites
	Cucumber peel
1	Sweet red pepper
¼ cup	Pitted ripe olives

Put pork in a pan, cover with water and bring to a boil. Drain off water. Peel onion and spike with clove. Chop celery. Peel garlic. Add vegetables to pan with 2 quarts water, the bouquet garni and seasoning. Bring to a boil and simmer for 1 hour.

Soak parsley in vinegar.

Lift pork out of pan. Remove meat from bone and chop. Reduce cooking liquid to 1¼ cups by boiling fast. Strain cooking liquid and return to pan. Add gelatin and herbs. Lightly beat egg whites and add. Leave for 30 minutes, then bring nearly to a boil, beating. Remove from heat and pour through a scalded jelly bag or several layers of cheesecloth.

Spoon a little gelatin into dampened mold. Chill till set.

Chop cucumber peel. Seed and slice pepper. Arrange decoratively in mold with olives. Add a little more gelatin and chill again till set. Arrange pork pieces and parsley in layers in mold. Pour remaining gelatin over, cover and chill overnight.

Sausages in cider sauce

Overall timing 50 minutes

Freezing Not suitable

To serve 4

1 lb	Boneless pork chops
8	Pork link sausages
2 tbsp	Lard
1	Large onion
1	Carrot
1	Stalk of celery
4	Large tomatoes
1	Garlic clove
½ cup	Dry hard cider
	Salt and pepper
2 tbsp	Butter
1½ cups	Long grain rice
1 quart	Chicken broth
3 tbsp	Grated Parmesan cheese

Cut the pork chops into bite-size pieces. Twist each sausage in half to make 16 small sausages. Melt the lard in a skillet and fry the pork and sausages gently, turning frequently, for 10 minutes.

Meanwhile, peel and chop the onion and carrot. Trim and chop the celery. Quarter the tomatoes. Peel and crush the garlic. Add the vegetables to the skillet with the cider and seasoning. Cover and simmer for 20 minutes.

Melt the butter in a saucepan, add the rice and fry, stirring, for 2 minutes. Add the broth and bring to a boil, stirring. Cover and simmer for about 15 minutes till rice is tender and liquid is absorbed.

Remove the rice from the heat and stir in the cheese. Taste and adjust the seasoning and fluff with a fork. Pile into a warmed serving dish and arrange sausages and pork on top. Spoon cider sauce over and serve immediately with a mixed salad.

Honey-glazed smoked pork

Overall timing 1 ½ hours

Freezing Not suitable

To serve 6-8

4 lb	Smoked pork shoulder roll
	Whole cloves
2 tbsp	Clear honey
3 tbsp	Brown sugar
2	Granny Smith apples
¼ cup	Butter

Place the pork in a large kettle and cover with cold water. Bring to a boil. Remove any scum. Reduce heat, cover and simmer gently for 1 hour. Preheat the oven to 350°. Remove pork from pan, allow to cool slightly, then cut off any rind. Score fat in a lattice pattern and put a clove in the center of each "diamond." Put in a roasting pan.

Gently heat honey and sugar in a small saucepan until melted. Brush over the surface of the pork. Cook in the oven for 20 minutes, basting from time to time. Take care not to let the glaze burn.

Five minutes before the pork is cooked, peel, core and slice apples into ¼ inch thick rings. Melt butter in a skillet and fry the apple rings on both sides until lightly golden and tender.

Serve pork on a dish surrounded by apple rings.

Alsatian chicken

Overall timing 1½ hours

Freezing Not suitable

To serve 4-6

8	Chicken pieces
1	Garlic clove
2oz	Slab bacon
¼ cup	Oil
2	Onions
1 cup	Dry white wine
¼lb	Mushrooms
2	Bay leaves
2 tbsp	Chopped parsley
2 tbsp	Chopped chives
	Salt and pepper
1 tbsp	Arrowroot
½ cup	Light cream
	Sprigs of fresh parsley

Rub the chicken all over with halved garlic clove. Dice bacon. Fry in flameproof casserole till brown. Add oil and when hot brown chicken pieces on all sides.

Peel and finely chop onions. Add to casserole and brown. Pour in half the wine, cover and cook for 35 minutes.

Slice mushrooms and add to casserole with bay leaves, half the chopped parsley and chives, and seasoning. Cover and cook for 10 minutes.

Discard bay leaves. Take out chicken pieces with a slotted spoon and place on warmed serving dish. Keep hot. If there's a lot of liquid in casserole, boil till reduced by half. Mix arrowroot with remaining wine and stir into pan juices. Cook, stirring, till sauce thickens, then gradually stir in cream. When hot (it must not boil) pour sauce over chicken. Garnish with remaining chopped parsley and chives and parsley sprigs.

Chicken croquettes

Overall timing 30 minutes

Freezing Suitable: reheat in 375° oven for 20 minutes.

To serve 4-6

¾lb (1½ cups)	Cooked chicken
6 tbsp	Butter
¾ cup + 2 tbsp	Flour
1¼ cups	Milk
	Salt and pepper
	Grated nutmeg
2	Egg yolks
1 tbsp	Grated cheese
1 tbsp	Chopped parsley
	Oil for frying
1	Egg
1⅓ cups	Dried bread crumbs
	Sprigs of parsley
	Lemon wedges

Finely chop or grind chicken.

To make sauce, melt the butter in a saucepan over a low heat and stir in 2 tbsp of the flour. When the mixture begins to froth, add the cold milk, salt, pepper and a pinch of grated nutmeg. Whisk until the sauce thickens.

Remove from heat and stir in egg yolks and cheese. Turn into a bowl and mix in chicken and chopped parsley. Cool.

Heat oil for frying to 340° or till a bread cube browns in 1 minute.

Using your hands, shape chicken mixture into small cylindrical croquettes. Roll them in the remaining flour, then in the lightly beaten egg to coat them completely and finally in the bread crumbs, pressing them on well with a palette knife.

Fry the croquettes, four or five at a time, in the hot oil until golden brown. Drain on paper towels and serve hot, garnished with parsley and lemon.

Chicken à la king

Overall timing 35 minutes

Freezing Suitable

To serve 4

1 lb	Cooked boneless chicken
1	Onion
1	Large green pepper
¼ cup	Butter
¼ cup	Flour
2 tbsp	Cold milk
1¼ cups	Warm milk
	Salt and pepper
	Grated nutmeg
2 tbsp	Sherry

Cut the chicken into small pieces. Peel and finely chop onion. Seed pepper and finely chop half of it.

Melt the butter in a saucepan and gently fry onion and pepper till onion is transparent.

Stir in the flour with a wooden spoon, then the cold milk. Remove from heat and gradually add the warm milk. Bring to a boil. Season with salt, pepper and a pinch of nutmeg. Reduce heat and simmer gently for 15 minutes.

Add chicken and sherry and cook for 5 minutes more. Stir frequently during this time to prevent mixture sticking.

Meanwhile, slice the remaining pepper and blanch in boiling water for 5 minutes.

Place chicken and sauce on a warmed serving plate and surround with the pepper slices. Serve with boiled rice or noodles.

Chicken baked in salt

Overall timing 1¾ hours

Freezing Not suitable

To serve 4-6

3½lb	Roaster chicken
1	Sprig of fresh
	tarragon
	Black pepper
8 cups	Coarse sea-salt

Preheat the oven to 450°.

Wipe the chicken, put the tarragon inside and sprinkle inside and out with pepper. Truss with string.

Line a casserole with a large sheet of foil and spread with one-third of the salt. Place chicken breast bone down on salt. Cover completely with remaining salt. Fold the foil over the top of the chicken and join together at top, sealing well. Bake, covered, for 1½ hours.

Take the chicken out of the oven, unwrap and remove the crust of salt. Brush off any salt that clings, then carve the chicken in the usual way.

Chicken Kiev

Overall timing 1 ½ hours

Freezing Suitable: fry after thawing.

To serve 4

½ cup	Softened butter
2 tbsp	Lemon juice
1	Garlic clove
1 tbsp	Chopped parsley
	Salt and pepper
4	Boneless chicken breasts
	Oil for frying
3 tbsp	Flour
1	Egg
2 cups	Soft white bread crumbs

Work together the butter and lemon juice until smooth. Peel and crush the garlic and add to the butter with the parsley and seasoning. Mix well. Shape into a cylinder, wrap in foil and place in freezer for 1 hour to firm.

Place the chicken breasts between two sheets of dampened wax paper on a flat surface and beat flat with a heavy knife or wooden mallet until thin.

Heat the oil in a deep-fryer to 350°.

Place a piece of butter on each chicken breast. Roll chicken around butter and secure with a toothpick. Coat each piece of chicken all over with the flour, then dip in the beaten egg to cover and finally in the bread crumbs, pressing them on well. Fry for 12-15 minutes until golden brown. Drain on paper towels, remove toothpicks and serve immediately with lemon wedges and a green salad.

Soufflé-topped chicken

Overall timing 1 1/4 hours

Freezing Not suitable

To serve 4-6

2 tbsp	Oil
3 lb	Chicken pieces
	Salt and pepper
1 lb	Can of whole kernel
	corn
2 tbsp	Soft bread crumbs
Sauce	
6 tbsp	Butter
1/4 cup	Flour
3/4 cup	Milk
2	Eggs
3/4 cup	Light cream
	Salt and pepper
	Grated nutmeg

Preheat the oven to 400°.

Heat oil in flameproof casserole. Add chicken and cook for about 10 minutes until pieces are browned on all sides. Season with salt and pepper.

Drain corn and add to the casserole with 1/4 cup of the liquid.

To make the sauce, melt 1/4 cup of the butter in a saucepan, sprinkle with the flour and cook till browned, stirring all the time. Gradually add milk and cook, stirring, for 5 minutes. Remove from heat.

Separate eggs. Mix cream, egg yolks, salt, pepper and a pinch of nutmeg in a bowl. Stir into the sauce and heat through but do not boil. Remove from heat and set aside.

Beat egg whites in a bowl until they hold stiff peaks. Fold into sauce with a metal spoon and pour over corn and chicken mixture, sprinkle with bread crumbs, dot with remaining butter and bake for 45 minutes. Serve with broccoli garnished with chopped hard-cooked eggs.

Chicken Maryland

Overall timing 1¾ hours

Freezing Not suitable

To serve 8

Corn fritters

1 cup	Flour
1	Egg
1 cup	Milk
11½oz	Whole kernel corn
1	Egg white

8	Boneless chicken breasts
	Salt
	Cayenne
½ cup	Flour
2	Eggs
2 cups	Soft bread crumbs
	Oil for frying
4	Bananas
12	Bacon slices

To make the fritter batter, sift flour and pinch of salt into a bowl and make a well in the center. Add the whole egg and gradually beat in the milk. Drain corn and add. Leave batter to stand.

Cut each chicken breast in half. Season with salt and cayenne. Dip into the flour, then into beaten eggs, then into bread crumbs.

Heat the oil in a deep-fryer until hot enough to brown a cube of bread in 30 seconds. Fry the chicken pieces a few at a time for about 10-15 minutes, depending on thickness. Remove from pan, drain on paper towels and keep hot. Skim surface of oil.

Peel bananas and cut into three, then halve each piece lengthwise. Stretch bacon slices and cut in half. Wrap a piece of bacon around each piece of banana and secure with a wooden toothpick. Fry in hot oil, then drain and keep hot.

Beat egg white till stiff and fold into fritter batter. Drop in spoonfuls into hot oil and fry till puffed and golden brown. Drain. Arrange fritters, chicken and bacon-wrapped bananas on plate and serve.

Chicken pineapple salad

Overall timing 30 minutes plus chilling

Freezing Not suitable

To serve 4-6

½ cup	Long grain rice
	Salt and pepper
1 cup	Frozen whole kernel corn
1	Celery heart
1	Cold roast chicken
8oz	Can of pineapple rings
4	Small firm tomatoes
½ cup	Ripe olives
3 tbsp	Salad oil
1 tbsp	Lemon juice
1 tbsp	Chopped chives
1	Bibb lettuce
1	Hard-cooked egg

Cook the rice in boiling salted water till tender, adding the corn for the last 5 minutes of cooking. Drain and rinse under cold water, then drain thoroughly.

Trim celery heart and cut into 2 inch lengths. Put into a large bowl with the celery leaves. Cut the chicken into bite-size pieces, discding the skin and bones. Add to the bowl.

Drain the pineapple; chop three of the rings. Quarter the tomatoes and add to the bowl with the chopped pineapple, olives, rice and corn.

Mix together the oil, lemon juice, chives and seasoning. Pour over the salad and toss lightly. Chill for 30 minutes.

Wash and dry the lettuce and use to line a salad bowl. Pile the salad into the center and garnish with the remaining pineapple rings and the hard-cooked egg quartered lengthwise. Serve with crusty bread.

Chicken pieces with nutty sauce

Overall timing 1 hour plus marination

Freezing Not suitable

To serve 4

5	Onions
1	Garlic clove
½ cup	Walnuts
	Salt
3 tbsp	Lemon juice
4	Boneless chicken breasts
2 tbsp	Groundnut oil
	Pinch of chili powder
½ cup	Roasted peanuts
2 tsp	Soy sauce
1¼ cups	Water

Peel and finely chop two onions. Peel and crush garlic. Place both in a mortar or blender with walnuts and salt. Crush or blend to a paste, gradually adding 2 tbsp lemon juice to give a creamy mixture. Cut chicken into bite-size pieces. Place in a shallow dish and pour walnut mixture over. Leave to marinate for 1 hour, turning occasionally.

Meanwhile, peel and finely chop two onions. Heat half oil in a skillet and fry onions till crisp and golden. Remove from pan and drain. Preheat the broiler.

Peel and finely chop remaining onion and purée in mortar or blender with chili powder, salt and peanuts till smooth. Heat remaining oil in skillet and fry peanut mixture for 3 minutes, stirring constantly. Stir in soy sauce, water and remaining lemon juice. Cook over low heat for 5 minutes.

Thread chicken pieces onto four oiled skewers. Broil for 10 minutes, turning frequently and brushing with walnut mixture. Add any remaining walnut mixture and fried onions to peanut sauce and heat through.

Poule-au-pot

Overall timing 4 hours

Freezing Not suitable

To serve 6

4	Bacon slices
¼lb	Bulk pork
	sausage meat
1 cup	Soft bread crumbs
2 tbsp	Chopped parsley
	Salt and pepper
2	Eggs
3½lb	Stewing chicken
4	Medium-size onions
4	Small white turnips
6	Large carrots
2	Leeks
4	Stalks of celery
¼ cup	Drippings
	Bouquet garni
1½ cups	Long grain rice

Chop bacon finely. Mix sausage meat, bacon, bread crumbs, parsley and seasoning and bind with eggs. Spoon into chicken and truss.

Peel onions, turnips and carrots. Trim leeks and celery. Heat drippings in a large pan and brown chicken all over. Add one each of the onions, turnips, leeks and celery stalks and two carrots and fry for 3 minutes. Pour off excess fat.

Add bouquet garni, giblets and col water to cover the chicken and bring to a boil. Skim off any scum. Cover and simmer for about 2¼ hours.

Discard vegetables and bouquet garni. Add remaining vegetables and seasoning. Cover and simmer for a further 45 minutes. Remove from heat. Strain 5½ cups of broth into another saucepan. Keep chicken hot.

Add rice to stock with salt and cover tightly. Bring to a boil and simmer for 15-20 minutes till rice is tender.

Fluff rice and arrange on a serving dish. Place chicken on rice and discard trussing strings. Arrange vegetables around chicken and serve.

Chicken supreme

Overall timing 2 hours

Freezing Not suitable

To serve 4

2	Carrots
2	Onions
2	Leeks
1	Stalk of celery
	Salt
1½ quarts	Water or broth
3lb	Roaster chicken
½	Lemon
1 cup	Rice
Sauce	
¼ cup	Butter
1 tbsp	Flour
2	Egg yolks
2 tbsp	Light cream
	Salt and pepper

Peel carrots and onions. Chop leeks and celery. Bring salted water or broth to a boil in a flameproof casserole, add prepared vegetables and cook for 15 minutes.

Rub chicken with the lemon. Add to casserole, cover and simmer gently for 1 hour. (If you prefer, chicken joints can be used instead of a whole chicken — they need only to be cooked for 45 minutes.)

Measure out 2½ cups broth from casserole and place in a saucepan. Continue cooking chicken for a further 15 minutes. Bring stock in saucepan to a boil, add rice and cook for 15 minutes.

Meanwhile, prepare sauce. Melt butter in a saucepan and stir in flour. Measure out another 2½ cups broth from casserole and gradually stir into pan. Cook, stirring till thickened. Remove from heat and stir in egg yolks and then cream. Season.

Drain rice and place on warmed serving dish. Remove chicken from casserole, cut into portions and arrange on top of rice. Pour sauce over and serve.

Chicken with eggplant and tomatoes

Overall timing 50 minutes

Freezing Not suitable

To serve 4

1	Eggplant
	Salt and pepper
1	Green pepper
2	Large onions
6 tbsp	Oil
4	Chicken pieces
2 cups	Tomato juice
¾lb	Ripe tomatoes

Slice the eggplant. Sprinkle with salt and leave for 15 minutes. Meanwhile, seed and slice the pepper. Peel and slice the onions.

Heat the oil in a flameproof casserole, add the chicken and fry over a moderate heat, turning frequently, till browned all over. Remove from the pan and reserve.

Add the onions and pepper and fry for 5 minutes. Return the chicken to the casserole, add the tomato juice and seasoning and bring to a boil.

Rinse the eggplant and pat dry on paper towels. Add to the chicken, cover and simmer for 25 minutes.

Blanch, peel and quarter the tomatoes. Add to the chicken and cook for a further 5 minutes. Serve with plain boiled rice and a green salad.

Chicken parcels

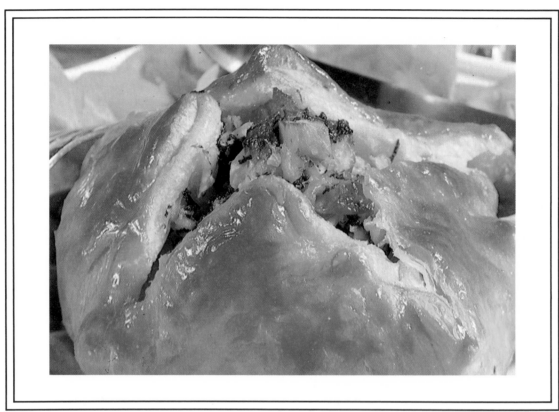

Overall timing 45 minutes

Freezing Suitable: bake from frozen,
allowing 35-45 minutes

To serve 6

¾lb	Frozen puff pastry
1	Medium-size onion
2 tbsp	Butter
1¼ cups	Cooked chicken meat
3 tbsp	Chopped parsley
¼ cup	Heavy cream
	Salt and pepper
3	Slices of cooked
	ham
1	Egg yolk
6	Lettuce leaves

Thaw pastry. Preheat oven to 400°.

Peel and chop onion and fry in the butter till transparent.

Set aside six fairly large pieces of chicken and finely chop the rest. Put chopped chicken into a bowl with the parsley and fried onion. Lightly beat the cream, then stir into the chicken with seasoning.

Roll out the dough on a lightly floured surface. Cut out six 5 inch squares. Cut ham slices in half and place one piece in center of each dough square. Top with a piece of chicken, then cover with chopped chicken mixture. Dampen dough edges with cold water. Fold corners to center to cover the filling, pinching the edges together, but leaving a small hole in the top. Place parcels on a greased baking sheet.

Beat the egg yolk with a pinch of salt and brush over the parcels. Bake for 25 minutes or until well risen and golden brown. Serve the parcels on lettuce leaves.

Chicken in a basket

Overall timing 40 minutes

Freezing Not suitable

To serve 2

2x1lb	Squab chickens
2 tbsp	Oil
	Salt and pepper
1lb	Potatoes
	Oil for frying
	Fresh parsley
1	Small onion

Preheat the oven to 400°.

Place the chickens in roasting pan. Brush with oil and season well. Roast for 30 minutes, or until juices from the legs run clear when pierced with skewer.

Meanwhile, peel potatoes and cut into thin, matchstick fries. Heat oil in a deep-fryer to 340°. Fry potatoes for 3-5 minutes till golden. Drain well.

Arrange napkins in two small baskets. Place fries in folds of cloth. Place chickens in baskets. Garnish with parsley sprigs and onion rings. Eat with your fingers or a knife and fork if preferred.

Variation

To make barbecue-style chickens, mix together 2 tbsp tomato paste, 1 tbsp Worcestershire sauce, 1 tbsp oil, 1 peeled and crushed garlic clove and seasoning. Spread over chickens, cover with foil and roast for 40 minutes. Serve as above.

Chicken with pineapple

Overall timing 45 minutes

Freezing Not suitable

To serve 2

1½lb	Chicken pieces	
2 tsp	Potato flour or	
	cornstarch	
3 tbsp	Oil	
1 tbsp	Soy sauce	
1½ tsp	Dry sherry wine	
	Salt and pepper	
4oz	Canned pineapple	
	rings or chunks	

Remove meat from chicken pieces and cut it into chunks.

Mix together potato flour or cornstarch, half the oil, the soy sauce, sherry and seasoning in a bowl. Add the chicken pieces and coat well. Leave to marinate for 15 minutes.

Heat the rest of the oil in a heavy-based saucepan. Drain the chicken, saving the marinade, and add to the pan. Cook over a fairly high heat for 5 minutes, stirring constantly.

Drain the pineapple, reserving ¼ cup of the syrup. Cut the rings into sections or halve the chunks. Add the reserved marinade from the chicken and the pineapple pieces to the pan and cook for a further 12 minutes, continually turning the chicken over.

When the chicken is golden brown, add the reserved pineapple syrup, adjust seasoning and cook for a further 5 minutes. Serve with saffron rice.

Roast ginger chicken

Overall timing 1 ¼ hours

Freezing Not suitable

To serve 4

1	Tart apple
1 inch	Piece of ginger root
⅔ cup	Cooked long grain rice
¾ cup	Plain yogurt
6 tbsp	Softened butter
	Salt and pepper
3lb	Roaster chicken

Preheat the oven to 400°.

Peel, core and grate apple. Grate or finely chop ginger and add to apple with rice, yogurt, ¼ cup of the butter and seasoning. Mix well together. Use to stuff chicken.

Place chicken on its side in a roasting pan and dot with remaining butter. Roast for 15 minutes, then turn chicken onto its other side and roast for 15 minutes. Turn chicken onto its back and continue roasting for a further 30 minutes or until tender. Baste frequently.

Remove chicken from roasting pan and place on warmed serving dish. Serve with gravy made from pan juices, green or mixed salad and sauté or creamed potatoes.

Turkey with lemon sauce

Overall timing 30 minutes

Freezing Not suitable

To serve 6

6	Slices of turkey breast (scaloppine)
	Salt and pepper
2 tbsp	Flour
2	Thick slices of Canadian bacon
6 tbsp	Butter
½ cup	Chicken broth
2 tbsp	Lemon juice
2 tbsp	Chopped parsley
	Lemon slices
	Sprigs of parsley

Place each slice of turkey between two sheets of damp wax paper and flatten with a rolling pin. Season the flour and use to coat the turkey. Cut bacon into strips.

Melt the butter in a skillet and cook the bacon for 5 minutes. Add turkey pieces and fry for 3-5 minutes on each side. Remove turkey and bacon from pan and arrange on a warmed serving plate. Keep hot.

Add any remaining seasoned flour to skillet and stir well with a wooden spoon, scraping the sediment from the bottom of the pan. Gradually add the broth and bring to a boil. Simmer gently for 5 minutes.

Remove pan from heat and stir in the lemon juice and chopped parsley. Taste and adjust seasoning. Pour over the turkey breasts and garnish with lemon slices and parsley sprigs. Serve immediately with a mixed salad.

Turkey fries

Overall timing 40 minutes plus marination

Freezing Not suitable

To serve 8

¼ cup	Oil
3 tbsp	Lemon juice
	Salt
8 x ¼lb	Slices of turkey breast (scaloppine)
4 tsp	Dijon-style mustard
2	Eggs
3 cups	Soft bread crumbs
¼ cup	Butter
	Chopped parsley
	Lemon wedges

Mix 2 tbsp of the oil with the lemon juice and a pinch of salt in a shallow dish. Add the turkey, mix well and leave to marinate for 1 hour.

Drain the turkey and pat dry on paper towels. Spread thinly with the mustard. Beat the eggs lightly on a plate and use to coat turkey. Dip turkey slices into the bread crumbs, pressing them on gently.

Melt the butter and remaining oil in a skillet and gently fry the turkey for about 10 minutes on each side, till tender and golden.

Drain on paper towels and arrange on a warmed dish. Garnish with chopped parsley and lemon wedges and serve immediately with a tomato and onion salad dressed with vinaigrette.

Roast squab with mushrooms

Overall timing 50 minutes

Freezing Not suitable

To serve 2

¼lb	Small onions
2	Squab
2	Sprigs of rosemary
4	Sage leaves
6	Bacon slices
2 tbsp	Butter
¼lb	Mushrooms
5 tbsp	Dry white wine
	Salt and pepper

Preheat the over to 450°.

Blanch the onions in boiling water for 5 minutes, then peel. Wipe the squab and put a sprig of rosemary, two sage leaves and a slice of bacon into each. Put into a roasting pan and spread half the butter over each. Roast for about 15 minutes till browned.

Meanwhile, chop the remaining bacon. Heat a flameproof casserole and fry the onions and bacon till just golden. Thickly slice the mushrooms. Add to onions and bacon and fry for 2 minutes.

Remove the squab from the oven and reduce the temperature to 400°. Put the squab into the casserole on top of the vegetables, pour the wine over and season.

Cover the casserole, place in the oven and cook for a further 15-20 minutes till the squab are tender. Adjust the seasoning before serving.

Pigeons with saffron

Overall timing 1 hour

Freezing Not suitable

To serve 6

3	Wild or wood pigeons
	Salt and pepper
1 tbsp	Flour
1 tbsp	Oil
¼ cup	Butter
6	Saffron strands
3 tbsp	Lemon juice
1	Small onion
2 tbsp	Chopped parsley

Quarter the pigeons. Lightly coat with seasoned flour. Heat the oil and butter in a saucepan, add the pigeon pieces and fry for about 10 minutes till lightly browned on all sides.

Meanwhile, pound the saffron in a small bowl. Add 2 tbsp warm water and leave to soak for 10 minutes.

Add saffron, soaking liquid and lemon juice to the pan. Cover and cook over a low heat for 20 minutes till meat is tender. Remove pigeons pieces from the pan, place on a warmed serving dish and keep hot.

Peel and finely chop the onion. Add to the liquid in the pan with parsley and seasoning. Cook for 3 minutes, then spoon over the pigeon quarters and serve immediately with boiled rice.

Duck with oranges

Overall timing 2 hours

Freezing Not suitable

To serve 4

4 lb	Duck
	Salt and pepper
1¼ cups	Hot chicken broth
2 tsp	Sugar
2 tbsp	White wine vinegar
4	Oranges

Preheat the oven to 400°.

Prick duck all over with a fork. Season well and place on rack in roasting pan. Roast for 45 minutes till brown and crisp.

Remove all but 1 tbsp of the fat from the pan. Pour hot broth over duck. Cover and roast for a further 30 minutes till cooked.

Heat sugar gently in a pan until it caramelizes, then remove from heat and add vinegar. Remove duck and strain juices from roasting pan into sugar mixture. Replace duck in pan and keep warm.

Cut the ring from one orange into thin matchsticks. Squeeze the juice from two oranges and add to the pan with the rind. Cook gently for 5 minutes till the rind has softened.

Remove duck from oven and cut into portions. Arrange on warmed serving dish and spoon over a little of the orange sauce. Peel and section remaining oranges and use to garnish duck. Serve with sautéed potatoes and peas, and with the rest of the sauce served in a sauce or gravy boat.

Duck with apples and cream

Overall timing 1 hour 20 minutes

Freezing Not suitable

To serve 4

4 lb	Duck
	Salt and pepper
6	Granny Smith apples
2 tbsp	Butter
1¼ cups	Light cream

Preheat the oven to 400°.

Sprinkle duck inside and out with salt and pepper. Prick all over with a fork and place on wire rack in roasting pan. Roast for 20 minutes, then reduce heat to 350°.

Peel and core the apples. Cut two of them into quarters and leave the rest whole. Arrange around the duck, dot with butter and continue roasting for 1 hour or till tender.

Remove duck and apples from the pan. Place duck on serving plate. Keep hot. Pour off excess fat from pan juices, then stir in the cream. Replace apples in pan and baste thoroughly with the sauce. Cook for a further 5 minutes.

Arrange apples around duck. Spoon some sauce over. Serve rest separately.

Chicken liver crêpes

Overall timing 45 minutes

Freezing Suitable: add cream and chesse and bake from frozen, covered, allowing 30-40 minutes

To serve 4

¼lb	Chicken livers
½lb	Button mushrooms
1	Small onion
¼ cup	Butter
	Salt and pepper
6	Slices of cooked ham
3 tbsp	Light cream
	Grated nutmeg
½ cup	Grated Cheddar cheese
Crêpes	
1¼ cups	Flour
¼ tsp	Salt
2	Eggs
1¾ cups	Beer
	Oil for frying
	Chopped parsley

Chop chicken livers. Chop mushrooms. Peel and finely chop onion. Melt butter in a saucepan and gently fry mushrooms and onion for 5 minutes. Add chopped livers ad fry for 3-4 minutes. Season with salt and pepper.

To make crêpes, sift flour and salt into a bowl and make a well in the center. Add eggs and beer and beat to a smooth batter. Heat a little oil in an 8 inch crêpe pan and make 12 crêpes.

Preheat oven to 400°.

Cut slices of ham in half. Place one half on each crêpe. Divide liver mixture between crêpes, then roll them up. Place side by side in greased baking dish. Pour cream over and sprinkle with nutmeg and grated cheese.

Bake for 15-20 minutes, or broil for 5 minutes. Sprinkle parsley over. Serve hot.

Rabbit carbonnade

Overall timing 2½ hours

Freezing Not suitable

To serve 4-6

2½lb	Rabbit
3 tbsp	Flour
2	Carrots
1	Onion
¼lb	Bacon slices
¼ cup	Butter
	Bouquet garni
1	Garlic clove
	Salt and pepper
2½ cups	Beer

Preheat the over to 350°.

Put the rabbit into neat pieces. Toss in the flour till lightly coated.

Peel and thinly slice the carrots. Peel and chop the onion. Cut the bacon into strips. Melt the butter in a flameproof casserole and fry the carrots, onion and bacon for 5 minutes. Add the rabbit pieces and fry till browned.

Add the bouquet garni, peeled and crushed garlic seasoning. Pour the beer over, cover tightly and cook in the oven for 1¾ − 2 hours till the rabbit is tender. Serve with boiled potatoes.

Quiche lorraine

Overall timing 1 ½ hours

Freezing Suitable: reheat in hot oven

To serve 4-6

2 cups	Flour
	Salt and pepper
½ cup	Butter
	Water
2	Thick bacon slices
¾ cup	Grated Cheddar cheese
2	Eggs
1 cup	Milk or light cream

Sift the flour, salt and pepper into a bowl. Rub in the butter till mixture resembles bread crumbs. Gradually add the water to bind and knead to a dough. Roll out and use to line a greased 8 inch pie or quiche pan. Leave to stand for 30 minutes.

Preheat the oven to 400°.

Dice the bacon, fry lightly. Sprinkle bacon and cheese over the bottom of the pastry case. Beat together the eggs, milk or cream and seasoning in a bowl. Pour mixture into pastry case. Do not overfill.

Bake for 15 minutes, then reduce heat to 325° and bake for further 25-30 minutes. Serve hot or cold with salad and potatoes.

Onion quiche

Overall timing 1 ½ hours

Freezing Suitable: reheat from frozen, covered, in 350° oven for 20 minutes.

To serve 4

1 lb	Medium-size onions
¼ cup	Lard
¼ lb	Slab bacon
6 oz	Rich pie pastry
3	Eggs
½ cup	Milk
½ cup	Light cream
	Salt and pepper

Preheat the oven to 400°.

Peel, halve and thinly slice the onions. Melt the lard in a skillet and fry the onions over a moderate heat till pale golden.

Dice the bacon and add to the pan. Fry for a further 4-5 minutes till the onions and bacon are golden brown.

Roll out the dough and use to line an 8½ inch quiche pan. Prick the bottom and bake blind for 15 minutes.

Spread the onion and bacon mixture over the pastry base. Mix the eggs with the milk and cream and seasoning. Pour over the onions.

Bake for a further 25 minutes till lightly set and golden. Serve hot with mixed salads.

Bacon and corn quiche

Overall timing 1 hour

Freezing Suitable: reheat in 425° oven for 10-15 minutes.

To serve 6-8

¼lb	Slab bacon
½lb	Pie pastry
2	Eggs
½ cup	Milk
	Salt and pepper
¼ tsp	Grated nutmeg
	Cayenne
16oz	Can of cream-style corn
1 cup	Grated sharp Cheddar cheese

Preheat the oven to 450°.

Finely chop bacon. Put into a small ovenproof dish in the oven to draw off the fat.

Roll out the dough and use to line a 9 inch quiche or pie p. Beat the eggs and milk together in a bowl and add salt, pepper, nutmeg and a pinch of cayenne. Blend in the corn. Mix three quarters of the cheese into the egg and corn mixture.

Remove bacon from oven and brush a little fat on the inside of the pastry case. Drain the bacon pieces and add half of them to the egg and corn mixture. Pour mixture into the pastry case. Sprinkle the rest of the cheese and remaining bacon on the top and bake for 20 minutes. Reduce the temperature to 350° and bake for a further 25 minutes. Serve hot or cold.

Asparagus quiche

Overall timing 1 ¼ hours

Freezing Suitable: thaw and refresh in hot oven for 10 minutes.

To serve 4

½ lb	Pie pastry
2 tbsp	Butter
2 tbsp	Flour
2 cups	Milk
	Salt and pepper
	Pinch of grated nutmeg
2	Eggs
1 cup	Grated sharp cheese
12 oz	Can of asparagus

Preheat the oven to 425°.

Roll out the dough to ¼ inch thick and use to line a greased 10 inch quiche or pie pan. Prick with fork. Bake blind for 5 minutes.

Melt the butter in a small saucepan. Stir in flour. Gradually stir in 1 ¼ cups of the milk. Season with salt, pepper and nutmeg. Bring to a boil, stirring constantly. Cook for 2 minutes. Remove pan from heat. Separate the eggs and stir one yolk into sauce. Add cheese to the sauce. Pour the sauce into pastry case. Return to the oven and bake for 15 minutes.

Remove quiche from oven. Reduce heat to 375°. Drain asparagus, cut into small lengths and arrange evenly over surface. Mix together the rest of the milk, the remaining egg yolk and 2 egg whites and pour this over top. Bake for 30 minutes more.

Tomato marjoram pizza

Overall timing 1 ½ hours

Freezing Suitable: cook in 450° oven for 35 minutes.

To serve 4

1 ½lb	Ripe tomatoes
1	Large onion
2	Garlic cloves
¼ cup	Oil
2 tsp	Dried marjoram
6	Basil leaves
1 tsp	Sugar
	Salt and pepper
Base	
10oz	Package of bread mix
1 cup	Grated Cheddar cheese
¼ tsp	Powdered mustard

Blanch, peel and roughly chop the tomatoes. Peel and finely chop the onion. Peel and crush the garlic. Heat 3 tbsp of the oil in a saucepan and fry the onion till transparent. Add the tomatoes, garlic, 1 tsp of the marjoram, the basil leaves, sugar and seasoning. Bring to a boil, stirring. Cover and simmer for 15 minutes.

Empty the bread mix into a large bowl. Stir the cheese into mix with powdered mustard. Add hot water (according to package instructions) and mix to a soft, but not sticky dough. Knead for 5 minutes, then roll out on a floured surface to a round 10 inches in diameter. Place on a greased 10 inch pizza pan or baking sheet. Pinch up the edges to make a slight lip.

Spread the tomato mixture over the pizza base and sprinkle with the remaining marjoram. Put pizza in a warm place to rise for about 30 minutes till base has almost doubled in size.

Preheat the oven to 425°.

Sprinkle the remaining oil over the pizza and bake for 25 minutes.

Pantry pizza

Overall timing 1 hour 10 minutes

Freezing Suitable: reheat from frozen in 400° oven for 40 minutes.

To serve 4-6

16oz	Can of tomatoes
2	Garlic cloves
1	Small onion
½ tsp	Dried basil
	Salt and pepper
4oz	Can of sardines
6oz	Cheddar cheese
1	Can of anchovy
	fillets
12	Small ripe olives
2 tbsp	Grated Parmesan
	cheese
Base	
2 cups	Self-rising flour
	Pinch of salt
3 tbsp	Oil

Preheat oven to 450°.

Mix together mashed tomatoes and juice, crushed garlic, chopped onion, herbs, seasoning and drained and chopped sardines. Leave for 15 minutes.

Meanwhile, for the base, sift flour and salt into a bowl. Stir in oil and sufficient water to mix to a soft dough. Roll out dough to a large round and place on a greased baking sheet. Pinch up edge to make a rim. Brush with oil.

Spread tomato mixture over base. Cover with grated or sliced cheddar and arrange anchovy fillets in a lattice shape on top. Garnish with olives and sprinkle with Parmesan.

Bake for 15 minutes. Reduce heat to 375° and bake for a further 20-25 minutes.

Olive and caper pizza

Overall timing 1¾ hours

Freezing Not suitable

To serve 2

6oz	Pot
	Salt and pepper
2 cups	Self-rising flour
¼ cup	Butter
¾lb	Tomatoes
4	Anchovy fillets
1 tbsp	Capers
1 cup	Ripe olives
¾ cup	Milk
2 tsp	Dried oregano
1 tbsp	Olive oil

Preheat the oven to 425°.

Peel potatoes and cut into small chunks. Cook in boiling salted water till tender.

Meanwhile, sift the flour into a bowl and rub in the butter till the mixture resembles fine bread crumbs. Blanch, peel and chop tomatoes. Chop anchovy fillets. Drain capers. Pit olives.

Drain potatoes and mash well. Stir into rubbed-in mixture. Add milk and mix to form a soft dough. Knead lightly till smooth. Roll out dough and use to line a greased 9 inch pizza pan.

Arrange tomatoes, anchovies, capers and olives on top. Sprinkle with salt, pepper and oregano. Sprinkle olive oil over and bake for about 35 minutes till well risen and golden. Cut into wedges to serve.

Ham, veal and pork pie

Overall timing 2½ hours plus
overnight marination and chilling
Freezing Suitable

To serve 6-8

¾lb	Veal for stew
2	Bay leaves
1 tbsp	Brandy
	Salt and pepper
½lb	Cooked ham
¾lb	Fresh pork sides
¼lb	Slab bacon
4 cups	Flour
10 tbsp	Butter
1¼ cups	Water
2	Egg yolks

Cut veal into thin strips and place in a bowl
with bay leaves, brandy and a pinch of salt.
Leave to marinate overnight. Cut ham into
thin strips, add to veal and leave to marinate
for another 2 hours.

Preheat the oven to 375°.
Pass pork and bacon through a grinder twice,
or process finely in a food processor. Mix with
a little of the marinade and seasoning.

Sift flour and 1 tsp salt into a large bowl and
make a well in the center. Melt butter in water
and bring to a boil. Pour quickly into the flour
and mix well. Add one egg yolk and knead to a
smooth dough.

Working quickly, roll out two-thirds of
dough and use to line a greased 9 x 5 x 3 inch
loaf pan. Spread half the pork mixture on
bottom, cover with ham and veal mixture and
spread remaining pork mixture on top. Roll
out remaining dough to fit pie. Seal edges.

Lightly beat remaining egg yolk with a
pinch of salt and brush over dough. Bake for
1 hour, then reduce heat to 325°, cover with
foil to prevent over-browning and bake for
another hour.

Savory strudel

Overall timing 1½ hours

Freezing Suitable: bake from frozen, allowing extra 10-15 minutes.

To serve 4-6

¾ lb	Frozen puff pastry
1	Onion
2	Tomatoes
1	Green pepper
3 tbsp	Oil
1 lb	Ground beef
3 tbsp	Tomato ketchup
½ tsp	Worcestershire sauce
	Salt and pepper
1 cup	Grated sharp Cheddar cheese
1	Egg yolk

Thaw pastry. Preheat oven to 425°. Grease baking sheet.

Peel and finely chop onion and tomatoes. Seed and finely chop pepper. Heat oil in a skillet. Cook onion till golden, then add beef and pepper. Cook for 5 minutes, then add tomatoes. Cook for 5 more minutes. Cool, then stir in tomato ketchup, Worcestershire sauce and seasoning.

Roll out dough thinly to a rectangle about 12 x 8 inches. Spread beef mixture over dough, leaving border clear. Scatter cheese over beef mixture, then fold borders on short sides over filling. Roll up from a long side and seal join.

Place strudel on baking sheet. Decorate with trimmings, then brush with beaten egg yolk. Bake for 20 minutes. Reduce heat to 350° and cook for a further 20 minutes. Cut into slices to serve.

Cottage spinach roll

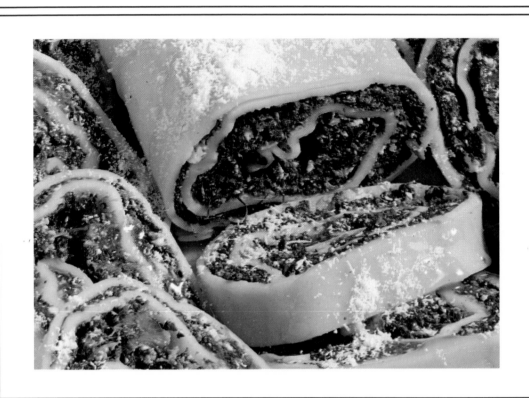

Overall timing 1¾ hours

Freezing Not suitable

To serve 4-6

2 cups	Flour
	Salt and pepper
2	Eggs
2 lb	Bulk spinach
6 tbsp	Butter
1 cup	Cottage cheese
¼ tsp	Grated nutmeg
6 tbsp	Grated Parmesan cheese

Sift the flour and ½ tsp salt into a bowl. Beat the eggs lightly in a bowl, pour half into the flour and mix with a palette knife. Add enough of the remaining egg to make a stiff dough. Knead till smooth, then chill for 30 minutes.

Meanwhile, wash and pick over the spinach. Put into a saucepan with only the water that clings to it. Cover and cook gently for 5 minutes. Drain thoroughly, then shred.

Melt 2 tbsp of the butter in a skillet, add the spinach and cook for 5 minutes, stirring occasionally. Pour into a bowl and add the cottage cheese, nutmeg, half the Parmesan and seasoning. Mix well. Leave to cool.

Roll out the dough on a floured surface to a rectangle about 15 x 12 inches. With a long side nearest you, spread the filling over the dough, leaving a 1 inch border. Fold the bottom border over the filling and roll up. Pinch the ends together to seal.

Wrap the roll in a double thickness of cheesecloth, tying the ends with string. Place in a large pan of boiling salted water, cover and simmer for 25 minutes.

Drain and unwrap the roll and place on a warmed serving dish. Melt the remaining butter. Cut the roll into thick slices, pour the butter over and sprinkle with the remaining Parmesan. Serve immediately.

Deep chicken and ham pie

Overall timing 2¾ hours plus cooling

Freezing Suitable

To serve 6

1 lb	Pie pastry
1½ lb	Boneless chicken
	Salt and pepper
1 tsp	Grated lemon rind
¼ tsp	Dried sage
¼ lb	Sliced cooked ham
1 tsp	Unflavored gelatin
6 tbsp	Chicken broth

Roll out two-thirds of pastry and use to line a greased 6 inch loose-bottomed cake pan. Reserve remaining pastry for lid. Preheat oven to 375°.

Finely dice chicken, keeping breast and dark meat separate. Season both well and add lemon rind and sage. Dice ham. Cover pastry case with half breast meat, then with half dark meat. Spread all ham on top, then repeat layering of dark and breast meats.

Roll reserved pastry to make lid. Moisten dough edges and place lid in position. Press down firmly to seal. Make a hole in center and decorate top. Glaze with lightly beaten egg.

Bake for 1 hour, then reduce oven temperature to 350° and bake for a further 1 – 1¼ hours. Remove pie from oven, cool for 30 minutes then remove from pan and leave until cold.

Meanwhile, dissolve gelatin in chicken broth. When the gelatin mixture begins to set, put a funnel or cone of foil or wax paper into the center hole in the pie. Pour in gelatin and chill in refrigerator till set. Serve cold with salad.

Brazilian meat turnovers

Overall timing 50 minutes

Freezing Suitable: omit hard-cooked eggs and bake from frozen in 425° oven for 30 minutes.

To serve 4

¾lb	Frozen puff pastry
1	Onion
¼lb	Thick bacon slices
2 tbsp	Butter
½lb	Ground beef
3 tbsp	Raisins
	Pinch of ground cloves
	Salt and pepper
¼ tsp	Paprika
2	Hard-cooked eggs
8	Pitted green olives
1	Egg

Thaw the pastry. Roll out to a rectangle 8 x 16 inches. Cut into eight 4 inch squares.

Preheat oven to 400°.

Peel and finely chop the onion. Grind or coarsely process the bacon. Melt the butter in a skillet and fry the onion and bacon till golden. Add the beef and fry briskly, stirring frequently, till brown.

Remove from heat and add the raisins, cloves, salt, pepper and paprika. Mix well. Shell and coarsely chop the hard-cooked eggs. Chop the olives, add to the pan with the eggs and mix well.

Place one eighth of the meat mixture on half of each dough square. Brush the edges with a little of the beaten egg and fold dough over. Crimp edges to seal.

Arrange on a dampened baking sheet and brush tops with beaten egg. Bake for about 25 minutes till well risen and golden.

Sausage in brioche

Overall timing 2½ hours plus rising

Freezing Not suitable

To serve 6-8

1 lb	Piece of fresh
	continental sausage
	Bouquet garni
1	Onion
2 cups	Flour
¼ tsp	Salt
1½ tsp	Active dry yeast
2 tbsp	Lukewarm water
1 tbsp	Sugar
2	Eggs
¼ cup	Butter
1	Egg yolk

Put sausage into a saucepan with bouquet garni and peeled onion and cover with cold water. Bring to a boil and simmer very gently for 1¾ hours.

Meanwhile, sift flour and salt into a bowl. Sprinkle yeast onto the water, add a pinch of the sugar and mix well. Leave in a warm place till frothy, then add to flour with remaining sugar. Add eggs and melted butter to flour and mix to a soft dough. Knead till glossy, cover with oiled plastic wrap and leave in a warm place to rise.

Drain sausage, discarding flavorings, and allow to cool slightly. Remove the skin.

Preheat the oven to 425°.

Roll out dough to a rectangle large enough to enclose the sausage. Place sausage in center and fold dough around it, pinching edges to seal. Place, join down, on a baking sheet. Leave to rise for 15 minutes.

Brush with beaten egg yolk and bake for about 25 minutes till crisp and golden. Serve hot, cut into thick slices.

Rich leek quiche

Overall timing 1 hour

Freezing Suitable: reheat from frozen, covered, in 375° oven for 35 minutes.

To serve 6-8

¾lb	Frozen puff pastry
2lb	Leeks
¼ cup	Butter
1 tbsp	Flour
1¼ cups	Light broth
	Salt and pepper
1	Egg
1	Egg yolk
1 cup	Light cream

Thaw pastry. Preheat the oven to 425°.

Trim leeks. cut into 1 inch lengths. Blanch in boiling water for 5 minutes, then drain thoroughly.

Melt butter in a skillet and fry the leeks for 5 minutes. Sprinkle with flour and cook until lightly browned. Gradually stir in the broth and bring to a boil. Season and cook gently for 10 minutes.

Meanwhile, roll out dough and use to line a 9 inch quiche pan. Prick bottom several times with a fork.

Beat the whole egg, yolk and cream together in a bowl. Remove leeks from heat and add cream mixture. Pour into pastry case and spread evenly. Bake for 30 minutes till lightly set and golden. Serve hot.

Club sandwiches

Overall timing 30 minutes

Freezing Not suitable

To serve 4

4-8	Bacon slices
12	Slices of bread
	Mayonnaise
4	Slices of cooked chicken or turkey
4	Lettuce leaves
5	Tomatoes

Preheat the broiler.

Broil the bacon until crisp. Toast four slices of bread on both sides, but toast the remaining slices of bread on one side only. Slice the tomatoes.

To assemble the sandwiches, spread the untoasted sides of bread with mayonnaise. Place four pieces, toasted side down, on a board and top with the chicken or turkey slices. Cover with the completely toasted bread. Add the lettuce, bacon, tomato slices (reserving some for the garnish) and remaining bread, mayonnaise side down. Press lightly together, then halve diagonally. Garnish with the reserved tomato slices.

Country-style liver pâté

Overall timing 3 hours plus maturing

Freezing Suitable

To serve 12

1½lb	Pork liver
1lb	Canadian bacon
½lb (1 cup)	Lard
1	Egg
1 tbsp	Flour
	Salt and pepper
½ tsp	Ground allspice
	Caul fat
	(optional)

Preheat the oven to 350°.

Chop the liver. Dice bacon. Put liver and bacon through a fine grinder or chop finely in a food processor. Melt the lard in a saucepan and gradually beat into ground liver and bacon in bowl. Beat egg and add with flour, seasoning and allspice. Mix well.

Line greased ovenproof dish with caul fat, if using, leaving edges hanging over sides. Add liver mixture and smooth top. Wrap caul edges over. Cover dish with lid or foil and place in a roasting pan containing 1 inch water. Bake for 1¾ hours.

Allow to cool, then leave in the refrigerator for 2-3 days to mature. Serve with crusty bread.

Blood sausage with apples

Overall timing 25 minutes

Freezing Not suitable

To serve 2

½lb	Blood sausage
¼ cup	Butter
1	Onion
2	Apples
	Fresh parsley

Thickly slice the sausage. Melt the butter in a skillet and add the sausage. Cook till crispy — if you cook them gently the slices will stay intact, instead of breaking away from the skin. Lift out with slotted spoon and keep hot.

Peel onion and slice into rings. Fry gently in the butter till brown and just tender.

Core and slice the apples. Add to pan and cook for 5 minutes, turning slices over halfway through. Add the sausage and cook the mixture for 2 minutes more.

Place sausage, onion and apples on two warmed plates. Garnish with parsley sprigs and serve hot.

Crusty mushroom bread

Overall timing 1 hour

Freezing Suitable: cook after thawing

To serve 6-8

1	Round loaf of bread
½ cup	Butter
1 lb	Mushrooms
	Salt and pepper
3 tbsp	Lemon juice
1 cup	White sauce
2	Eggs

Preheat the oven to 350°.

Slice the top off the bread and scoop out most of the crumbs, leaving a ½ inch thick shell. Spread the inside with half the butter, place on a baking sheet and bake for 10 minutes.

Meanwhile, finely chop the mushrooms. Melt the remaining butter in a saucepan and fry the mushrooms for 5 minutes, stirring frequently. Add salt, pepper and lemon juice. Stir the mushrooms into the white sauce. Separate the eggs and beat the egg yolks, one at a time, into the sauce. Return to the heat and heat through gently. Beat the egg whites till stiff but not dry. Gently fold into the mushroom mixture.

Pour the mixture into the bread shell and sprinkle the top with a few of the scooped out bread crumbs, grated finely. Bake for 30 minutes till well risen and crisp. Serve hot.

Provençal sandwiches

Overall timing 15 minutes

Freezing Not suitable

To serve 4

4	Crusty rolls
1	Garlic clove
4	Large lettuce leaves
2	Large tomatoes
2	Hard-cooked eggs
	Pickled vegetables
	or gherkins
	Ripe olives
	Cooked green beans
	Anchovy fillets
	Sweet green or red
	pepper
	Olive oil
	Vinegar

Halve the rolls and the garlic clove. Rub the cut surfaces of the rolls with the garlic. Place the lettuce leaves on the bottom halves of the rolls.

Slice the tomatoes. Shell and slice the eggs. Place the tomatoes and eggs on the lettuce, then add pickled vegetables or gherkins, olives, beans, anchovies and pepper strips, according to taste. Sprinkle with oil and vinegar, then place the tops of the rolls on the filling. Press gently together and serve.

Ham and potato cake

Overall timing 1 ¼ hours

Freezing Not suitable

To serve 4

1 ½ lb	Medium-size potatoes
	Salt and pepper
½ lb	Sliced cooked ham
6 tbsp	Butter
3 tbsp	Soft bread crumbs
2 cups	Grated cheese
½ cup	Milk

Cook potatoes in boiling salted water for 20 minutes. Meanwhile, chop the ham. Grease a 7 inch springform pan with a little of the butter and sprinkle breadcrumbs over the bottom and sides, shaking off any excess. Preheat oven to 350°.

Drain and peel the potatoes, then cut into ¼ inch thick slices. Arrange a few of the slices, slightly overlapping, in the bottom of the pan. Melt the remaining butter and brush a little over the potatoes. Scatter some of the ham, then some of the cheese over and season. Continue layering, reserving a little of the butter, and finishing with a layer of potato topped with cheese. Pour the milk over and brush with remaining butter.

Bake for about 30 minutes till potatoes are tender and cheese has melted. Unmold cake from pan to serve.

Ham and vegetable bake

Overall timing 1 hour 10 minutes

Freezing Suitable: top with egg after reheating in 350° oven for 1 ¼ hours

To serve 4

½lb	Frozen spinach
1lb	Celeriac
2lb	Potatoes
	Salt and pepper
5 tbsp	Butter
3 tbsp	Light cream
6 tbsp	Hot milk
1	Small head of celery
½lb	Sliced cooked ham
1 cup	Grated Cheddar cheese
2	Eggs

Place spinach in a strainer to thaw. Peel celeriac and potatoes and cut into small chunks. Put prepared vegetable chunks into saucepan of cold salted water and bring to a boil. Cook for 20 minutes till tender. Drain well and mash or purée with ¼ cup of the butter, the cream and enough milk to give a creamy purée. Season to taste.

Preheat over to 400°.

Wash and trim celery. Blanch in boiling water for 5 minutes. Drain well and cut into pieces.

Grease ovenproof dish with remaining butter. Spread the well-drained spinach over, arrange the chopped celery on top and cover with ham slices. Sprinkle over half the cheese and cover with the celeriac and potato purée. Bake for 15 minutes.

In a bowl, lightly beat the eggs with salt and pepper. Pour over the purée, top with remaining cheese and return to oven. Bake for another 15 minutes till golden. Serve immediately.

Curried clams with rice

Overall timing 30 minutes

Freezing Not suitable

To serve 2

½ cup	Long grain rice
	Salt
1 lb	Small clams
Curry sauce	
1	Small onion
1	Garlic clove
2 tbsp	Butter
1 tbsp	Curry powder
	Ground cinnamon
	Ground ginger
	Sugar
¼ cup	Boiling water
	Salt and pepper

Cook the rice in boiling salted water till tender.

Meanwhile, scrub the clams well under cold running water. Place them in a saucepan of salted water. Bring to a boil, cover and cook gently till the shells open. Discard any that do not open. Remove clams from their shells and set aside. Strain the cooking liquid through a cheesecloth-lined sieve into bowl.

Peel and finely chop onion and garlic. Melt butter in a skillet and fry the onion and garlic till transparent. Add the curry powder and cook for a further 2 minutes. Add a large pinch each of cinnamon, ginger and sugar and the boiling water. Add 5 tbsp of the cooking liquid from the clams. Taste, and season if necessary.

Stir the clams into the sauce and heat through quickly. Put the drained rice on a warmed serving dish and pour the clams and sauce over. Serve hot.

Shrimp pilaf

Overall timing 1 hour

Freezing Not suitable

To serve 4

2	Large onions
2	Fresh green chilies
2	Garlic cloves
½lb	Bacon slices
1 cup	Long-grain rice
16oz	Can of tomatoes
	Salt
2 cups	Chicken broth
1lb	Shelled shrimp
2 tbsp	Chopp
d parsley	
2 tbspu5	Grated Parmesan cheese

Peel and slice onions. Seed and slice chilies. Peel and crush garlic. Chop bacon.

Heat a flameproof casserole. Add bacon and fry until well browned. Add the onions, chilies and garlic to the casserole. Cook until onions are soft and transparent but not brown, stirring occasionally.

Add the rice and stir for 2-3 minutes until grains are coated with fat. Add the tomatoes with their juice, salt and chicken broth. Bring rapidly to a boil, then reduce heat, cover and simmer for 15 minutes on a very low heat.

Stir and add the shrimp. Cover and cook for a further 5 minutes.

Turn mixture into warmed serving dish. Sprinkle with parsley and cheese and serve immediately.

Fish paella

Overall timing 45 minutes

Freezing Not suitable

To serve 6

1	Large onion
2	Garlic cloves
¼ cup	Oil
2 cups	Long grain rice
16oz	Can of tomatoes
4	Saffron strands
2 quarts	Chicken broth or
	water
	Salt and pepper
1½lb	White fish fillets
1	Sweet red pepper
16oz	Can of artichoke
	hearts
16oz	Can of kidney beans
2 cups	Frozen peas

Peel and chop the onion. Peel and crush the garlic. Heat the oil in a flameproof casserole, add the onion and fry till transparent. Add the rice and garlic and fry, stirring, for 2 minutes.

Add the tomatoes and juice, the saffron, broth or water and seasoning and bring to a boil. Reduce the heat and simmer for 10 minutes.

Meanwhile, cut the fish into chunks. Halve and seed the pepper and cut into 1 inch pieces. Drain the artichoke hearts and cut in half lengthwise. Drain the beans.

Add all these ingredients to the pan with the peas and mix lightly. Cover and cook for a further 10 minutes till the rice is tender and the liquid is absorbed. Fluff the mixture with a fork. Taste and adjust seasoning. Serve immediately.

Pilau rice

Overall timing 45 minutes plus soaking

Freezing Not suitable

To serve 4-6

1 lb	Patna rice
1	Large onion
1	Garlic clove
6	Whole allspice
8	Cardamom pods
½ cup	Butter or ghee
2 inch	Cinnamon stick
8	Cloves
1 tsp	Ground turmeric
	Salt
½ cup	Flaked almonds
⅔ cup	Golden raisins

Soak rice in cold water for 1 hour, then drain thoroughly.

Peel and finely chop the onion. Peel and crush garlic. Lightly crush allspice and cardamom pods. Melt 6 tbsp of the fat in a saucepan. Add onion, garlic and spices and fry till onion is transparent but not browned.

Add rice and cook over a low heat, stirring for 3-4 minutes. Add salt to taste and enough boiling water to come 1 inch above the rice. Cover pan tightly and simmer over a very low heat for about 20 minutes till water is absorbed and rice is tender.

Melt remaining fat in skillet and fry almonds and raisins for 3-5 minutes. Mix lightly into rice and serve immediately.

Eggplant and pasta casserole

Overall timing 1 hour

Freezing Not suitable

To serve 4-6

1	Large eggplant
	Salt and pepper
1	Onion
1	Garlic clove
6 tbsp	Butter
1lb	Tomatoes
2 tsp	Chopped fresh basil
6 tbsp	Oil
¾lb	Rigatoni pasta
3oz	Mozzarella cheese

Preheat oven to 400°.

Cut eggplant into thin slices lengthwise. Arrange slices on a plate, sprinkle with salt and leave for 30 minutes.

Meanwhile, peel and chop onion. Peel and crush garlic. Melt ¼ cup of the butter in a saucepan, add onion and garlic and fry till transparent.

Blanch, peel and finely chop tomatoes. Add to onion with seasoning. Simmer gently for 15 minutes. Remove from heat and stir in basil.

Rinse eggplant slices under running cold water and pat dry with paper towels. Heat oil in skillet, add slices and cook for 4-5 minutes each side. Drain on paper towels.

Cook rigatoni in boiling salted water till tender. Drain and mix with tomato sauce. Season to taste. Put half the rigatoni mixture into greased ovenproof dish and arrange eggplant slices on top. Add remaining rigatoni mixture. Thinly slice cheese and arrange on top. Dot with remaining butter and bake for 15 minutes. Serve hot.

Seafood spaghetti

Overall timing 20 minutes

Freezing Not suitable

To serve 4

¾lb	Spaghetti
	Salt and pepper
1	Garlic clove
3 tbsp	Oil
½lb	Large shelled shrimp
10oz	Can of baby clams or mussels
8oz	Can of tomatoes
1 tbsp	Chopped parsley

Cook spaghetti in boiling salted water till tender.

Meanwhile, peel and crush garlic. Heat oil in a large saucepan, add garlic and fry for 1 minute. Add shrimp and fry, stirring, for 2-3 minutes.

Drain clams or mussels and add to pan with tomatoes and their juice and seasoning. Cook for about 3 minutes, stirring to break up tomatoes.

Drain spaghetti thoroughly. Add to seafood sauce with parsley and toss lightly over a low heat till well coated. Serve immediately.

Spaghetti with goat's cheese

Overall timing 35 minutes

Freezing Not suitable

To serve 2

1	Garlic clove
2	Anchovy fillets
2 tbsp	Olive oil
1 tbsp	Chopped parsley
	Salt and pepper
½lb	Spaghetti
¼lb	Firm goat's cheese
2 tbsp	Butter

Peel and crush the garlic into a bowl. Add the anchovy fillets and pound to a paste with a wooden spoon. Beat in the oil, parsley and seasoning. Leave to stand for 15 minutes.

Meanwhile, cook the spaghetti in boiling salted water till tender. Derind the cheese and cut into small cubes.

Drain the spaghetti in a colander. Melt the butter in the spaghetti pan and add the cheese. Cook, stirring, over a low heat for 2 minutes.

Return spaghetti to the pan and toss lightly till coated with butter. Arrange in a warmed serving dish, pour the anchovy dressing over and toss lightly before serving with crusty bread.

Crisp-topped macaroni with tuna

Overall timing 35 minutes

Freezing Not suitable

To serve 4

1	Onion
6 tbsp	Butter
½ cup	Chicken broth
	Salt and pepper
1	Medium-size cauliflower
½ lb	Short-cut macaroni
6	Anchovy fillets
½ cup	Soft bread crumbs
7 oz	Can of tuna
¼ cup	Grated Parmesan cheese

Peel and chop the onion. Melt 2 tbsp of the butter in a large saucepan and fry the onion till golden. Add the chicken broth and seasoning. Bring to a boil and simmer for 5 minutes.

Divide cauliflower into florets and cook in boiling salted water for 4 minutes. Remove with a slotted spoon and reserve. Add macaroni to boiling water and cook till tender.

Meanwhile, melt remaining butter in a skillet and fry cauliflower till golden. Roughly chop anchovies and add to pan with bread crumbs. Fry till crisp. Remove from heat.

Preheat the broiler.

Drain the macaroni and add to the broth mixture. Drain and flake tuna and stir carefully into the macaroni with half the Parmesan. Taste and adjust seasoning and heat through gently.

Pour the macaroni mixture into a flameproof dish and scatter cauliflower and bread crumb mixture over it. Sprinkle with remaining cheese, then broil for 5 minutes till golden.

Lasagne alla bolognese

Overall timing 2 hours

Freezing Suitable: reheat in 350° oven for 1 hour.

To serve 6

1	Onion
1	Carrot
1	Stalk of celery
¼lb	Slab bacon
¼lb	Chuck steak
¼lb	Fresh pork sides
6 tbsp	Butter
1 tbsp	Tomato paste
½ cup	Hot broth
3 tbsp	Dry white wine
½ cup	Milk
1 lb	Fresh bulk spinach
	Salt and pepper
¾lb	Green lasagne
2½ cups	White sauce
¾ cup	Grated Parmesan cheese

Peel and chop onion and carrot. Chop celery. Chop bacon. Grind meats. Melt 2 tbsp of butter in a saucepan, add bacon and meats and brown. Add vegetables, tomato paste, broth, wine and milk. Simmer gently for 45 minutes, stirring occasionally.

Meanwhile, wash spinach and remove coarse stalks. Place in a saucepan with 2 tbsp of the butter and seasoning. Cook gently for 5-10 minutes. Chop finely and add to meat mixture.

Preheat oven to 375°.
Cook lasagne in boiling, salted water till tender. Drain on damp dish-towel.

Cover bottom of greased ovenproof dish with a quarter of the lasagne. Spread half the meat mixture on top, then another quarter of the lasagne, half the white sauce and Parmesan. Repeat layers, finishing with white sauce and Parmesan. Dot with remaining butter. Bake for 20 minutes.

Spaghetti alla carbonara

Overall timing 20 minutes

Freezing Not suitable

To serve 4

¾lb	Spaghetti
	Salt and pepper
2	Eggs
2 tbsp	Half-and-half
¼lb	Bacon slices
1 tbsp	Oil
½ cup	Grated Parmesan
	cheese

Cook the spaghetti in boiling water till tender.

Meanwhile, beat eggs, half-and-half and pepper in a bowl. Dice the bacon. Heat the oil in a large skillet, add the bacon and fry till crisp.

Drain the spaghetti and add to the bacon. Pour in the egg mixture, stirring, and toss over a gentle heat till the egs just begin to set. Serve immediately, sprinkled with grated Parmesan.

Spaghetti with chicken sauce

Overall timing 1 hour

Freezing Suitable: cook spaghetti and almonds after reheating sauce

To serve 4

2	Thick bacon slices
¾ lb	Boneless chicken breasts
¼ cup	Butter
1 lb	Ripe tomatoes
1	Garlic clove
2 tbsp	Tomato paste
½ tsp	Sugar
	Salt and pepper
½ cup	Dry white wine
¾ lb	Spaghetti
¼ cup	Chopped almonds

Dice the bacon. Wipe and trim the chicken, discarding skin. Cut the meat into strips. Heat half the butter in a flameproof casserole, add the bacon and chicken and fry for 5 minutes till browned all over.

Blanch, peel and chop the tomatoes. Add to the pan with the peeled and crushed garlic, tomato paste, sugar and salt and pepper. Add the wine and bring to a boil, stirring. Reduce the heat, cover the pan tightly and simmer for 20 minutes.

Meanwhile, cook the spaghetti in boiling salted water till just tender. Drain in a colander.

Melt remaining butter in the saucepan, add the almonds and fry over a high heat till golden. Return the spaghetti to the pan with half the tomato chicken sauce, toss lightly and adjust seasoning to taste. Place in a warmed serving dish.

Season remaining sauce, pour into a warmed sauceboat and serve separately.

Turkey noodle bake

Overall timing 1 ½ hours

Freezing Not suitable

To serve 4

¼ lb	Button mushrooms
½ lb	Noodles
	Salt and pepper
3 tbsp	Flour
1	Chicken bouillon cube
¼ tsp	Paprika
5 tbsp	Light cream
1 cup	Diced cooked turkey meat
½ cup	Grated Cheddar cheese
½ cup	Soft bread crumbs
1 tbsp	Butter

Wipe and slice the mushrooms. Cook the noodles in boiling salted water for about 5 minutes, till tender. Drain the noodles thoroughly, reserving 2½ cups of the cooking water.

Blend the flour in a small bowl with a little of the measured cooking water. Put rest of the measured cooking water into a saucepan, stir in blended flour, crumbled bouillon cube, salt, pepper and paprika. Bring to a boil, stirring. Reduce the heat and add the mushrooms. Simmer for 10 minutes.

Preheat the oven to 350°. Grease an 8 inch soufflé dish.

Remove pan from heat and stir in cream.

Spread half the drained noodles over the bottom of the souffle dish. Arrange half the turkey over the noodles. Cover with half the sauce. Repeat the layers, finishing with sauce. Scatter cheese over top. Sprinkle with bread crumbs and dot with butter. Bake for 30 minutes.

Cheesy macaroni

Overall timing 30 minutes

Freezing Not suitable

To serve 4

½lb	Long macaroni
	Salt and pepper
2	Eggs
¼lb	Cooked ham
1½ cups	Grated Cheddar cheese
6 tbsp	Butter
	Cayenne

Preheat the oven to 425°. Grease an 8 inch soufflé dish.

Place macaroni in saucepan of boiling salted water and cook till tender.

Meanwhile, lightly beat the eggs. Coarsely chop the ham. Drain macaroni and place in soufflé dish. Add ¼ cup of the butter, 1¼ cups of the cheese, the eggs and ham to the dish. Add a pinch of cayenne and season to taste. Mix well. Sprinkle with remaining cheese and dot with the rest of the butter.

Bake for 10 minutes or till golden and lightly set. Serve immediately with a tomato salad.

Cheesy noodles with ham

Overall timing 1 hour

Freezing Not suitable

To serve 4

½lb	Tagliatelle
	Salt and pepper
1 cup	Grated cheese
3	Eggs
2 cups	White sauce
¼lb	Sliced cooked ham

Preheat the oven to 400°.

Cook the noodles in boiling salted water for about 10 minutes till tender.

Separate eggs. Stir yolks, ¾ cup of the cheese and seasoning into sauce.

Cut ham into strips and stir into the sauce. Drain noodles thoroughly and fold into sauce. Season to taste. Beat the egg whites in a bowl till stiff but not dry and fold into the mixture with metal spoon.

Pour the mixture into a greased ovenproof dish. Sprinkle remaining grated cheese over and bake for about 30 minutes till set and golden. Serve immediately with whole green beans mixed with flaked almonds and butter.

Spaghetti with eggplant

Overall timing 45 minutes plus draining

Freezing Not suitable

To serve 4

1	Large eggplant
	Salt and pepper
1 lb	Ripe tomatoes
1	Garlic clove
	Oil
2 tsp	Chopped fresh basil
¾ lb	Spaghetti
½ cup	Grated Parmesan cheese
	Sprig of basil

Wash and thinly slice the eggplant. Put into a colander and sprinkle with salt. Leave to drain for 1 hour.

Blanch, peel and chop the tomatoes. Peel and crush garlic. Heat 3 tbsp oil in a saucepan, add garlic and fry for 1 minute. Add tomatoes, basil and seasoning, stir well and cook over a low heat for 15 minutes.

Cook spaghetti in boiling salted water till tender.

Meanwhile, rinse eggplant slices under running water and gently squeeze dry. Heat ½ inch oil in a skillet and fry eggplant slices, a few at a time, till crisp on both sides. Drain on paper towels and keep hot.

Drain spaghetti thoroughly. Put into a warmed serving dish and pour tomato sauce over. Add eggplant slices, sprinkle with cheese, garnish with sprig of basil and serve.

Macaroni niçoise

Overall timing 30 minutes

Freezing Not suitable

To serve 4

3	Anchovy fillets
¾lb	Tomatoes
1	Garlic clove
¾lb	Rigatoni pasta
	Salt
¼ cup	Butter
½ cup	Grated Parmesan cheese
1 tbsp	Chopped fresh basil

Chop the anchovies. Blanch, peel and cut tomatoes into thin slices. Place in a serving bowl with the anchovies and peeled and crushed garlic.

Cook the rigatoni in a large saucepan of boiling salted water till just tender. When cooked, drain in colander.

Melt butter in the saucepan and when frothy, add rigatoni and toss well. Add to the tomatoes and garlic, toss, then sprinkle with Parmesan and basil and serve immediately.

Spaghetti with bacon sauce

Overall timing 45 minutes

Freezing Not suitable

To serve 4

¾lb	Slab bacon
1	Small sweet red pepper
16oz.	Can of tomatoes
	Salt and pepper
¾lb	Spaghetti
6 tbsp	Grated Parmesan cheese

Cut the bacon into ¼ inch thick slices, then cut across into strips. Heat a saucepan, add the bacon and fry till golden all over.

Seed and finely chop the pepper. Add to the pan and fry for 1 minute. Press the tomatoes and juice through a sieve into the pan and bring to a boil, stirring. Add seasoning, cover and simmer for 15 minutes.

Meanwhile, cook the spaghetti in boiling salted water till tender. Drain thoroughly and return to the pan. Add the sauce and all but 1 tbsp of the cheese. Toss lightly over a low heat for 2 minutes. Adjust the seasoning to taste.

Place spaghetti in a warmed serving dish and sprinkle with the remaining cheese. Serve immediately with fresh crusty bread.

Spaghetti with piquant sauce

Overall timing 50 minutes

Freezing Not suitable

To serve 4

1	Can of anchovy
	fillets
¼ cup	Milk
1 lb	Ripe tomatoes
1	Garlic clove
1	Dried red chili pepper
6 tbsp	Olive oil
1 tbsp	Tomato paste
2 tbsp	Capers
¾ lb	Spaghetti
	Salt and pepper
1 cup	Pitted ripe olives

Drain the anchovies and put into a small bowl with the milk. Soak for 10 minutes. Blanch, peel and chop tomatoes. Peel and crush the garlic; seed and finely chop the chili.

Heat the oil in a saucepan, add the garlic and cook for 2 minutes. Drain the anchovies, discarding the milk. Chop and add to the pan with the chili. Fry for 3 minutes, pressing the anchovies with the back of a wooden spoon to break them up.

Add the tomatoes, tomato paste and capers. Bring to a boil, then cover and simmer for 15 minutes.

Meanwhile, cook the spaghetti in boiling salted water till tender. Drain thoroughly. Return to the pan and add the tomato and anchovy sauce and the olives. Stir over a low heat for 3 minutes. Adjust seasoning to taste and serve hot.

Mushroom ravioli

Overall timing 45 minutes

Freezing Suitable: Cook from frozen

To serve 4

3 cups	Flour
	Salt and pepper
3	Eggs
1 lb	Mushrooms
1	Onion
¼ cup	Butter

Sift flour and 1 tsp salt into a bowl. Add eggs and mix to a smooth, glossy dough. Add a little water if necessary.

Chop the mushrooms. Peel and finely chop onion. Melt half the butter in a skillet and fry the onion for 5 minutes till transparent. Add mushrooms and seasoning and stir-fry over a high heat for about 5 minutes to evaporate any liquid. Reduce heat and cook gently for a further 5 minutes. Remove from heat and leave to cool.

Roll out the dough on a lightly floured surface and cut into 3 inch squares with a pastry wheel. Divide the mushroom mixture between the squares, then fold them over, pressing the edges together well to seal.

Put plenty of lightly salted water in a large saucepan and bring to a boil. Add the ravioli and cook for 10-15 minutes, then drain and place in a warmed serving dish. Melt the remaining butter, pour over the ravioli and toss well.

Neapolitan cannelloni

Overall timing 1½ hours

Freezing Suitable: reheat from frozen in 350° oven for 1 hour

To serve 4

12	Sheets of lasagne
½lb	Mozzarella cheese
2oz	Cooked ham
½lb	Cream cheese
2	Eggs
	Salt and pepper
6 tbsp	Grated Parmesan cheese
Tomato sauce	
1	Onion
1	Garlic clove
1 tbsp	Oil
16oz	Can of tomatoes
1 tbsp	Chopped fresh basil

Cook lasagne in boiling salted water for 10-15 minutes till tender. Drain and spread on a damp cloth to cool.

Thinly slice the Mozzarella. Dice ham. Place in a bowl with the cream cheese, eggs and seasoning. Mix well.

For the sauce, peel and finely chop onion. Peel and crush garlic and fry until golden. Add tomatoes in their juice, basil, salt and pepper. Cook for 10 minutes, stirring occasionally.

Preheat oven to 425°.

Divide cheese mixture between lasagne sheets. Roll lasagne around filling and arrange, joins down, in greased ovenproof dish. Pour the tomato sauce over. Sprinkle half the Parmesan on top and bake for 15 minutes or until golden. Sprinkle with the rest of the Parmesan and serve immediately.

Spaghetti with sardine dressing

Overall timing 20 minutes

Freezing Not suitable

To serve 4

¾lb	Spaghetti
	Salt and pepper
11½oz	Can of sardines
2	Garlic cloves
6 tbsp	Butter

Cook the spaghetti in boiling salted water till tender.

Drain the sardines and put into a mortar. Peel and crush garlic and add to sardines. Pound to a paste with a pestle. Add the butter and mix well. Season to taste.

Drain the spaghetti and return to the pan. Add the sardine paste and toss lightly over a low heat till the spaghetti is coated. Place in a warmed serving dish and serve immediately with wedges of lemon.

Spaghetti with tomato sauce

Overall timing 30 minutes

Freezing Not suitable

To serve 4

1	Onion
2lb	Cherry or plum
	tomatoes
	Bouquet garni
	Pinch of sugar
	Cayenne or
	hot pepper sauce
	Salt and pepper
1 tbsp	Chopped fresh basil
	or parsley
¾lb	Spaghetti

Peel and chop the onion. Halve the tomatoes. Put the onion and tomatoes in a saucepan with the bouquet garni and simmer gently until mushy.

Discard the bouquet garni, then rub the tomato sauce through a sieve, or purée in a blender. Return to the pan and add the sugar, a little cayenne or pepper sauce and seasoning. Stir in the herbs and reheat gently.

Meanwhile, cook the spaghetti in boiling salted water till just tender. Drain well and turn into a warmed serving dish. Pile the tomato sauce on top and serve.

Pasta with lamb and tomato sauce

Overall timing 1 ¼ hours

Freezing Not suitable

To serve 2

2	Bacon slices
½lb	Tomatoes
1	Onion
1	Garlic clove
6oz	Ground lamb
½ cup	Red wine
	Salt and pepper
½lb	Pasta shapes

Chop bacon. Blanch, peel and chop tomatoes. Peel and chop onion and garlic. Heat a saucepan, add the bacon and fry for 5 minutes. Add onion and garlic and fry gently till transparent. Add the ground lamb and fry for about 15 minutes till browned.

Stir in the red wine, tomatoes and seasoning. Cover and simmer for 40 minutes.

Meanwhile, cook pasta in boiling salted water till tender. Drain and place in a warmed serving dish.

Spoon meat sauce over pasta and serve hot with a green salad.

Cannelloni with tuna fish

Overall timing 1 ½ hours

Freezing Suitable: reheat in 350° oven for 1 hour

To serve 4

12	Sheets of lasagne
	Salt and pepper
2	Onions
2	Garlic cloves
2oz	Capers
7oz	Can of tuna fish
1 cup	Soft bread crumbs
1 tbsp	Lemon juice
1	Egg
2 tbsp	Chopped parsley
16oz	Can of tomatoes
2 tbsp	Grated Parmesan cheese

Place lasagne in saucepan of boiling, salted water and cook for 10-15 minutes or until tender. Drain in a colander, rinse with boiling water and spread out on a damp dishtowel to cool for a few minutes.

Peel and chop onions. Peel and crush garlic. Drain capers. Drain tuna fish oil into a skillet, heat, add onions and fry until golden. Add garlic, tuna fish and capers and cook over low heat for 5 minutes, stirring. Remove from heat.

Preheat oven to 400°. Grease ovenproof dish.

Add bread crumbs (reserving 2 tbsp) to fish mixture with lemon juice, egg, parsley and seasoning. Mix well. Place some of the fish mixture in center of each lasagne sheet and roll around filling. Arrange rolls, joins down, in ovenproof dish.

Press tomatoes in their juice through a sieve, season and spread over cannelloni. Sprinkle with reserved bread crumbs and then with Parmesan. Bake for 30 minutes.

Eggplant cheese bake

Overall timing 2¼ hours

Freezing Suitable: bake from frozen in 350° oven for 45 minutes

To serve 4

1¼lb	Eggplants
	Salt and pepper
2 tbsp	Flour
	Oil
1	Small onion
16oz	Can of tomatoes
½ tsp	Dried basil
½lb	Mozzarella cheese
¾ cup	Grated Parmesan cheese

Remove stalks from eggplant and cut lengthwise in ½ inch thick slices. Sprinkle with salt. Leave for 1 hour, then rinse and pat dry. Coat with flour.

Preheat the oven to 350°. Heat oil in a large skillet and fry eggplant slices on both sides till golden. Drain on paper towels and keep warm.

Peel and finely chop onion. Fry till transparent, adding more oil to pan if necessary. Mash tomatoes and juice and add to pan with seasoning. Cook for 10 minutes. Stir in basil and simmer for a further 5 minutes.

Place a layer of eggplant in oiled ovenproof dish. Cover with slices of Mozzarella and spoon on a little tomato sauce. Sprinkle with Parmesan and a pinch of salt. Repeat layering, ending with Parmesan. Sprinkle a little oil over surface and bake for 15 minutes or until top begins to brown.

Eggplant boxes

Overall timing 1 ½ hours

Freezing Not suitable

To serve 4

4 small	Eggplants
	Salt and pepper
3	Anchovy fillets
2oz	Mozzarella cheese
1 tsp	Dried basil
2 tsp	Capers
1	Large onion
2	Garlic cloves
2 tbsp	Oil
16oz	Can of tomatoes
1 tbsp	Worcestershire sauce
4-5	Fresh tomatoes
	(optional)

Cook eggplants in boiling salted water for 5 minutes. Drain and leave to cool, then cut off stalks and make a lengthwise cut through the eggplants leaving the halves still attached at one side. Ease open and remove most of the flesh with a teaspoon. Finely chop or mash the flesh and put into a bowl.

Drain and chop anchovies. Dice Mozzarella. Mix together eggplant flesh, anchovies, basil, Mozzarella, capers and seasoning. Stuff the hollowed-out eggplant shells with mixture.

Preheat the oven to 350°.

Peel and chop onion. Peel and crush garlic. Heat oil in flameproof casserole and fry onion till brown. Stir in garlic, tomatoes, Worcestershire sauce and seasoning. Simmer gently for about 10 minutes or until the sauce has become quite pulpy.

Arrange the stuffed eggplants on top of sauce and bake for 45 minutes. You can add 4-5 fresh tomatoes about 15 minutes before the end of the cooking time − they add attractive colour as well as taste.

Tomatoes stuffed with vegetables

Overall timing 30 minutes

Freezing Not suitable

To serve 4

3	Large waxy potatoes
3	Large carrots
¼lb	Green beans
2	Stalks of celery
	Salt and pepper
1 cup	Frozen peas
6 tbsp	Mayonnaise
	Lemon juice
4	Large tomatoes
	Basil leaves
	Hard-cooked eggs

Peel the potatoes. Scrape the carrots. Trim the beans. Wash and trim the celery. Dice all the vegetables. Cook in boiling salted water for 5 minutes. Add the peas and cook for a further 5 minutes or until tender. Drain well and cool.

Add the mayonnaise to the vegetables with a few drops of lemon juice and seasoning and mix well.

Halve the tomatoes and scoop out the seeds and centers. Fill with the vegetable mixture and arrange on a serving plate. Serve garnished with basil leaves and sliced hard-cooked egg.

Endive rolls in cheese sauce

Overall timing 1 ¼ hours

Freezing Suitable: bake from frozen in cold oven set to 350° for 1 hour; increase to 450° for extra 10 minutes

To serve 4-6

½ cup	Butter
8	Large heads of Belgian endive
2 tbsp	Lemon juice
1 tsp	Sugar
	Salt and pepper
2 tbsp	Flour
1 ¼ cups	Milk
	Grated nutmeg
2	Egg yolks
½ cup	Grated Parmesan cheese
8	Thin slices of cooked ham

Melt half butter in a saucepan and add endive, lemon juice, sugar and seasoning. Cover and cook gently for about 30 minutes, turning the endive occasionally.

Meanwhile, make the sauce. Melt 2 tbsp of remaining butter in another saucepan and stir in the flour. Remove from heat and gradually add milk. Return to heat and bring to a boil, stirring until thickened. Remove from heat and stir in a pinch of nutmeg, egg yolks, cheese and seasoning.

Preheat the broiler.

Lift out endive with slotted spoon. Reserve cooking liquid. Wrap each endive head in a slice of ham and arrange in a greased ovenproof dish. Add reserved liquid to sauce, heat well, then pour over endive. Dot with the rest of the butter and broil for 5-10 minutes till golden on top. Serve immediately.

Swiss-style potatoes

Overall timing 1 hour

Freezing Not suitable

To serve 4

2lb	Potatoes
3 tbsp	Caraway seeds
1 tbsp	Sea-salt
¼ cup	Butter
1 cup	Cottage cheese
½ cup	Milk
1	Onion
2 tbsp	Chopped parsley
2 tbsp	Chopped garden cress
	Salt and pepper
Garnish	
	Parsley sprigs
	Garden cress

Preheat the oven to 350°.

Halve potatoes. Mix caraway seeds and sea-salt together in a bowl. Dip the cut sides of potatoes into mixture. Place potatoes in greased ovenproof dish with the caraway seeds facing up.

Melt the butter and pour a little over each potato half. Bake for 45 minutes.

Mix cheese with milk in a bowl. Peel and finely chop onion and add to bowl with parsley, cress and seasoning.

Divide cheese mixture between warmed serving plates and place the potatoes on top. Garnish with parsley and cress.

Zucchini with Mozzarella

Overall timing 30 minutes plus chilling

Freezing Not suitable

To serve 2

1	Onion
1	Garlic clove
2 tbsp	Butter
3 tbsp	Oil
8oz	Can of tomatoes
¼ tsp	Dried basil
4	Zucchini
2 tbsp	Flour
	Salt and pepper
¼lb	Mozzarella cheese

Peel and finely chop onion. Peel and crush garlic. Heat butter and 1 tbsp oil in a skillet and fry onion and garlic till transparent.

Drain tomatoes. Add to pan with basil and cook over a low heat for 20 minutes. Purée mixture in a blender or food processor.

Trim and slice zucchini. Coat slices with flour. Heat remaining oil in another skillet and fry zucchini till lightly golden and tender. Drain on paper towels and season with salt and pepper.

Thinly slice Mozzarella. Layer zucchini, Mozzarella and tomato sauce in serving dish. Chill for 2-3 hours. Serve with hot garlic bread or toast and butter curls.

Deep-fried zucchini

Overall timing 2¼ hours including salting

Freezing Not suitable

To serve 4

1¼lb	Zucchini
	Salt
3 tbsp	Flour
	Oil for frying

Trim zucchini and cut into thin strips. Sprinkle with salt and leave for 1½ hours.

Dry zucchini well on paper towels and coat in flour. Shake in a strainer to remove excess flour.

Heat oil in a deep-fryer

Fry zucchini till lightly golden, then drain well on paper towels. Serve hot with tartare sauce

Variation

Season the flour with a little paprika or ground coriander before coating zucchini.

Braised fennel

Overall timing 1 hour

Freezing Suitable

To serve 6

5	Bulbs of fennel
	Salt and pepper
¼ lb	Slab bacon
1	Onion
¼ cup	Butter
1 cup	Chicken broth
	Bouquet garni
	Sprigs of parsley

Trim fennel. Cut each bulb in half and blanch in boiling water for 10 minutes. Drain.

Finely chop bacon. Peel and chop onion. Melt butter in flameproof casserole and fry bacon for 5 minutes.

Arrange onion and fennel pieces on top of bacon. Cover with broth and add bouquet garni and seasoning. Cover and simmer for about 45 minutes till tender.

Remove bouquet garni. If liked, sprinkle fennel with grated Parmesan cheese. Garnish with parsley and serve with chicken or a baked ham.

Tunisian stuffed zucchini

Overall timing 1¼ hours

Freezing Suitable: bake from frozen, covered, in 350° oven for about 45 minutes

To serve 4

1 lb	Zucchini
1	Onion
½ lb	Ground lamb
1 tbsp	Chopped parsley
2	Eggs
	Cayenne
	Salt and pepper
¼ cup	Flour
¼ cup	Oil
8 oz	Can of tomatoes
	Parsley

Trim zucchini. Using a long thin knife or melon-baller, scoop out center of each whole zucchini, working from both ends if necessary and trying to keep the sides an even thickness. Reserve cut-out flesh.

Peel and finely chop onion and mix with chopped zucchini flesh, ground lamb, parsley, 1 egg, a pinch of cayenne and seasoning.

Fill zucchini with prepared mixture. Roll any leftover mixture into little meat balls. Beat remaining egg in a bowl and dip stuffed zucchini and meat balls in in. Coat lightly with flour.

Heat oil in a large skillet. Add zucchini and meat balls and cook for about 20 minutes, turning to brown all sides. Remove from pan and drain on paper towels.

Sieve tomatoes and their juice. Add to pan juices with seasoning and cook over a moderate heat for about 15 minutes.

Return zucchini and meat balls to pan and cook for a further 15 minutes. Serve hot sprinkled with chopped parsley.

Avocado and pepper omelettes

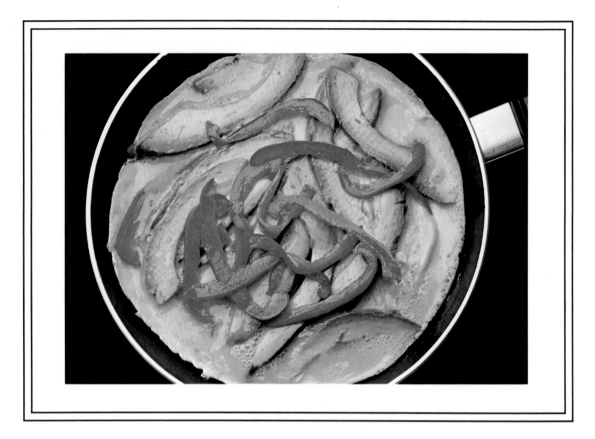

Overall timing 15 minutes

Freezing Not Suitable

To serve 4

1	Sweet red pepper
6 tbsp	Butter
2	Ripe avocados
1 tbsp	Lemon jice
12	Eggs
1 tbsp	Water
	Salt and pepper

Seed pepper and cut into long strips. Melt 2 tbsp of the butter in a omelette pan and fry pepper till just tender. Remove from pan and set aside.

Cut avocados in half lengthwise and lift out seeds. Peel, then cut avocado flesh into thick strips. Sprinkle with lemon juice to prevent discoloration.

Lightly beat together eggs, water and seasoning in a pitcher. Divide remaining butter into four pieces. Melt one piece in omelette pan.

Pour one-quarter of egg mixture into pan and cook till omelette starts to set. Run a spatula around the edge to loosen it and tilt the pan to the the uncooked egg run underneath. Continue to cook till the omelette is just soft and creamy.

Spread one-quarter of the pepper and avocado strips on top. Cook for 1 further minute, then fold over the omelette and slide it onto a warm serving plate. Serve immediately or keep it warm while you cook three more omelettes in the same way.

Baked sweet potatoes

Overall timing 1 hour

Freezing Not suitable

To serve 4

4 x ½lb	Sweet potaotes
	Salt and pepper
¼ cup	Butter

Preheat the oven to 400°.

Wash the sweet potatoes gently to avoid breaking the skin. Arrange on a greased baking sheet and bake for about 45 minutes till tender when pierced with a skewer.

Arrange the sweet potatoes on a warmed serving dish and cut open along the top. Sprinkle a little salt and pepper into each and top with a pat of butter. Serve immediately.

Cauliflower ring

Overall timing 1 ¼ hours

Freezing Not suitable

To serve 4-6

1	Large cauliflower
	Salt and pepper
½ cup	Butter
¼ cup	Flour
2 cups	Milk
¼ tsp	Grated nutmeg
1 cup	Grated Gruyère or
	Cheddar cheese
3	Eggs
1 tbsp	Dried bread crumbs
	Sprigs of parsley

Preheat oven to 375°.

Trim cauliflower and divide into florets. Cook for 7-10 minutes in boiling salted water. Drain, chop and put in a bowl. To make sauce, melt ¼ cup of the butter in a pan, stir in flour and cook for 1 minute. Gradually stir in milk. Bring to a boil, stirring, and cook for 1 minute. Add seasoning and nutmeg. Stir ¾ cup of cheese into sauce.

Remove pan from heat. Pour about two-thirds of the sauce into a bowl and set aside. Stir eggs into sauce left in pan. Mix sauce thoroughly into cauliflower.

Grease a 9½ inch ring mold with half remaining butter. Sprinkle bread crumbs on bottom. Fill with cauliflower mixture, pressing down well, and bake for 30-35 minutes.

Remove from oven and immerse mold up to rim in cold water. Turn up oven to 450°. Run a knife blade around the sides of the mold, then carefully turn out on to ovenproof dish (if any of the mixture sticks to mould, quickly smooth it back into position with a knife and a little of remaining sauce).

Spread reserved sauce over cauliflower ring and sprinkle with remaining cheese. Melt remaining 2 tbsp butter and pour over. Return to oven and bake for about 15 minutes until golden brown. Serve hot.

Broccoli vinaigrette

Overall timing 20 minutes plus marination

Freezing Not suitable

To serve 6

1 lb	Broccoli
	Salt and pepper
10 tbsp	Oil
1 tsp	Powdered mustard
¼ cup	White wine vinegar
1 tsp	Brown sugar
1	Onion
2 tbsp	Chopped chives
2 tbsp	Chopped parsley
1 tbsp	Chopped fresh tarragon
5	Small gherkins
2	Hard-cooked eggs
2	Tomatoes
5	Radishes

Trim broccoli leaves and coarse stems, then cook in boiling salted water for about 10 minutes. Drain well, then chop and divide pieces between six serving dishes or place in salad bowl.

Beat together oil, mustard, vinegar, sugar and seasoning. Peel and finely chop the onion and add to dressing with herbs. Finely chop gherkins and eggs and stir into dressing.

Blanch, peel and finely chop tomatoes. Chop radishes and stir both into dressing. Pour over broccoli and mix well. Leave for 20 minutes until completely cold. Serve with buttered toast.

Stuffed tomatoes au gratin

Overall timing 50 minutes

Freezing Not suitable

To serve 4

4	Large tomatoes
1½lb	Fresh peas
1	Onion
2 tbsp	Oil
	Salt and pepper
¼ cup	Butter
2 tbsp	Flour
1 cup	Milk
1 cup	Grated cheese
1 tbsp	Soft bread crumbs

Preheat the oven to 400°.

Halve the tomatoes and scoop out the flesh. Discard the seeds and chop the flesh. Shell the peas. Peel and finely chop the onion.

Heat the oil in a skillet and fry the onion till transparent. Add the peas, cover and cook for 5 minutes. Stir in the chopped tomato flesh, season and continue cooking, covered, for 10 minutes.

Meanwhile, melt the butter in a saucepan. Stir in the flour and cook for 1 minute. Gradually stir in the milk and bring to a boil, stirring until thickened.

Mix three-quarters of the cheese into the sauce with the pea mixture. Use to fill the tomato halves and arrange in an ovenproof dish. Mix the remaining cheese with the bread crumbs and sprinkle over the tomatoes. Bake for 20 minutes and serve hot.

Vegetable croquettes

Overall timing 1¼ hours plus chilling

Freezing Suitable: deep fry after thawing

To serve 4

1½lb	Floury potatoes
1	Large parsnip
	Salt and pepper
2	Large leeks
1	Stalk of celery
2	Large carrots
¼ cup	Butter
2 tbsp	Chopped parsley
¼ tsp	Grated nutmeg
2	Eggs
	Oil for deep frying
¼ cup	Flour
	Sprigs of parsley

Peel and chop the potatoes and parsnip. Cook in boiling salted water for 15-20 minutes till tender.

Meanwhile, trim and finely shred leeks and celery. Peel and grate carrots. Melt butter in a skillet, add leeks and celery and fry till golden.

Drain potatoes and parsnip, return to pan and shake over a low heat to dry thoroughly. Remove from heat and mash to a smooth purée. Stir in fried vegetables and any pan juices. Add carrots, parsley, nutmeg and seasoning. Beat in eggs. spread the mixture on a plate, cool, then chill for 2-3 hours till firm.

Heat oil in a deep-fryer to 340°. Shape vegetable mixture into 20 balls with floured hands. Fry, a few at a time, for 5-6 minutes, till crisp and golden. Drain on paper towels. Serve hot, garnished with parsley.

Brussels sprouts with chestnuts

Overall timing 1 hour

Freezing Not suitable

To serve 4-6

¾lb	Chestnuts
2 cups	Hot beef broth
1½lbs	Brussels sprouts
	Salt
	Grated nutmeg
¼ cup	Butter

Make a cut in each chestnut with a sharp knife, then place them in a saucepan. Cover with cold water, bring to a boil and cook for 10 minutes.

Drain chestnuts and peel off both outer and inner skins. Add to the broth and simmer gently for about 20 minutes till tender.

Meanwhile, trim the sprouts and cut a cross in the base of each one. Cook in boiling salted water for 10-12 minutes till tender. Drain and season with nutmeg.

Melt the butter in a pan, then add the drained chestnuts and sprouts. Gently shake the pan to coat the vegetables with butter. Turn into a warmed serving dish and serve.

Potato and onion bake

Overall timing 1 hour

Freezing Not suitable

To serve 4

1½lb	Potatoes
¾lb	Onions
6 tbsp	Butter
	Salt and pepper

Preheat the oven to 400°.

Peel the potatoes and slice very thinly (use a mandolin for best results). Put into a bowl of cold water to prevent discoloration. Peel and thinly slice the onions.

Drain the potatoes and dry with paper towels. Butter an ovenproof dish and cover the bottom with a layer of potato. Dot with butter, season and cover with a layer of onion. Dot with butter, season and repeat the layers till all ingredients have been used, finishing with potato. Dot the top with the remaining butter.

Bake for about 40 minutes till the potatoes are tender and golden. Serve immediately.

Venetian green beans

Overall timing 1 ¼ hours

Freezing Suitable

To serve 4-6

1 ¼ lb	Green beans
1 lb	Fresh tomatoes or
16 oz	Can of tomatoes
1	Medium-size onion
1	Garlic clove
¼ cup	Butter or
2 tbsp	Oil
	Bouquet garni
¼ tsp	Dried oregano or
	marjoram
	Salt and pepper

Trim beans and remove strings if necessary. If using fresh tomatoes, blanch, peel and chop them; drain and chop canned tomatoes. Peel and chop the onion. Peel and crush garlic.

Heat the butter or oil in a saucepan and fry the onion till browned. Add beans, tomatoes, garlic, bouquet garni, oregano or marjoram and seasoning. Cover and simmer over a very low heat for 1 hour. If necessary add a little boiling water during cooking to prevent sticking. Serve hot.

Potato gnocchi

Overall timing 1 ½ hours plus chilling

Freezing Not suitable

To serve 6

2lb	Floury potatoes
	Salt and pepper
2 cups	Flour
1 tsp	Baking powder
2	Eggs
6oz	Sliced cheese
¼ cup	Butter
3 tbsp	Grated Parmesan cheese
	Grated nutmeg

Scrub the potatoes and cook in boiling salted water for about 30 minutes till tender. Drain, peel and press through a ricer into a large bowl.

Sift the flour and baking powder together, add to the potatoes and mix in with a wooden spoon. Beat in the eggs and seasoning. Spread out on a plate and chill for 2-3 hours till firm.

Preheat the oven to 425°.

Bring a large pan of salted water to a boil, then reduce heat till simmering. Put teaspoonfuls of the potato mixture into the water and cook for about 4 minutes or till they rise to the surface. Remove with a slotted spoon and keep hot while you cook the rest.

Layer cooked dumplings in an ovenproof dish with slices of cheese and butter and sprinkle Parmesan on top. Brown in the oven for 5-10 minutes. Sprinkle nutmeg over.

Fried ham and spinach

Overall timing 30 minutes

Freezing Not suitable

To serve 4

2lb	Bulk spinach
	Salt and pepper
6oz	Slice of cooked ham
1	Garlic clove
3 tbsp	Oil
2	Hard-cooked eggs
2 tbsp	Pine nuts
	(optional)

Wash and pick over the spinach, discarding any withered leaves or coarse stalks. Drain thoroughly and blanch in lightly salted boiling water for 1 minute. Remove from heat, rinse under cold water and drain thoroughly. Chop coarsely.

Dice the ham and peel the garlic. Heat the oil in a large skillet, add ham and garlic and fry for 2-3 minutes. Stir in the spinach, add plenty of pepper and fry gently for 5 minutes, stirring occasionally.

Meanwhile, shell and finely chop the eggs. Add to the pan with the pine nuts, if used, and cook for 2 minutes.

Discard garlic clove. Adjust seasoning to taste and arrange on a warmed serving dish. Serve immediately with thick slices of crusty bread.

Bubble and squeak

Overall timing 15 minutes

Freezing Not suitable

To serve 4-6

2 cups	Mashed potatoes
3 cups	Cooked shredded cabbage
¼ cup	Butter
	Salt and pepper
2 cups	Diced leftover cooked meat

Beat together mashed potatoes and cabbage with a wooden spoon, adding plenty of seasoning.

Melt the butter in a heavy skillet and add the potato and cabbage mixture, spreading it over the bottom of the pan. Mix in meat. Fry, turning the mixture occasionally, until crisp and golden brown. Serve immediately.

Potato pancakes

Overall timing 45 minutes

Freezing Not suitable

To serve 4

1¼lb	Waxy potatoes
2	Eggs
1 tbsp	Flour
	Salt and pepper
¼ cup	Oil

Peel the potatoes and grate coarsely into a bowl of cold water. Drain and squeeze dry in a cloth, then put into a dry bowl. Add the eggs, flour and seasoning and mix well.

Heat a little of the oil in a skillet and add one-quarter of the potato mixture. Flatten into a pancake with the back of a spatula and fry over a moderate heat for about 5 minutes till the edges are golden. Turn carefully and brown the other side. Remove from the pan and keep hot while rest of mixture is cooked.

Serve hot with roast or broiled meats and a green vegetable.

Rumanian vegetable casserole

Overall timing 1¼ hours

Freezing Not suitable

To serve 6-8

2	Waxy potatoes
2	White turnips
2	Medium-size onions
2	Garlic cloves
2	Carrots
1	Medium-size eggplant
2	Zucchini
2	Small leeks
¼ lb	Green beans
3	Large tomatoes
2 tbsp	Butter
2 tbsp	Oil
1 cup	Shelled fresh peas
2 tbsp	Tomato paste
	Bouquet garni
	Salt and pepper

Peel the potatoes, turnips, onions, garlic and carrots. Cut the potatoes, turnips, carrots, eggplant and zucchini into ¾ inch chunks. Cut the leeks and beans into 1 inch lengths. Quarter the tomatoes; slice the onions.

Heat the butter and oil in a flameproof casserole and fry the onions, leeks and garlic till golden. Add the remaining vegetables, tomato paste, bouquet garni and 2½ cups water and mix well. Season and bring to a boil. Simmer gently for 45 minutes till the vegetables are tender.

Rutabaga purée

Overall timing 35 minutes

Freezing Not suitable

To serve 4-6

2lb	Rutabaga
	Salt and pepper
6 tbsp	Butter

Peel the rutabaga thickly, wash and cut into 1 inch chunks. Put into a saucepan of lightly salted cold water and bring to a boil. Reduce the heat, cover and simmer for 15-20 minutes till tender.

Drain thoroughly, then mash well till smooth with two-thirds of the butter. Season to taste.

Arrange in a warmed serving dish, top with the remaining butter and grind a little pepper over. Serve immediately.

Variations

"Clapshot" is a traditional mixed rutabaga and potato dish from the Orkney Islands, off the north coast of Scotland. Cook equal quantities of rutabaga and floury potatoes in separate pans till tender. Drain well, then mash together with butter and seasoning and 1 small finely chopped onion or 2 tbsp chopped chives. Any leftovers can be fried in butter.

To turn clapshot into a tasty lunch or supper dish, spread the mashed rutabaga, potato and onion mixture in a shallow ovenproof dish. Make 4 hollows with the back of a spoon and break an egg into each one. Season and dot with butter, then bake in the oven, preheated to 425° for 8-10 minutes till the eggs are lightly set. Serve immediately with strips of crispy fried bacon.

German broad beans

Overall timing 45 minutes

Freezing Suitable

To serve 4

2lb	Unshelled broad or fava beans
	Salt and pepper
1	Chicken bouillon cube
4	Bacon slices
2	Onions
3 tbsp	Flour
	Pinch of grated nutmeg
1 cup	Light cream
1 tbsp	Chopped parsley

Shell beans. Place in boiling, salted water and cook for 20 minutes or until tender. Drain cooking liquid into measuring cup and make up to 1 cup with water. Crumble in bouillon cube. Set beans and liquid in cup aside for the moment.

Dice bacon; peel and chop onions. Put bacon and onions into a saucepan and fry gently for about 10 minutes. Remove pan from heat and stir in the flour. Gradually stir in the liquid from the cup. Return pan to heat and cook gently for about 5 minutes, stirring constantly until sauce thickens. Remove from heat and season to taste with salt, pepper and nutmeg.

Stir in beans and cream and heat gently for a further 5 minutes, stirring. Transfer to warmed serving dish, garnish with parsley and serve.

Stuffed cucumbers

Overall timing 1 hour

Freezing Not suitable

To serve 6

3	Large cucumbers
¼ cup	Diced cooked ham
¼ lb	Ground beef
2 tbsp	Soft bread crumbs
1 tbsp	Chopped parsley
3 tbsp	Milk
1	Egg
	Salt and pepper
Sauce	
1	Onion
1	Leek
¼ cup	Butter
2 tbsp	Flour
1 cup	Broth
1 tbsp	Chopped parsley
	Paprika
	Salt
1 tbsp	Vinegar
½ cup	Half-and-half

Peel cucumbers. Halve them lengthwise and scoop out seeds. Mix ham with beef, bread crumbs, parsley, milk, egg and seasoning. Stuff cucumbers with mixture.

To make sauce, peel and finely chop onion. Trim and finely chop leek. Melt butter in a saucepan and fry onion and leek till golden. Sprinkle flour into pan and cook for 1 minute, stirring. Gradually stir in broth, then add parsley, a pinch each of paprika and salt and the vinegar. Bring to a boil, stirring.

Arrange cucumbers on top of sauce and surround with any leftover stuffing. Cover and cook gently for 30 minutes. Turn cucumbers over halfway through cooking time.

Stir half-and-half into sauce and heat through uncovered for 2 minutes.

Romanian peppers

Overall timing 1 ¼ hours

Freezing Not suitable

To serve 6

1 lb	Lean boneless pork
2	Onions
¼ cup	Butter
¼ lb	Button mushrooms
½ lb	Tomatoes
1 cup	Water
	Salt and pepper
½ tsp	Paprika
6	Green peppers
2 tsp	Cornstarch
¼ cup	Half-and-half
	Hot pepper sauce

Dice the pork. Peel and finely chop onions. Melt the butter in saucepan. Fry onions and pork for 10 minutes.

Slice mushrooms. Blanch, peel and chop tomatoes. Add mushrooms and tomatoes to the saucepan. Pour in water and cook for 40 minutes over a low heat. Season with salt, pepper and paprika.

Cut tops off peppers. Remove seeds. Place peppers and their tops in a saucepan of boiling water and cook for 5 minutes or until just soft. Lift out and drain. Keep warm.

Blend cornstarch with half-and-half. Stir into pork mixture, then bring just to a boil to thicken. Season with a few drops of hot pepper sauce. Mix well, then use mixture to fill peppers. Place tops on peppers to serve.

Leeks with mustard sauce

Overall timing 30 minutes

Freezing Not suitable

To serve 4-6

2lb	Leeks
	Salt and pepper
1	Small onion
1	Garlic clove
¼ cup	Butter
1 tbsp	Flour
2 cups	Milk
1 tbsp	Prepared mustard
1 cup	Grated cheese

Trim leeks. Cook in boiling salted water for 15-20 minutes till tender. Drain, saving ½ cup cooking liquid. Arrange leeks in warmed serving dish. Keep hot.

Peel and chop onion and garlic. Melt the butter in a saucepan and fry the onion and garlic till golden. Stir in the flour and cook for 1 minute. Gradually add reserved cooking liquid and milk. Bring to a boil, stirring, and cook for 3 minutes. Stir in mustard, cheese and seasoning and heat through gently without boiling. Pour over the leeks and serve immediately.

Stuffed mushrooms

Overall timing 1 hour

Freezing Suitable: reheat in 375° oven for 10 minutes

To serve 4

8	Cup mushrooms
1 cup	Soft bread crumbs
½ cup	Warm mlk
1	Garlic clove
	Salt and pepper
1	Egg
1	Egg yolk
1 cup	Grated Parmesan cheese
2 tsp	Chopped fresh marjoram
3 tbsp	Oil
	Fresh parsley

Preheat the oven to 350°.

Carefully detach mushroom caps from stalks. Wipe caps and reserve. Chop stalks.

Soak bread crumbs in warm milk, then squeeze out well, reserving milk. Peel garlic and place in mortar or blender with mushrooms stalks, a little of the reserved milk and seasoning. Pound or blend till well combined. Put mixture into a bowl and add egg, egg yolk, grated Parmesan, marjoram and 2 tsp of oil. Mix well until creamy, then add salt.

Spread stuffing into hollow of each mushroom cap using a dampened knife. Arrange the stuffed mushrooms in an oiled baking dish. Sprinkle the top with the remaining oil and pepper and bake for about 30 minutes. Garnish with parsley and serve hot.

Corn fritters

Overall timing 30 minutes

Freezing Not suitable

To serve 4

1 lb	Can of whole kernel corn
1	Egg
½ cup	Flour
	Salt
1 tbsp	Oil
½	Grated rind of
	lemon
	Oil for deep frying
	Grated Parmesan
	cheese

Drain corn. Separate egg. Sift flour and pinch of salt into a mixing bowl. Make a well in center, then put in egg yolk, oil and grated lemon rind. Stir until a smooth batter forms. Add a little water if necessary.

In another bowl, beat egg white until stiff. Fold into batter with corn.

Heat oil in deep-fryer to 340°.

Drop spoonfuls of batter into the hot oil — be careful because corn can burst — a few at a time, and fry for 5 minutes on each side or until golden. Remove with a spatula and drain on paper towels. Keep warm while frying the rest.

Sprinkle grated Parmesan over and serve hot.

Russian potatoes with cream

Overall timing 1 ¼ hours

Freezing Not suitable

To serve 4

1 ½ lb	Waxy potatoes
	Salt and pepper
½ cup	Button mushrooms
1	Small onion
¼ cup	Butter
½ cup	Sour cream
2 tbsp	Chopped parsley

Cook the potatoes in boiling salted water for about 30 minutes till tender. Drain and peel the potatoes, then cut into ¼ inch thick slices. Slice the mushrooms. Peel and thinly slice the onion.

Melt the butter in a skillet and fry the onion till transparent. Add the mushrooms and fry for 2-3 minutes, stirring. Add the sliced potatoes and fry for 5 minutes, turning once.

Pour the cream over and season well. Turn potatoes gently till coated and continue cooking over a low heat for about 10 minutes till the potatoes have absorbed most of the cream.

Stir in the parsley, adjust the seasoning and serve hot.

Lettuce and ham supper

Overall timing 40 minutes

Freezing Not suitable

To serve 4

4	Heads romaine lettuce
1	Onion
2 tbsp	Butter
1 cup	Chicken broth
	Salt and pepper
4	Thick slices of cooked ham
1 tsp	Cornstarch
2 tbsp	Water
½ cup	Sherry wine

Trim and wash lettuces. Drain well and cut in half lengthwise. Peel and chop the onion.

Melt the butter in a saucepan and fry onions till golden. Add lettuces and fry for 3 minutes. Add broth, salt and pepper. Tightly cover pan and simmer for 15-20 minutes.

Cut ham slices in half and add to pan. Heat through gently for 3 minutes.

Carefully lift out the lettuce halves and ham, draining thoroughly. Arrange on a warmed serving dish and keep hot.

Blend cornstarch with water, then stir into cooking liquid. Bring to a boil, stirring continuously. Remove from heat and stir in sherry. Taste and adjust seasoning. Pour over lettuce and ham and serve immediately with mashed potatoes and wholewheat bread.

Savory pumpkin

Overall timing 1 ¼ hours plus
30 minutes standing

Freezing Not suitable

To serve 4-6

2lb	Pumpkin
	Salt and pepper
2 cups	Grated cheese
¼ teasp	Ground cumin
3	Eggs
1 cup	Soft bread crumbs
2 tbsp	Chopped parsley
2 tbsp	Butter

Scrape the seeds and fibrous center out of the pumpkin. Remove the skin and grate the flesh into a bowl. Sprinkle with salt, mix well and leave to stand for 30 minutes.

Preheat the oven to 350°.

Press the pumpkin with the back of a spoon to squeeze out as much liquid as possible. Add the cheese to the pumpkin with cumin, eggs, bread crumbs, parsley and seasoning and beat the mixture till smooth.

Pour into a greased ovenproof dish and smooth the top. Dot with butter and bake for about 45 minutes till set. Serve immediately with a tomato salad and fresh crusty bread and butter.

Lyonnaise beans

Overall timing 1 hour plus soaking

Freezing Not suitable

To serve 6

1½ cups	Dried lima beans
	Salt and pepper
2	Medium-size onions
¼ cup	Butter
1 tbsp	Chopped parsley

Soak beans in water to cover overnight. Drain.

Place beans in saucepan and add 1 quart fresh water. Cover and cook for about 1 hour till tender. Add a little salt toward the end of cooking time.

Peel and finely chop onions. Melt the butter in a saucepan and add the onions, parsley and seasoning. Cook gently till onions are transparent.

Drain beans well, then toss them in the onion and parsley mixture. Transfer to a warmed dish and serve.

Scalloped Chinese cabbage

Overall timing 45 minutes

Freezing Not suitable

To serve 4

2lb	Chinese cabbage
	(bok choy)
1	Onion
2½ cups	Milk
	Salt and pepper
1	Egg
2 tbsp	Chopped parsley
2 tbsp	Butter
1 cup	Grated cheese

Preheat the oven to 375°.

Trim stalk end of Chinese cabbage. Remove any damaged outer leaves, then separate remaining leaves. Rinse and drain.

Peel and slice the onion and put into a large saucepan with the milk and a little salt. Bring just to a boil, then add the Chinese cabbage. Cover and simmer for 5 minutes.

Lift the Chinese cabbage out of the milk with a slotted spoon and arrange in a shallow ovenproof dish. Beat the egg in a bowl with the parsley and gradually add the milk, beating constantly. Add pepper and the butter and stir till melted. Pour over the Chinese cabbage. Sprinkle the cheese over the top. Bake for about 30 minutes till golden. Serve immediately with brown bread rolls.

Spinach dumplings

Overall timing 40 minutes plus setting

Freezing Suitable: cook from frozen for 12-15 minutes, then add melted butter and cheese

To serve 6

2lb	Bulk spinach
½	Chicken bouillon cube
5 tbsp	Warm milk
3 cups	Flour
3	Eggs
	Salt and pepper
½ cup	Butter
4 cups	Soft bread crumbs
¼ tsp	Grated nutmeg
1 tbsp	Chopped parsley
1 tbsp	Chopped chives
1 cup	Grated Swiss cheese

Wash spinach and put into a saucepan with only water that clings to it. Cover and cook for 5 minutes.

Dissolve bouillon cube in milk. Sift flour into a bowl, add eggs, milk and seasoning and mix to a soft dough.

Drain spinach thoroughly and chop finely. Melt half the butter in a skillet, add bread crumbs and fry till crisp and golden. Add to dough with nutmeg, parsley and chives. Add spinach and mix to a stiff dough.

Roll dough between floured hands into long sausage-shapes about ½ inch in diameter. Leave to set.

Cut across dough into 1 inch lengths. Cook in boiling salted water for about 10 minutes till they float to the surface.

Lift out dumplings with a slotted spoon, drain thoroughly and arrange in a warmed serving dish. Melt remaining butter, pour over dumplings and sprinkle with grated cheese. Toss lightly before serving with casseroles.

Marseilles squash

Overall timing 45 minutes

Freezing Not suitable

To serve 6

1½lb	Summer squash
	Salt and pepper
¾lb	Ripe tomatoes
2	Large onions
3 tbsp	Olive oil
½ cup	Long grain rice
2½ cups	Water
1 tbsp	Chopped parsley

Blanch whole squash in boiling salted water for 10 minutes. Drain thoroughly. Cut in half lengthwise, then cut across each half into 1 inch thick slices, removing the seeds.

Blanch, peel and halve the tomatoes. Peel and slice the onions. Heat the oil in a flameproof casserole and fry onions till pale golden.

Add the rice to the casserole and fry, stirring, for 2 minutes till the oil is absorbed. Add the water, tomatoes, squash and seasoning. Bring to a boil, then cover and simmer gently for 15-20 minutes till rice is tender and most of the water has been absorbed.

Taste and adjust the seasoning, sprinkle with parsley and serve hot.

Stir-fried celery

Overall timing 15 minutes

Freezing Not suitable

To serve 4

1	Large head of celery
2 tsp	Salt
3 tbsp	Oil
2 tbsp	Soy sauce
½ tsp	Sugar

Cut off leaves from celery, then chop into 2 inch pieces. Sprinkle with salt.

Heat oil in skillet or wok. When oil is very hot, add the celery and stir-fry for 5 minutes. Add soy sauce and sugar, mix well and serve immediately.

Mushrooms in batter

Overall timing 30 minutes

Freezing Not suitable

To serve 2-4

¾ lb	Large open mushrooms
1 cup + 2 tbsp	Flour
1 tsp	Salt
1	Egg
1 tbsp	Oil
¾ cup	Milk or water
2	Egg whites
	Oil for frying
	Sprigs of parsley

Trim the mushrooms, then toss in 2 tbsp of the flour.

Sift the remaining flour and salt into a bowl and make a well in the center. Add the egg and oil and begin to mix with a wooden spoon, drawing the flour into the liquid. Gradually stir in the milk or water to make a thick smooth batter. Add more liquid if necessary. Beat the egg whites in a bowl till stiff but not dry and fold gently into the batter.

Heat oil in a deep-fryer to 340°.

Spear a mushroom on a long skewer and dip into the batter. Using a second skewer, carefully push the mushroom off the first skewer into the oil. Fry the mushrooms, a few at a time, for 3-4 minutes till crisp and golden. Remove from the pan with a slotted spoon and drain on paper towels. Pile onto a warmed serving plate and garnish with sprigs of parsley.

Sweet-sour red cabbage

Overall timing 1 hour 20 minutes

Freezing Suitable

To serve 4

2lb	Head red cabbage
4	Bacon slices
1	Onion
1	Tart apple
6	Whole allspice
½ tsp	Salt
2 tsp	Honey
6 tbsp	Red wine or wine vinegar

Discard any damaged outer leaves from the cabbage. Quarter, cut away core and thick ribs and shred leaves.

Chop bacon. Peel and chop onion. Cook bacon in flameproof casserole over a low heat until fat starts to run. Add onion and cook for 5 minutes, stirring.

Peel, core and chop apple and add to casserole with cabbage. Crush allspice and add to casserole with salt, honey and wine or vinegar. Mix well, then cover and simmer for 1 hour.

If there's too much liquid at the end of the cooking time, remove the lid and continue simmering. Serve hot.

Mushroom loaf

Overall timing 1 hour

Freezing Not suitable

To serve 4

1½lb	Button mushrooms
3 tbsp	Butter
1 cup	White sauce
	Salt and pepper
	Grated nutmeg
3	Eggs

Preheat the oven to 350°.

Trim the mushrooms. Reserve four for decoration and finely chop the rest. Melt 2 tbsp butter in a saucepan and cook the chopped mushrooms for 5 minutes. Stir in the white sauce, then season with salt, pepper and a little grated nutmeg to taste.

Remove pan from heat and allow to cool slightly, then beat in the eggs one at a time. Pour the mixture into a greased 6 inch soufflé dish and bake for about 45 minutes till set.

Meanwhile, flute one of the reserved mushrooms and thinly slice the other three. Melt remaining butter in a saucepan and fry mushrooms till golden.

Unmold mushroom loaf and serve hot, garnished with fried mushrooms, on a bed of lettuce leaves.

Bean gratin

Overall timing 40 minutes

Freezing Not suitable

To serve 6

4 slices	Bread
	Milk
1	Garlic clove
1 tbsp	Chopped parsley
1 cup	Chopped leftover cooked lamb or beef
	Salt and pepper
2x16oz	Cans of green beans
	or
1 lb	Cooked frozen beans
	or
1¼lb	Cooked fresh beans
2 tbsp	Butter
2 tbsp	Flour
2 cups	Milk
¾ cup	Grated cheese
1	Egg

Preheat oven to 450°.

Soak the bread in a little milk. Squeeze out, then put through a grinder or food processor with the peeled garlic, parsley and meat. Season with salt and pepper.

If using canned beans, drain them. Fill a well-greased gratin dish with alternate layers of beans and meat mixture, finishing with a bean layer.

Melt butter in a saucepan. Stir in flour and cook for 1 minute, then gradually add milk. Bring to a boil, stirring until thickened. Add cheese to sauce. Cool slightly, then mix in beaten egg and seasoning.

Cover bean mixture in gratin dish with the sauce. Bake for about 10 minutes until the sauce is lightly browned.

Beans with egg sauce

Overall timing 25 minutes

Freezing Not suitable

To serve 6

1½lb	Fresh green beans
	or
2x16oz	Cans of whole or
	cut green beans
	Salt
6 tbsp	Butter
¼ cup	Soft bread crumbs
2 tbsp	Flour
	Nutmeg
1 tsp	Lemon juice
¼ tsp	Dried mixed herbs
3 tbsp	White wine or hard
	cider
2	Hard-cooked eggs
1 tsp	Chopped chives

If using fresh beans wash, trim them and remove strings. Break or cut into short lengths. Cook for 10-15 minutes in boiling salted water until tender. Drain, saving 1 cup of the cooking liquid, and put beans into a warmed serving dish. Heat canned beans in their liquid and use this, made up to required amount with water, for sauce.

Melt ¼ cup of the butter in a saucepan, add the bread crumbs and lightly brown. Sprinkle over beans and keep warm.

To make the sauce, melt the remaining butter in the saucepan then stir in the flour. Remove pan from heat and blend in the reserved cooking liquid. Stir sauce over a medium heat until it comes to a boil and thickens, then add pinches of salt and nutmeg, the lemon juice and mixed herbs.

Remove pan from heat and stir in wine or cider, chopped hard-cooked eggs and chives. Pour sauce over beans. Serve with lamb steaks and potato croquettes.

Celeriac with onions

Overall timing 50 minutes

Freezing Not suitable

To serve 4-6

1½lb	Celeriac	
	Salt and pepper	
1 tbsp	Lemon juice	
2	Medium-size onions	
¼ cup	Butter	
2 tbsp	Pork drippings or	
	oil	
2 tbsp	Flour	
2 cups	Chicken broth	

Peel celeriac and cut into ⅛ inch slices. Blanch in boiling salted water with the lemon juice for 5 minutes, then drain.

Peel and finely chop onions. Heat half the butter and all the drippings or oil in a large skillet. Add onions and celeriac and cook till onions are transparent, turning the celeriac over once with tongs — take care not to break up the fragile slices.

Tilt the pan, sprinkle the flour over the fat and stir. Add the broth and seasoning. Move the pan to distribute the liquids evenly, then cover and cook over a very low heat for 30 minutes.

Transfer celeriac to a warmed serving dish. Strain the cooking juices, stir in remaining butter and seasoning to taste and pour over the celeriac.

Ratatouille

Overall timing 1 ½ hours

Freezing Suitable

To serve 8

2	Large eggplants
1 lb	Zucchini
	Salt and pepper
3	Large onions
2-3	Garlic cloves
2	Green peppers
1 lb	Ripe tomatoes
5 tbsp	Olive oil
1 tsp	Sugar

Cut the eggplants into 1 inch chunks. Cut zucchini into quarters lengthwise, then into 1 inch lengths. Put the vegetables into a colander, sprinkle with salt and leave to drain for 30 minutes.

Meanwhile, peel and slice the onions. Peel and crush the garlic. Seed and thinly slice the peppers. Blanch, peel and halve the tomatoes.

Heat the oil in a flameproof casserole, add the onions and garlic and fry gently till transparent. Dry the eggplants and zucchini on paper towels and add to the pan with the peppers, tomatoes, sugar and plenty of pepper. Cook for about 45 minutes till the vegetables are tender but not mushy. Adjust the seasoning and serve hot, or cool and chill before serving.

Bacon and potato salad

Overall timing 55 minutes

Freezing Not suitable

To serve 6-8

2lb	Medium-size waxy potatoes
	Salt and pepper
½lb	Bacon slices
1	Large onion
¼ cup	White wine vinegar
¼ cup	Water
1 tsp	Powdered mustard
1 tbsp	Chopped chives

Scrub the potatoes, cover with cold salted water and bring to a boil. Cook for about 30 minutes till tender.

Meanwhile, dice the bacon and fry over a moderate heat till crisp and brown. Lift out of the pan with a slotted spoon and put into a warmed serving dish. Cover with foil to keep hot.

Drain the potatoes and cut into ½ inch thick slices. Add to the bacon and cover again.

Peel and roughly chop the onion, add to the bacon fat in the pan and fry over a moderate heat till golden. Add the vinegar, water, salt, pepper and mustard and bring to a boil.

Pour over the potatoes and bacon, turning them carefully till coated. Sprinkle with chives and serve immediately with fresh crusty bread.

Tropical salad

Overall timing 25 minutes plus cooling

Freezing Not suitable

To serve 2

½ cup	Long grain rice
1	Leek
½ lb	Cooked chicken meat
1	Small onion
¼ lb	Shelled shrimp
Dressing	
2 tbsp	Mango chutney
2 tbsp	Oil
2 tbsp	Lemon juice
1 tsp	Vinegar
½ tsp	Worcestershire sauce
½ tsp	Curry powder
	Salt and pepper

Garnish	
	Lettuce leaves
1	Banana

Put rice in a pan of boiling salted water and cook for 10 minutes.

Wash, trim and finely slice the leek. Add to the pan and cook for a further 5 minutes or until rice is cooked. Drain and leave to cool.

Slice cooked chicken into thin strips. Peel and finely slice the onion. Add both to the rice with the shrimp and mix.

To make the dressing, finely chop the mango chutney and put into a bowl with the oil, lemon juice, vinegar, Worcestershire sauce, curry powder and salt and pepper. Mix well.

Arrange rice mixture on top of lettuce leaves in a serving dish. Garnish with slices of banana and pour dresssing over.

Apple and salami salad

Overall timing 40 minutes

Freezing Not suitable

To serve 4

3	Small onions
3	Apples
½lb	Salami
2	Large gherkins
1 tbsp	Vinegar
1 tbsp	Lemon juice
3 tbsp	Oil
	Salt and pepper
	Pinch of sugar
¼ tsp	Celery or mustard
	seeds

Peel onions and cut into thin rings. Peel, core and chop apples. Dice salami and gherkins. Put them all in a salad bowl and mix well together.

Combine all remaining ingredients to make the dressing and pour over salad, mixing it in well. Leave for 20 minutes to blend the flavors before serving with crusty bread and butter.

Spinach and avocado salad

Overall timing 20 minutes plus cooling

Freezing Not suitable

To serve 6

½lb	Bulk spinach
½	Head lettuce
1	Avocado
1 tbsp	Oil
1 tbsp	Lemon juice
	Salt and pepper
¼ cup	Thick mayonnaise
1	Hard-cooked egg

Trim spinach and wash thoroughly. Put into a pan with no extra water, cover and cook for 8-10 minutes till tender. Turn into a colander and press with wooden spoon to remove excess liquid. Leave to cool.

Wash, trim and dry lettuce. Reserve six medium-size leaves and finely shred the rest. Cut avocado in half and remove seed. Scoop out flesh and chop finely. Place in bowl with cooled spinach, shredded lettuce, oil and lemon juice. Mix together well and season to taste.

Arrange reserved lettuce leaves on serving plate and divide spinach mixture between them. Pipe or spoon mayonnaise on top. Cut hard-cooked egg into wedges and use to garnish.

Avocado and pine nut salad

Overall timing 15 minutes plus chilling

Freezing Not suitable

To serve 2

1	Large ripe avocado
1½ tsp	Lemon juice
2	Gherkins
1 tbsp	Pine nuts
1½ tbsp	Olive oil
	Salt and pepper
1	Garlic clove
4	Fresh mint leaves
2 tbsp	Plain yogurt

Cut the avocado in half and remove the seed. Peel away the skin, dice the flesh and put into a bowl. Sprinkle with lemon juice and toss lightly till the avocado is coated.

Slice the gherkins thinly and add to the avocado with the pine nuts. Sprinkle with oil, season and toss.

Peel and crush the garlic into a small bowl. Wash the mint leaves and shred finely. Add to the garlic with the yogurt and mix well. Pour over the avocado and toss lightly. Chill for 1 hour.

Divide salad between two individual dishes and serve immediately with crusty rolls.

Fennel and tomato salad

Overall timing 30 minutes

Freezing Not suitable

To serve 4

1	Large bulb of fennel
	Salt and pepper
1	Onion
4	Tomatoes
3 tbsp	Oil
1 tbsp	Wine vinegar or lemon juice

Trim fennel. Cut into thin slices and blanch in boiling salted water for 5 minutes. Drain. Peel onion and cut into rings. Slice tomatoes. Arrange fennel, onion and tomatoes in layers in salad bowl.

In another bowl, mix together oil, vinegar or lemon juice and seasoning. Pour over salad. Chill for 15 minutes before serving.

Florida salad

Overall timing 20 minutes plus chilling

Freezing Not suitable

To serve 4

1	Fresh red chili pepper
3 tbsp	Olive oil
2 tsp	Vinegar
	Salt and pepper
4	Slices of fresh
	pineapple
	or
8oz	Can of pineapple
	slices in natural
	juice
1	Sweet red pepper
1	Sweet yellow or green
	pepper
3	Medium-size bananas
1	Large avocado

Seed and finely chop the chili. Put into a bowl with the oil, vinegar and seasoning and mix well with a fork.

Peel and chop the fresh pineapple, or drain and chop the canned pineapple, and add to the bowl. Seed and chop the peppers and add to the bowl. Peel and slice the bananas. Halve the avocado, discard the seed, peel and cut into chunks. Add to the bowl with the bananas.

Toss the salad lightly and put into a serving dish. Chill for 30 minutes before serving with chicken or seafood.

Walnut cabbage salad

Overall timing 30 minutes plus maceration

Freezing Not suitable

To serve 4

½	Head red cabbage
¼ cup	Walnut or olive oil
2 tbsp	Lemon juice
2	Large oranges
1	Large apple
1	Banana
½ cup	Walnut halves
3 tbsp	Raisins

Shred the cabbage and toss with the oil and lemon juice. Leave to macerate in the refrigerator for 1 hour.

Peel the oranges and separate into sections. Peel, core and chop the apple. Peel and thickly slice the banana. Add the fruit to the cabbage with the walnuts and raisins. Toss together well, then serve.

Asparagus and ham salad

Overall timing 20 minutes plus chilling

Freezing Not suitable

To serve 4

12oz	Can of asparagus spears	
¼lb	Cooked ham	
4	Pineapple rings	
	Lettuce leaves	
½ cup	Mayonnaise	
½ tsp	Brandy (optional)	
2 tbsp	Lemon juice	
	Pinch of cayenne	
Garnish		
2	Tomatoes	
2	Hard-cooked eggs	
	Chopped parsley	

Drain and chop asparagus and place in a mixing bowl. Dice ham. Chop the pineapple rings. Add both to asparagus and mix together well.

Place lettuce in the bottom of individual glasses. Divide asparagus mixture evenly between them.

Mix mayonnaise with brandy, if using, lemon juice and cayenne. Divide dressing equally between glasses. Garnish with sliced tomato, sliced hard-cooked egg and chopped parsley. Chill for 10 minutes before serving.

Caesar salad

Overall timing 15 minutes plus chilling

Freezing Not suitable

To serve 4

6 tbsp	Oil
2 tbsp	Vinegar
2	Garlic cloves
	Salt and pepper
½	Head romaine lettuce
4	Eggs
2	Slices of bread
½ cup	Crumbled Roquefort or
	grated Parmesan cheese
4	Anchovy fillets

Beat together ¼ cup of the oil, the vinegar, 1 peeled and crushed garlic clove and seasoning in a bowl. Cover and chill for 30 minutes.

Wash and dry lettuce. Tear leaves into pieces, put in a bowl and leave in the refrigerator to crisp.

Put eggs in a pan of cold water, bring to a boil and cook for 4-5 minutes. Drain and place in a bowl of cold water. Shell.

Rub bread slices all over with remaining halved garlic clove, then cut into 1 inch cubes. Fry in rest of oil till golden. Drain croûtons on paper towels.

Divide lettuce and croûtons between serving plates. Arrange eggs on top of lettuce, sprinkle over crumbled or grated cheese, then spoon dressing over. Garnish with rolled anchovy fillets and serve with crusty bread.

Chef's salad

Overall timing 20 minutes

Freezing Not suitable

To serve 4-6

1	Head Boston lettuce
2	Heads of radicchio
	or
¼	Head red cabbage
¼lb	Cooked ham
3oz	Gruyère or
	Swiss cheese
1	Small onion
2	Tomatoes
Dressing	
2 tbsp	Oil
1 tbsp	Wine vinegar
1 tsp	Dijon-style mustard or
	prepared English
	mustard
	Salt and pepper

Wash and dry lettuce. Line salad bowl with crisp whole leaves. Tear the rest into bite-size pieces and arrange on top.

Wash and dry radicchio and tear into pieces, or shred cabbage. Cut ham into ½ inch dice. Slice cheese, then cut into small strips. Peel and slice onion and separate into individual rings. Cut tomatoes into wedges. Arrange all the prepared ingredients on top of the lettuce.

Mix together the dressing ingredients and pour over the salad. Toss thoroughly but gently.

Tunisian tuna salad

Overall timing 25 minutes plus chilling

Freezing Not suitable

To serve 6

2	Green peppers
1	Small onion
2x7oz	Cans of tuna in oil
	Olive oil
2 tsp	Red wine vinegar
1 tsp	Lemon juice
	Salt and pepper
1	Garlic clove
¼lb	Gruyère or Cheddar cheese
¾ cup	Pitted green olives
1lb	Large firm tomatoes

Seed the peppers and cut into thin strips. Peel the onion and slice thinly into rings.

Drain the oil from the tuna and put into a small bowl with enough olive oil to make it up to ¼ cup. Add the vinegar, lemon juice, seasoning and peeled and crushed garlic.

Flake the tuna; slice the cheese thickly, then cut into thin strips. Put into a large bowl with the onion, pepper and olives. Pour the dressing over and toss lightly till ingredients are evenly coated.

Wash and thinly slice the tomatoes and use to line the salad bowl. Arrange the tuna mixture on top, cover and chill for 30 minutes before serving.

Beet and apple salad

Overall timing 1 hour 40 minutes plus cooling

Freezing Not suitable

To serve 4-6

1¾lb	Fresh beets
	Salt
¼ cup	Oil
2 tbsp	Wine vinegar or
	lemon juice
1 tsp	Sugar
½lb	Apples
1	Onion

Wash beets, then cut off green tops. Take care not to pierce the skin when you are preparing beets or the color will boil out, leaving them a rather washed out pink. Place prepared beets in saucepan and cover with water. Add a little salt, cover and simmer for 1¼ hours over a low heat. Leave to cool.

Drain beets, cut off root and pull off skin. Slice with a mandolin or fluted grater. Dry slices and put them in layers in a salad bowl.

Mix together oil, wine vinegar or lemon juice and sugar and pour over beets. Chill for 2 hours.

Peel, core and chop apples. Peel and finely chop onion. Mix into beets and serve before the beets color the apple and onion.

Smoked trout and potato salad

Overall timing 30 minutes

Freezing Not suitable

To serve 4-6

3	Smoked trout
½lb	Cold boiled potatoes
½lb	Red apples
¼ cup	Olive oil
3 tbsp	Lemon juice
	Salt and pepper
2	Tomatoes
2	Hard-cooked eggs
	Sprig of dill or fennel

Slice trout along backbone. Skin and fillet. Break fish into large pieces and place in serving bowl.

Cut the potatoes into cubes and add to bowl. Core and dice apples. Add to fish and potatoes.

Mix the olive oil, lemon juice and seasoning together to make a dressing. Pour over the fish mixture. Toss carefully and leave for 15 minutes for the flavors to develop.

Wash tomatoes and cut into eighths. Shell and slice eggs and arrange with the tomatoes and herbs around the salad. Serve with hot, crusty bread.

Salade Béatrice

Overall timing 10 minutes plus chilling

Freezing Not suitable

To serve 4

1 lb	Cooked green beans
	Salt and pepper
3 tbsp	Oil
1 tbsp	White wine vinegar
2	Tomatoes
1	Bunch of watercress
1	Hard-cooked egg yolk

Break or cut the beans into short lengths and put into a salad bowl. Season, add oil and vinegar and mix together well. Chill for 15 minutes.

Cut tomatoes into quarters and arrange around the edge of the salad bowl with the watercress.

Just before serving, garnish with sieved or finely chopped egg yolk. Toss salad at the table.

Salade niçoise

Overall timing 25 minutes

Freezing Not suitable

To serve 4

1 lb	Waxy potatoes
	Salt and pepper
½ lb	Green beans
¾ cup	Large ripe olives
2 tbsp	Drained capers
1	Garlic clove
¼ cup	Olive oil
1 tbsp	Tarragon vinegar
1 tsp	Lemon juice
1 tbsp	Chopped parsley
1	Large firm tomato
6	Anchovy fillets

Peel and dice the potatoes. Cook in boiling salted water for about 5 minutes till just tender. Trim the beans and cut into 1 inch lengths. Cook in another pan of boiling salted water for 5 minutes till tender.

Drain the vegetables and rinse under cold water. Drain thoroughly and put into a salad bowl. Add half the olives and the capers.

Peel and crush the garlic clove into a bowl. Add the oil, vinegar, lemon juice, parsley and pepper to taste and mix well, then pour over vegetables. Toss lightly till evenly coated.

Cut the tomato into thin wedges. Arrange on the salad with the remaining olives. Cut the anchovies into strips and arrange in a lattice on top of the salad. Serve immediately with French bread.

Spanish salad

Overall timing 45 minutes plus 1 hour refrigeration

Freezing Not suitable

To serve 4

½	Cucumber
	Salt and pepper
¾lb	Potatoes
12oz	Can of asparagus spears
1 cup	Mayonnaise
1 tbsp	Dijon-style mustard
½ tsp	Dried tarragon
½	Sweet red pepper

Peel and slice cucumber. Sprinkle with salt and chill for 1 hour.

Peel and dice potatoes, then cook in boiling salted water for 10 minutes. Drain and leave to cool.

Drain asparagus and dry spears on paper towels.

Mix together potatoes, mayonnaise, mustard, tarragon and seasoning and put into a shallow dish. Arrange asparagus on top like the spokes of a wheel. Drain cucumber slices and put one between each asparagus spear and one in the center. Seed and dice pepper and place on top of cucumber to add color.

Rice salad with anchovy dressing

Overall timing 40 minutes plus chilling

Freezing Not suitable

To serve 4

1 cup	Long grain rice
	Salt and pepper
1	Can of anchovy fillets
2	Large hard-cooked eggs
1 tsp	Powdered mustard
5 tbsp	Olive oil
1	Carrot
1	Small onion
1	Green chili pepper
1	Sweet red pepper
1	Small bulb of fennel
½ cup	Pitted ripe olives
1 tsp	Chopped chives

Cook rice in boiling salted water for 15 minutes till tender. Drain and rinse under cold water to cool.

Drain anchovies and reserve half for garnish. Put the rest into a mortar and pound to a paste with the pestle. Shell and finely chop eggs. Add to mortar with mustard and pound together, gradually adding oil a few drops at a time. Season.

Peel carrot and cut shallow grooves at intervals along its length. Slice thinly and place in large bowl with rice.

Peel and finely chop onion; thinly slice chili pepper; seed and slice pepper. Add these to the rice. Thinly slice fennel; chop fennel tops and add to salad. Toss lightly. Chill salad and dressing for 30 minutes.

Put salad into a serving dish and arrange reserved anchovies on top with olives and chives. Serve with dressing.

Greek salad

Overall timing 40 minutes including chilling

Freezing Not suitable

To serve 2

2	Large tomatoes
¼	Cucumber
1	Small onion
¼ cup	Ripe olives
8	Anchovy fillets
¼lb	Feta cheese
Dressing	
3 tbsp	Olive oil
1 tbsp	Lemon juice
	Salt and pepper
	Pinch of dried
	marjoram

Quarter tomatoes. Slice cucumber. Peel onion and cut into rings. Pit olives (optional). Roll up anchovy fillets. Cut cheese into chunks. Place all these ingredients in a serving bowl or divide them between two serving dishes.

To make the dressing, mix the oil and lemon juice with a pinch of salt, pepper to taste and marjoram. Pour over salad, mix well and chill for another 30 minutes before serving.

Other cheeses may be used instead of feta, but the important thing is to use a crumbly white cheese with a slightly sour taste. As in the authentic Greek version, it will absorb all the flavour of the oil dressing.

Israeli sweet-sour salad

Overall timing 20 minutes plus chilling

Freezing Not suitable

To serve 4

2 tbsp	Golden raisins
1 lb	Carrots
4	Oranges
2	Avocados
2 tbsp	Lemon juice
3 tbsp	Oil
1 tbsp	Wine or cider vinegar
	Salt and pepper
	Ground ginger

Put the raisins into a bowl, cover with warm water and leave to soak.

Peel carrots and grate into serving dish. Add the juice of two of the oranges and mix well. Peel remaining oranges and separate into sections.

Peel avocados and remove seeds. Cut flesh into chunks and sprinkle with lemon juice.

Drain raisins and add to serving dish with oranges and avocados.

In a small bowl, beat the oil and vinegar with a pinch each of salt, pepper and ground ginger. Pour over salad and toss. Chill for 15 minutes before serving.

Russian salad

Overall timing 30 minutes

Freezing Not suitable

To serve 4

3	Medium-size potatoes
2	Carrots
¼lb	Green beans
2	Stalks of celery
	Salt and pepper
1 cup	Frozen peas
2 tbsp	Capers
	Juice of ½ lemon
1 cup	Heavy cream
2	Hard-cooked eggs

Peel and dice potatoes and carrots. Trim beans and remove strings. Cut beans into small pieces. Trim and finely dice celery.

Place potatoes in boiling salted water and cook for 5 minutes. Remove with slotted spoon, place in colander and rinse under cold water. Add carrots to pan and cook for 5 minutes. Remove and rinse. Add beans, peas and celery to pan and cook for 4 minutes. Remove and rinse.

Drain cooled vegetables and place in bowl with capers. Add lemon juice and salt and pepper. Pour cream over and mix carefully. Pile salad onto a serving plate.

Shell and quarter eggs and arrange around the edge of the plate.

Goat's cheese salad

Overall timing 15 minutes plus 1 hour chilling

Freezing Not suitable

To serve 4

¾lb	Goat's cheese
	Salt and pepper
¼ cup	Olive oil
2 tbsp	Wine vinegar
4	Stalks of celery
⅔ cup	Walnut halves
	Fennel seed
	(optional)

Slice cheese and put into serving bowl. Grind black pepper over it. Beat 2 tbsp oil and 1 tbsp vinegar together and pour over cheese.

Chop celery. Add celery and nuts to bowl. Toss lightly.

Beat together the rest of the oil and vinegar and pour over. Sprinkle with salt and crushed fennel seed, if used, and chill for 1 hour. Serve with crusty French bread.

Gouda salad

Overall timing 15 minutes

Freezing Not suitable

To serve 4-6

Salad

1	Head iceberg lettuce
2oz	Corn salad or watercress
1	Head of Belgian endive
4	Tomatoes
1	Hard-cooked egg
1	Onion
½ cup	Ripe olives
¼lb	Gouda cheese

Dressing

2 tbsp	Oil
1 tbsp	Wine vinegar
1 tbsp	Chopped fresh mixed herbs
	or
1 tsp	Dried mixed herbs
	Salt and pepper

Trim and wash lettuce and corn salad or watercress. Dry thoroughly. Trim, wash and shred endive. Arrange lettuce leaves in salad bowl, scatter the endive over and arrange corn salad or watercress in the center.

Wipe and slice tomatoes. Shell and quarter hard-cooked egg. Peel and finely slice onion. Arrange on top of lettuce with the olives.

Cut cheese into thin matchstick strips. Sprinkle over top of salad.

To make dressing, put the oil, vinegar, herbs, salt and pepper into a bowl and mix well together. Pour over salad just before serving and toss.

Normandy salad

Overall timing 10 minutes plus chilling

Freezing Not suitable

To serve 4

1	Head Boston lettuce
2	Apples
½	Lemon
3 tbsp	Light cream
1 tbsp	Cider vinegar
	Grated nutmeg
	Salt and pepper
⅔ cup	Walnut halves

Wash and dry lettuce. Peel and core apples. Cut into thin rings. Rub cut surface of the lemon half over both sides of the apple rings to prevent browning. Place lettuce leaves and apple in a salad bowl and chill for 15 minutes.

Mix together the cream, cider vinegar, a pinch of grated nutmeg and seasoning in a small bowl. Just before serving, pour dressing over salad and toss. Garnish with walnut halves.

Pepper salad

Overall timing 30 minutes including cooling

Freezing Not suitable

To serve 4

4	Large sweet red and yellow peppers
½ cup	Olive oil
¼ cup	Grated Parmesan or sharp Cheddar cheese
1 tbsp	Dried bread crumbs
2 tbsp	Capers
	Pinch of dried marjoram or mint
	Sea-salt
1 tbsp	Vinegar

Preheat the broiler.
Halve peppers and place, rounded side up, under broiler. Cook for a few minutes till skins are charred, then peel. Cut in half again and remove seeds.

Heat oil in skillet and fry peppers gently for 7 minutes on each side. Arrange peppers in serving dish, alternating colors to achieve a spoked effect.

Sprinkle cheese over peppers with breadcrumbs, capers, marjoram or mint and sea-salt. Leave to cool slightly, then pour vinegar over. Serve immediately or cool and serve chilled.

Shrimp and endive salad

Overall timing 30 minutes plus chilling

Freezing Not suitable

To serve 4

2	Small heads of Belgian endive
3 tbsp	Lemon juice
4	Tomatoes
1	Fresh green chili pepper
½lb	Shelled shrimp
1 tbsp	White wine vinegar
	Salt and pepper
½ cup	Cream cheese
3 tbsp	Plain yogurt
1	Garlic clove
¼ tsp	Powdered mustard
2 tbsp	Oil

Remove any wilted outside leaves from the endive, cut off the bases and scoop out the cores. Cut across into ½ inch thick slices. Put into a bowl, add 2 tbsp of the lemon juice and toss.

Blanch, peel and quarter the tomatoes. Seed and thinly slice the chili. Put into a salad bowl with the tomatoes, shrimp, vinegar and seasoning. Add the endive and toss together lightly.

Put the cheese and yogurt into a bowl and beat till smooth. Add the peeled and crushed garlic, mustard, oil and remaining lemon juice. Season to taste and trickle over the salad. Chill for 15 minutes.

Just before serving, toss salad lightly till ingredients are evenly coated.

Cucumber and fruit salad

Overall timing 15 minutes

Freezing Not suitable

To serve 2

½	Cucumber
1	Orange
¼	Honeydew melon
½ cup	Purple grapes
	Sprigs of dill
Dressing	
3 tbsp	Sour cream
1½ tsp	Lemon juice
1 tbsp	Sugar
1 tbsp	Chopped fresh dill
	Salt and pepper

Thinly slice cucumber. Put into a bowl. Peel orange, remove seeds and cut flesh into pieces. Peel melon, remove seeds and cut flesh into thin slices. Add orange and melon to cucumber with grapes. Chill for 20 minutes.

To make the dressing, beat sour cream, lemon juice, sugar, dill and seasoning in a bowl.

Divide salad between two serving glasses and spoon a little of the dressing over each. Garnish with dill sprigs and keep in refrigerator till ready to serve.

Carrot and cabbage slaw

Overall timing 15 minutes plus chilling

Freezing Not suitable

To serve 4

½lb	Carrots
½lb	Head white cabbage
¼ cup	Wine vinegar
¼ cup	Oil
½ tsp	Caraway seeds
¼ tsp	Sugar
	Salt and pepper
2oz	Slab bacon
1	Large onion

Peel and grate carrots. Shred cabbage. In a salad bowl, mix together vinegar, 4 tbsp of the oil, caraway seeds, sugar and seasoning. Add carrots and cabbage and mix well. Cover the bowl and chill for 30 minutes.

Chop the bacon. Heat a skillet and fry bacon for 3 minutes till crisp. Peel and finely chop onion, saving a few rings for garnish. Add chopped onion to pan and fry for a few minutes.

Remove salad from refrigerator. Put the hot bacon and onion mixture on top and garnish with onion rings. Serve with roasts or cold meat.

Sunshine salad

Overall timing 15 minutes plus chilling

Freezing Not suitable

To serve 2

½lb	Poached smoked haddock (finnan haddie)
1	Orange
1	Grapefruit
1	Green pepper
1	Onion
1 tbsp	Chopped parsley
3 tbsp	Olive oil
1 tbsp	Lemon juice
	Salt and pepper
½ cup	Ripe olives

Cut the haddock into small strips. Peel orange and grapefruit and slice or chop the flesh. Seed and slice pepper. Peel onion and cut into thin rings.

Put prepared ingredients into salad bowl with the parsley. Add oil, lemon juice and seasoning. Toss salad well and chill. Garnish with olives just before serving.

Sweet and sour corn salad

Overall timing 45 minutes including chilling

Freezing Not suitable

To serve 6

8oz	Can of whole kernel corn
2 tbsp	Wine vinegar
3 tbsp	Oil
	Salt and pepper
1lb	Cold boiled potatoes
½lb	Tomatoes
8oz	Can of pineapple chunks
2	Bananas
5 tbsp	Lemon juice
1	Small head lettuce
Dressing	
1 tbsp	Dijon-style mustard
½ cup	Sour cream or plain yogurt
2 tbsp	Milk
	Salt and pepper
1 tsp	Paprika

Drain corn and place in a bowl. Mix together vinegar, oil and seasoning and add to bowl. Mix well. Cover and chill.

Peel and dice potatoes. Slice tomatoes. Drain pineapple, reserving 2 tbsp of the juice. Peel and slice bananas. Put all these in a bowl and pour lemon juice over.

Mix together dressing ingredients with reserved pineapple juice. Add to potato mixture. Chill for 30 minutes.

Line serving dish with lettuce leaves and spoon potato mixture in a ring around the edge. Pile corn in the middle and serve.

Upside-down cheesecake

Overall timing 1¼ hours plus chilling

Freezing Suitable

To serve 8

½ cup	Butter
3 tbsp	Light brown sugar
1 tsp	Ground cinnamon
2 cups	Crushed graham crackers
Filling	
12	Petit suisse cheeses
¼ cup	Light cream
4 tsp	Flour
6 tbsp	Sugar
1 tsp	Vanilla
1	Lemon
4	Eggs

Preheat the oven to 350°.

Put butter, sugar and cinnamon into a saucepan and heat gently till sugar dissolves. Remove from heat and stir in cracker crumbs. Press all but 4 tbsp over bottom and sides of a greased 9 inch loose-bottomed cake pan.

Beat cheese with cream, flour, sugar, vanilla, grated rind of the lemon and 1 tbsp of the juice. Separate eggs. Beat yolks into the cheese mixture. Beat whites till stiff and fold into cheese mixture. Pour into crumb case and smooth the top. Sprinkle remaining crumbs on top and press down lightly.

Bake for 45 minutes till set. Switch off the oven, open the door slightly and leave cheesecake in oven till cold. Chill for 2-3 hours, then unmold onto a serving dish.

Raspberries jubilee

Overall timing 10 minutes plus 2 hours maceration

Freezing Not suitable

To serve 6

¾lb (3 cups)	Fresh or frozen raspberries
¼-½ cup	Sugar
3 tbsp	Lemon juice
	Vanilla ice cream
3 tbsp	Kirsch or brandy

Put raspberries, sugar (add according to taste) and lemon juice in a bowl and macerate for 2 hours in the refrigerator. Chill serving plate.

Transfer raspberries and soaking juices to a saucepan and heat through gently.

Remove ice cream from freezer and place on serving plate. Spoon raspberries and syrup over. Warm Kirsch or brandy in ladle. Set alight and pour over ice cream. Serve immediately.

Strawberries and cream

Overall timing 15 minutes plus chilling

Freezing Not suitable

To serve 4

1 lb (3-4 cups)	Strawberries
1 cup	Heavy cream
¼ tsp	Vanilla
	Confectioners' sugar

Hull and wipe the strawberries. Divide between individual serving dishes and chill for 1 hour.

Whip the cream till stiff peaks form, then fold in the vanilla and sugar to taste. Pipe the cream on top of the strawberries and serve immediately.

Variation

Sprinkle the strawberries with fresh orange juice, or an orange liqueur such as Cointreau, before chilling.

Strawberries Melba

Overall timing 15 minutes plus maceration

Freezing Not suitable

To serve 4-6

1lb (3-4 cups)	Strawberries
1 cup	Raspberries
¼ cup	Sugar
2 tsp	Lemon juice
¼ cup	Slivered almonds

Hull the strawberries and pile in a serving dish.

Sieve the raspberries, then stir in the sugar and lemon juice until the sugar has dissolved. Pour over the strawberries and toss gently to coat. Leave to macerate for 1 hour.

Scatter the almonds over the top and serve.

Peach sundae

Overall timing 40 minutes plus
maceration

Freezing Not suitable

To serve 2

2	Large ripe peaches
1 tbsp	Maraschino or peach brandy
3 tbsp	Sugar
1 tbsp	Apricot jam
	Peach or vanilla ice cream

Peel, halve and pit one of the peaches. Roughly chop the flesh and put into a bowl with the Maraschino or peach brandy and sugar. Macerate in the refrigerator for 30 minutes.

In a saucepan, melt the apricot jam with 1 tbsp of macerating liquid. Peel, halve and pit remaining peach. Divide chopped fruit and juices between two serving dishes and top each with cubes of ice cream and a peach half. Spoon the warmed jam over and serve immediately.

Pineapple gelatin cream

Overall timing 20 minutes plus chilling

Freezing Suitable

To serve 2

½	Package pineapple-flavored gelatin
½ cup	Boiling water
7 oz	Canned crushed pineapple
6 tbsp	Whipping cream
1	Egg white

Dissolve the gelatin in the boiling water.

Add the crushed pineapple, mix well and chill till beginning to set.

Whip the cream till soft peaks form. Beat the egg white till stiff but not dry. Fold the cream into the pineapple mixture with a metal spoon, then carefully fold in the egg white.

Pour into two small dishes, smooth the top and chill till lightly set.

Coffee water ice

Overall timing 2 hours

Freezing See method

To serve 6-8

1 cup	Sugar
1 tbsp	Vanilla sugar
2½ cups	Water
8 tsp	Instant coffee granules
1 cup	Whipping cream
	Peppermint extract (optional)

Put granulated and vanilla sugar and water in a saucepan. Stir until sugar has completely dissolved, then bring to a boil and boil for 5 minutes. Skim if necessary. Stir in the coffee granules and remove pan from heat. Allow mixture to cool completely.

Pour coffee mixture through a fine sieve into a freezer tray. Place in freezer or freezing compartment of refrigerator and leave for about 1 hour or until the mixture forms a granular mass. Do not stir.

In a bowl whip cream till just holding soft peaks, then add a few drops of peppermint extract, if using, to taste. Scrape out contents of freezer tray with a fork and divide ice between chilled serving glasses. Top each glass with peppermint-flavored cream and serve with cookies.

Sherry trifle

Overall timing 1 ½ hours including chilling time

Freezing Not suitable

To serve 6-8

2½ cups	Milk
3 tbsp	Imported custard powder
2 tbsp	Sugar
6 slices	Sponge cake
2 tbsp	Raspberry jam
1lb 13oz	Can of sliced peaches
6 tbsp	Sherry
½ cup	Heavy or whipping cream
¼ cup	Toasted split almonds

Blend 6 tbsp of the milk with the custard powder and sugar. Bring remaining milk to a boil, then pour onto powder and stir well. Return to pan and bring back to a boil, stirring continuously until thickened. Put to one side to cool, covering surface with wet wax paper to prevent a skin forming.

Cut sponge into small pieces and spread with jam. Arrange around the bottom and sides of serving dish.

Drain peaches. Mix 3 tbsp of syrup from can with the sherry and sprinkle over the sponge. Reserve a few peaches for decoration and arrange the rest on top of sponge.

Remove wax paper and beat cooled custard well. Pour over fruit and chill for 1 hour.

Whip cream until stiff, then pipe onto trifle. Decorate with reserved peaches and sprinkle with toasted almonds.

Lemon sherbet

Overall timing 20 minutes plus freezing

Freezing See method

To serve 6

1 cup	Sugar
2½ cups	Water
½ cup	Fresh lemon juice
1	Egg white

Put the sugar and water in a pan and heat slowly, stirring until sugar dissolves. Bring to a boil and simmer for 10 minutes without stirring — do not let the syrup color. Remove from heat and leave to cool.

Add lemon juice to syrup, then strain into freezer tray and freeze until mushy.

Remove mixture from freezer, turn into a bowl and beat well to break down crystals. Beat egg white till soft peaks form. Fold into frozen mixture. Return to freezer tray and freeze till firm.

Chocolate mousse

Overall timing 15 minutes plus 3 hours chilling

Freezing Not suitable

To serve 4

1	Orange
4 x 1oz	Squares semisweet chocolate
2 tbsp	Butter
4	Eggs
	Pinch of salt

Grate the orange rind finely, being careful not to remove any pith. Break the chocolate into pieces and melt in the top of a double boiler over gently simmering water. Immediately the chocolate has melted pour into a heavy-based pan and add the butter and orange rind.

Separate the eggs. Add the yolks to the chocolate, stirring vigorously with a wooden spoon to prevent the mixture from boiling. Remove from heat. Cool.

Add pinch of salt to egg whites and beat till stiff peaks form. Fold one or two spoonfuls into the chocolate mixture, to make it more liquid, then gently fold in the rest of the whites with a spatula or metal spoon. Take care not to let the mixture become flat and heavy.

Pour into a serving bowl and chill for 3 hours before serving.

Black currant sorbet

Overall timing 4½ hours including refrigeration

Freezing See method

To serve 8

2lbs (4 pints)	Black currants or
	blueberries
	Black currant
	cordial or liqueur
1 cup	Sugar
2	Egg whites

Reserve a handful of black currants, and put the rest through a food mill or sieve to make a purée. Measure the purée — you should have about 2½ cups. Top up with blackcurrant cordial or liqueur and/or water if necessary.

Add the sugar to the purée and mix well to dissolve sugar. Pour into a freezer tray and freeze for about 2 hours till mushy.

Beat the egg whites till stiff. Turn black currant mixture into a bowl, mash lightly with a fork, then fold in the beaten egg whites, stirring to distribute evenly through purée. Turn into lightly oiled or dampened shallow container or 1 quart mold. Freeze for 2 hours till firmly set.

Immerse mold in hot water up to the rim, then quickly unmold sorbet onto a serving dish. Decorate sorbet with remaining black currants, and allow to soften at room temperature for 20 minutes before serving.

Candied fruit bombe

Overall timing 15 minutes plus
maceration and freezing

Freezing See method

To serve 6-8

⅔ cup	Chopped candied fruit
¼ cup	Apricot brandy or sweet sherry wine
1 quart	Vanilla ice cream
¾ cup	Apricot jam

Put a 9 x 5 x 3 inch loaf pan in the freezer. Place fruit in a bowl, add apricot brandy or sherry and leave to macerate for 30 minutes.

Put softened ice cream into a bowl, add fruit and liqueur and quickly mix well with a wooden spoon.

Remove pan from freezer and coat bottom and sides with a thick layer of the ice cream mixture. Spoon jam into the center of the pan, then cover with remaining ice cream. Smooth surface with a dampened knife.

Freeze for at least 2 hours. Unmold and cut into slices to serve.

Coffee charlotte

Overall timing 50 minutes plus chilling

Freezing Suitable

To serve 8

2 tbsp	Brandy
30	Ladyfingers
10 tbsp	Sugar
½ cup	Strong black coffee
2 tsp	Unflavored gelatin
4	Egg yolks
2 tbsp	Vanilla sugar
1 cup	Heavy cream
16	Sugar coffee beans

Mix brandy with ½ cup water in a shallow dish. Dip ladyfingers quickly in mixture to moisten them, then use them to line sides of greased 10 inch springform pan. Place cookies upright, sugared sides against pan, and trim ends to height of pan. Press lightly into place.

Put sugar and 3 tbsp water in heavy-based saucepan. Stir to dissolve sugar, then heat until golden brown. Stir in coffee and simmer for 2 minutes till caramel dissolves. Cool.

Dissolve gelatin in 2 tbsp cold water.

Put egg yolks and vanilla sugar in a bowl over a pan of hot water and beat together till light and foamy. Stir coffee caramel into egg mixture and beat till it starts to thicken. Stir in gelatin, then leave to cool until just on the point of setting.

Whip two-thirds of the cream until it holds soft peaks. Using a metal spoon, fold lightly into coffee mixture. Pour into center of ladyfinger-lined pan and chill till set.

Unclip pan and carefully transfer charlotte to a serving plate. Whip remaining cream until it holds stiff peaks. Pipe 16 rosettes around edge of charlotte. Place a coffee bean on top of each one. Pipe smaller rosettes around base.

Strawberry vacherin

Overall timing 2¼ hours plus cooling

Freezing Not suitable

To serve 8

6	Egg whites
1½ cups	Sugar
1 lb (3-4 cups)	Strawberries
Crème Chantilly	
1 cup	Heavy cream
1 tbsp	Cold milk
1	Ice cube
1 tbsp	Sugar
¼ tsp	Vanilla

Preheat the oven to 300°.

Line two baking sheets with non-stick paper. Draw a 10 inch square on one, and a 6 inch square on the other.

Beat egg whites till stiff and dry. Sprinkle over 2 tbsp of the sugar and beat in, then gradually beat in remaining sugar to make a stiff, glossy meringue.

Using the marked squares as a guide, put large spoonfuls of meringue onto paper to make two squares with scalloped edges. Swirl into peaks. Place large square in center of oven with small square below. Bake for about 1¼ hours till slightly browned and crisp. Cool.

Meanwhile, hull strawberries. To make the Crème Chantilly, whip cream with milk, ice cube, sugar and vanilla till it forms soft peaks. Chill till required.

Just before serving, carefully peel the paper from the meringue squares and place the large one on a flat board or serving dish. Spread or pipe two-thirds of the Crème Chantilly over and arrange two-thirds of the strawberries on top. Place the small meringue square on top and spread with the remaining crème. Decorate with remaining strawberries and serve immediately.

Strawberry milk ring

Overall timing 30 minutes plus setting

Freezing Not suitable

To serve 6

1	Lemon
5 tsp	Unflavored gelatin
5 tbsp	Sugar
1	Large can of evaporated milk
1 cup	Buttermilk
	Pink food coloring
1	Egg white
½ cup	Heavy cream
1 lb (3-4 cups)	Fresh strawberries

Grate the rind from the lemon and reserve. Squeeze out the juice and place in a small bowl. Sprinkle the gelatin over and dissolve. Stir in the sugar. Allow to cool slightly.

Pour the well-chilled evaporated milk into a large bowl and beat till very thick and foamy. Beat in the buttermilk, gelatin mixture, reserved lemon rind and a few drops of food coloring. Pour into a dampened 1-quart ring mold and chill for 3-4 hours till set.

Dip the mold up to the rim in hot water for a few seconds and unmold onto a serving plate.

Beat the egg white till stiff. Whip the cream till stiff and fold into the beaten egg white. Hull the strawberries and pile half in the center of the ring. Pipe the cream mixture on top and around the base of the ring. Decorate with the remaining strawberries and serve immediately.

Crème caramel

Overall timing 45 minutes

Freezing Not suitable

To serve 6

2½ cups	Milk
½	Vanilla bean
1	Piece lemon rind
4	Eggs
½ cup	Sugar

Preheat the oven to 350°.

Put the milk, vanilla bean and lemon rind in a saucepan and bring to a boil. Remove from heat and lift out the vanilla bean and lemon rind.

In a bowl, beat eggs with half the sugar and gradually pour in the hot milk, stirring constantly.

Melt the remaining sugar in a saucepan over a moderate heat till golden brown. Divide between six small molds and turn them so the caramel coats the bottoms and sides.

Strain the custard mixture into the molds and place them in a roasting pan half-filled with hot water. Bake for 45 minutes till set. Allow to cool in molds and chill before unmolding.

Cider and grape ring

Overall timing 15 minutes plus setting

Freezing Not suitable

To serve 4-6

2½ cups	Medium-sweet hard cider
1 tbsp	Unflavored gelatin
1 tbsp	Lemon juice
½lb	Green grapes
½lb	Purple grapes
2 tbsp	Sugar

Put 6 tbsp of the cider in a bowl, sprinkle over the gelatin and dissolve over a pan of hot water.

Stir in the remaining cider and lemon juice. Remove bowl from the heat. Spoon enough of the cider gelatin into a dampened 1-quart ring mold just to cover it. Leave it to set in the refrigerator.

Reserve half of each kind of grape. Wash and cut remainder in half and remove seeds. Arrange halves over the set gelatin, then cover with more liquid gelatin and leave to set.

Continue layers, ending with gelatin, then chill in refrigerator till set. Wash remaining grapes and remove most of the moisture. Toss in sugar.

Dip the mold quickly in and out of hot water and invert over a serving plate so gelatin slides out. Fill center with sugared grapes. Serve with whipped cream and gingersnaps.

Caramel cornmeal mold

Overall timing 1 hour

Freezing Not suitable

To serve 6-8

2 cups	Milk
	Pinch of salt
½ cup	Sugar
1	Bay leaf
18	Sugar cubes
½ cup	Warm water
1 tbsp	Lemon juice
5	Eggs
⅔ cup	Fine cornmeal

Preheat the oven to 400°.

Put the milk in a saucepan with the salt, sugar and bay leaf. Bring to a boil. Remove from the heat, cover and leave to infuse for 10 minutes.

Put the sugar cubes, water and lemon juice into a small saucepan and heat gently, stirring, till sugar dissolves. Bring to a boil and boil without stirring till a deep golden caramel color. Watch pan carefully to see that caramel does not burn. Pour into an 8 inch round deep cake pan, turning it so that the bottom and sides are coated with the caramel.

Separate the eggs. Put the egg yolks and cornmeal into a bowl and mix together with a wooden spoon. Remove bay leaf from the milk. Gradually pour the hot milk onto the egg yolks, stirring continuously. Beat the egg whites till stiff and fold into the mixture.

Pour the mixture into the prepared pan and place in a roasting pan containing 1 inch hot water. Bake for 35-40 minutes. While still warm, run knife around edge of pan and unmold onto serving plate. Serve warm or cold, with pouring cream.

Fruit salad with prunes

Overall timing 15 minutes plus
maceration and chilling

Freezing Not suitable

To serve 6

½lb (1½ cups)	Plump prunes
2 cups	Hot strong tea
3	Oranges
1	Grapefruit
2	Bananas
1 tbsp	Lemon juice
8oz	Can of pineapple slices
2 tbsp	Brandy or sherry

Put pitted prunes in a bowl and cover with
strained tea. Soak for 30 minutes.

Cut the rind and pith away from the
oranges and grapefruit with a serrated knife.
Cut into slices across the sections, cutting
large slices in halves or quarters. Place in glass
serving bowl.

Peel and cut the bananas into thick slices
and sprinkle with lemon juice to prevent
discoloration. Add to bowl with drained
prunes, lemon juice and pineapple slices with
their syrup. Stir in the brandy or sherry and
chill for at least 1 hour before serving.

Spicy fruit purée

Overall timing 1 ½ hours plus overnight maceration and cooling

Freezing Suitable

To serve 2

½lb	Mixed dried fruit
	(figs, apricots,
	peaches, pears,
	prunes)
2½ cups	Water
6 tbsp	Sugar
1	Apple
1 tsp	Ground cinnamon
1 tbsp	Cornstarch

Put the dried fruit in a large bowl with three-quarters of the water and the sugar and leave to soak overnight.

Pit the prunes. Transfer fruit to a saucepan, add remaining water and bring to a boil. Cook over a low heat for about 15 minutes.

Peel, core and slice the apple and add with cinnamon to the pan. Cook for a further 45 minutes.

Drain fruit and return liquid to the pan. Process or blend to a purée, then return to the pan.

Mix cornstarch with 1 tbsp cold water in a bowl, then stir into fruit mixture. Bring to a boil and boil for 5 minutes, stirring, until thick. Remove from heat and allow to cool. Pour into two serving glasses and chill for 2 hours before serving.

Pears in chocolate sauce

Overall timing 40 minutes plus chilling

Freezing Not suitable

To serve 6

6	Firm pears
2 cups	Water
1 tbsp	Lemon juice
½ cup	Sugar
1	Vanilla bean
4 x 1oz	Squares semisweet chocolate
1 tbsp	Butter
	Vanilla ice cream
	Crystallized violets (optional)

Peel the pears and remove the stalks. Put the water, lemon juice, sugar and vanilla bean into a saucepan and heat gently till the sugar dissolves. Bring the syrup to a boil, add the pears and simmer for about 15 minutes till just tender. Leave pears to cool in the syrup, then lift them out with a slotted spoon and chill for several hours. Reserve the syrup.

Break the chocolate into small pieces and put into the top of a double boiler with the butter. Place over simmering water and stir till melted. Remove from the heat and beat in 2 tbsp of the pear syrup.

Arrange the pears in a serving dish and place scoops of ice cream between them. Decorate with crystallized violets, if liked. Spoon the chocolate sauce over the pears and serve.

Black currant crêpe tower

Overall timing 45 minutes

Freezing Suitable: assemble tower and make sauce after reheating crêpes

To serve 4-6

1½lb	Black currants
10 tbsp	Sugar
Crêpes	
6	Eggs
	Pinch of salt
½ cup	Milk
1 cup	Flour
2 tbsp	Sugar
6 tbsp	Oil

Put black currants into a bowl and sprinkle with sugar.

To make crêpes, separate eggs. Beat yolks with salt and milk, then gradually beat in flour.

In another bowl, beat egg whites till frothy. Add sugar and beat until stiff. Fold whites into yolk mixture.

Heat 1 tbsp of the oil in an 8 inch skillet. Add one-sixth of the batter and cook till crêpe is golden brown underneath. Turn and cook other side. Place on serving dish and top with some of the fruit. Cook five more crepes in the same way, placing each one on the "tower" as it is cooked with a layer of fruit.

Serve hot with custard sauce.

Almond apricot desserts

Overall timing 1 ¼ hours

Freezing Not suitable

To serve 6

2 tbsp	Butter
2 tbsp	Sugar
⅔ cup	Apricot jam
3 tbsp	Lemon juice
3	Eggs
½ cup	Ground almonds

Preheat the oven to 300°.

Melt the butter in a saucepan and use to grease six small ovenproof dishes. Coat the inside of each dish with sugar.

Put the apricot jam and lemon juice into a saucepan and heat gently, stirring. Put pan into water to cool mixture slightly.

Separate the eggs. Stir the yolks and almonds into the jam mixture. Beat the egg whites in a mixing bowl until very stiff. Gently fold in the jam mixture.

Fill each dish to the top with the mixture. Place on a baking sheet and bake for about 45 minutes.

Serve in the dishes with custard sauce, whipped cream or ice cream.

Raisin and macaroon pudding

Overall timing 1 hour 20 minutes

Freezing Suitable: serve cold

To serve 6

2½ cups	Milk
2 cups	Soft bread crumbs
6 tbsp	Butter
3	Eggs
¼ cup	Sugar
1 cup	Golden raisins
½lb	Macaroons
Rum cream	
4	Eggs
6 tbsp	Sugar
¼ cup	Rum
	Juice of ½ lemon

Preheat the oven to 400°.

Put the milk into a saucepan and bring to a boil. Add the bread crumbs and cook gently – just simmering – for 10 minutes.

Meanwhile, cream butter in a bowl till softened. Separate the eggs. Beat the yolks with the sugar till light and fluffy, then gradually beat into the butter. Add the milk and bread crumbs and the raisins and mix well. Beat the egg whites till stiff and fold into the mixture.

Arrange the raisin mixture and the macaroons in layers in a greased 8 inch brioche or kugelhopf mold, beginning and ending with the raisin mixture. Bake for 1 hour.

To make the rum cream, mix the eggs, sugar, rum, lemon juice and 6 tbsp water in the top of a double boiler. Place over simmering water and cook, stirring constantly, till the mixture is thick enough to coat the back of a spoon. Strain into a warmed sauceboat or serving dish.

Unmold the pudding onto a warmed serving plate and serve hot, cut into thick wedges with the rum cream.

Coconut and cherry surprise

Overall timing 1 hour

Freezing Suitable: reheat in 375° oven for 10 minutes.

To serve 8-10

½lb	Pie pastry
10 tbsp	Ground almonds
16oz	Can of cherry pie filling
⅓ cup	Shredded coconut
Filling	
6 tbsp	Butter
6 tbsp	Sugar
2	Eggs
¼ tsp	Almond extract
2 tbsp	Milk
½ cup	Self-rising flour
⅔ cup	Shredded coconut
10 tbsp	Ground almonds

Topping	
3 tbsp	Shredded cocnut
1	Egg yolk
1 tsp	Milk

Roll out dough and use to line a greased 10 inch springform pan. Sprinkle ground almonds over. Spread pie filling to within 1 inch of edge, then cover with coconut.

Preheat the oven to 400°.

Make filling by creaming butter with sugar till pale and fluffy. Add eggs, almond extract and 1 tbsp milk and beat well. Fold in flour, followed by remaining milk, coconut and almonds.

Place mixture in blobs over pie filling and smooth evenly so no fruit is visible. Sprinkle with coconut and bake for 30 minutes.

Mix egg yolk and milk together. Brush over tart and bake for a further 10 minutes. Serve hot.

Flamed fruit salad

Overall timing 30 minutes

Freezing Not suitable

To serve 4

	Selection of any firm fresh fruit: apple, banana, cherries, orange, clementine, pear, peach, strawberries and grapes
1	Lemon
2 tbsp	Butter
3 tbsp	Sugar
½ cup	Flaked almonds
3 tbsp	Rum

Prepare the fruit and chop it into pieces. Mix these together in a bowl. Grate lemon and squeeze out juice. Add juice to fruit.

Put the butter and sugar into a saucepan. Heat without stirring, until the sugar caramelizes and becomes light brown. This will take about 5 minutes. Add the grated lemon rind and almonds. Cook for about 5 minutes, stirring occasionally, until the caramel and nuts are golden brown.

Remove pan from the heat. Add juices from mixed fruits and stir until caramel becomes a smooth syrup. Add the fruit and heat through for about 5 minutes, turning the mixture over frequently to distribute the syrup. Remove from heat.

Warm rum in a metal ladle, then set alight and pour over fruit. Serve immediately with whipped cream or ice cream.

Fruit brochettes

Overall timing 20 minutes

Freezing Not suitable

To serve 6

3	Bananas
2	Oranges
1	Lemon
8oz	Can of pineapple chunks
2 tbsp	Rum
½ cup	Sugar
2 tbsp	Butter
3	Thick slices of bread

Peel the fruit. Cut bananas into 1 inch pieces; divide oranges and lemon into sections; drain pineapple chunks. Place fruit in a bowl, pour rum over and sprinkle with 2 tbsp of the sugar.

Preheat the broiler or a charcoal grill.

Butter the bread on both sides, cut into small cubes and roll in sugar to coat. Thread fruit and bread cubes onto skewers.

Broil or grill for 10 minutes, turning brochettes over from time to time and sprinkling them with any remaining sugar. Serve immediately with whipped cream or vanilla ice cream.

Apricot crêpes

Overall timing 45 minutes

Freezing Suitable: fill crêpes after thawing and reheating

To serve 4

2	Eggs
¾ cup	Milk
¼ cup	Water
¾ cup	Flour
2 tbsp	Sugar
	Vanilla
	Pinch of salt
7 tbsp	Butter
½ cup	Apricot jam
	Confectioners' sugar
¼ cup	Ground hazelnuts

Put eggs, milk and water into a bowl. Add the flour, sugar, a few drops of vanilla and salt. Beat well together until creamy and smooth.

Melt a pat of butter in a small crêpe pan. Pour in a little of the batter and spread in a thin layer over the pan. When underside is cooked, flip the crêpe over to brown the other side.

As soon as each crêpe is ready, spread with apricot jam and roll up. Put onto a dish and keep warm in the oven while you cook the other crêpes, adding more butter to the pan as necessary.

Before serving, dredge with confectioners' sugar and sprinkle with ground hazelnuts or chopped nuts of your choice.

Blackberry crêpes

Overall timing 30 minutes

Freezing Not suitable

To serve 2

6 tbsp	Flour
2 tsp	Sugar
	Pinch of salt
1	Egg
½ cup	Milk
	Oil for frying
Topping	
1 cup	Canned blackberries
3 tbsp	Honey
1½ tbsp	Brandy
	Vanilla ice cream
¼ cup	Chopped walnuts

Sift flour, sugar and salt into a bowl. Make a well in the center and add egg and milk. Beat till smooth. Pour into a pitcher and leave to stand for 5 minutes.

Lightly oil an 8 inch crêpe pan and heat. Make four thin crêpes. Fold into quarters, arrange on a warmed serving plate and keep hot.

Place drained blackberries in a sieve. Drain on paper towels.

Gently heat honey with brandy in a saucepan. Remove from heat before it boils.

To assemble crêpes, put a cube of ice cream on top of each and scatter with blackberries. Pour over hot honey mixture and sprinkle with chopped walnuts. Serve immediately.

Fruity crêpes

Overall timing 1 hour

Freezing Not suitable

To serve 2

6 tbsp	Flour
2 tsp	Sugar
	Pinch of salt
1	Egg
½ cup	Milk
2 tbsp	Hard cider or white wine
	Grated rind of ½ orange
	Vanilla
3	Sugar cubes
1	Orange
½ tsp	Ground cinnamon
2	Apples
	Oil for frying

Sift flour, sugar and salt into a bowl. Make a well in the center and add egg, milk, cider or wine, orange rind and a few drops of vanilla. Beat till smooth. Pour batter into a pitcher.

Rub sugar cubes over surface of orange to absorb zest. Crush them and add cinnamon.

Peel orange, then chop flesh roughly. Place in a bowl. Peel, core and cube apples, then mix well with orange.

Preheat the broiler.

Lightly oil an 8 inch crêpe pan and heat. Pour in one-quarter of the batter and cook for 1-2 minutes till base bubbles and is firm. Spoon over one-quarter of the fruit and crushed sugar and cinnamon mixtures. Place under broiler and cook for a few minutes till bubbling. Fold crêpe and lift out onto a warmed serving dish. Cover and keep hot while you cook three more crêpes in the same way.

Serve whipped cream flavored with orange juice separately, or serve with vanilla ice cream.

Honey-baked bananas

Overall timing 40 minutes

Freezing Not suitable

To serve 4

4	Bananas
¼ cup	Lemon juice
3 tbsp	Honey
½ cup	Blanched almonds
3 tbsp	Soft bread crumbs
¼ cup	Butter
½ cup	Sour cream
3 tbsp	Orange juice

Preheat the oven to 400°.

Peel bananas. Arrange side by side in a greased ovenproof dish. Pour over lemon juice and honey. Mix the chopped almonds with the bread crumbs and sprinkle over bananas. Cut butter into small pieces and scatter over bananas.

Bake for 30 minutes. Serve with sour cream mixed with orange juice.

Apple and marmalade charlotte

Overall timing 1 hour

Freezing Suitable: reheat in 400° oven for 10 minutes

To serve 8

2½lb	Tart apples
¼ cup	Water
2 tbsp	Sugar
⅓ cup	Marmalade
1	Large stale loaf sliced bread
6 tbsp	Butter

Preheat the oven to 400°.

To make the filling, peel apples, core and slice into a large saucepan. Add water, cover and bring to a boil. Cook over medium heat for 12 minutes without removing the lid during cooking. Remove from heat and beat in sugar and marmalade with a wooden spoon.

Remove crusts and butter bread. Cut a third of slices into triangles and the rest into wide fingers.

Grease a 1 quart charlotte mold and line the bottom with some of the bread triangles, buttered-side out. Overlap the slices as the bread tends to shrink during cooking. Line sides of mold with overlapping bread fingers, butter-side out.

Pour in apple mixture and top with remaining bread triangles, butter-side up. Bake for 30-40 minutes till golden brown.

Remove from oven. Leave to cool slightly in the mold. Run a knife around the edge and unmold onto a warmed serving plate. Serve hot with custard sauce or cream.

Fruity rice pudding

Overall timing 1 ¼ hours

Freezing Suitable: reheat in 300° oven for 30 minutes

To serve 6-8

3 cups	Milk
	Salt
4	Strips of lemon rind
⅔ cup	Round grain rice
1½lb	Apples
2	Bananas
2 tbsp	Butter
½ cup	Sugar
1 tsp	Ground cinnamon
4oz	Bottle of Maraschino cherries
½ cup	Chopped walnuts
3	Eggs

Preheat oven to 350°.

Put the milk, pinch of salt and strips of lemon rind into a saucepan and bring to a boil. Add the rice. Cover and cook for 40 minutes on a low heat, stirring occasionally.

Meanwhile, peel and slice the apples and bananas. Melt the butter and ¼ cup of the sugar in a saucepan until golden brown. Add the apples and cook for 5 minutes, then add the bananas and cook for 2-3 minutes more. Sprinkle on the cinnamon, then stir in drained cherries and chopped walnuts.

Remove from heat, put mixture into a greased ovenproof dish and smooth over. Work quickly to prevent caramel setting.

Separate the eggs. Cream together the yolks and 2 tbsp sugar in one bowl. In another, beat the whites and remaining sugar together until mixture is very stiff. Fold both mixtures into the cooked rice (take out the lemon rind first) then pour over the fruit. Bake for 30 minutes. Serve hot with cream.

Nutty apple pudding

Overall timing 50 minutes

Freezing Not suitable

To serve 4-6

1½lb	Tart apples
½ cup	Water
½ cup	Flaked almonds
⅓ cup	Golden raisins
7 slices	Wholewheat bread
⅔ cup	Light brown sugar
¼ cup	Butter

Preheat the oven to 425°.

Peel and core apples and slice into a saucepan. Add water, almonds and raisins. Cover and cook over a gentle heat for 10 minutes. Remove from heat.

Crumble the bread into a bowl and mix in half the sugar. Grease an ovenproof dish with some of the butter and spread half the bread mixture over the bottom. Cover with apple mixture, then top with remaining bread. Sprinkle on rest of sugar and dot with remaining butter. Bake for about 20 minutes.

Peach meringue pudding

Overall timing 50 minutes

Freezing Not suitable

To serve 6

2½ cups	Milk
¼ cup	Semolina
2	Eggs
6 tbsp	Sugar
4	Ripe peaches
3 tbsp	Peach or raspberry jam
¼ cup	Toasted flaked almonds

Preheat the oven to 350°.

Heat the milk in a saucepan and sprinkle in the semolina, stirring constantly. Bring to a boil and cook, stirring, for 3 minutes till thickened. Remove from the heat.

Separate the eggs. Beat the yolks into the semolina with 2 tbsp of the sugar. Pour mixture into a 7 inch soufflé dish and smooth surface.

Peel and halve the peaches. Remove pits. Place a little jam in each peach half. Arrange in soufflé dish, some with the cut sides pressing against the sides of the dish and the rest jam-side down on the semolina.

Beat the egg whites till stiff, then beat in half the remaining sugar. Fold in the finely chopped almonds and the rest of the sugar. Pipe or spoon the meringue over the peaches.

Bake for 20 minutes till the meringue is lightly browned. Serve hot or leave to cool completely and chill before serving.

Pear brown betty

Overall timing 1 hour

Freezing Not suitable

To serve 6-8

2lb	Ripe pears
3 cups	Stale bread crumbs
½ cup	Sugar
¼ cup	Butter

Preheat the oven to 375°.

Peel and halve the pears. Remove the cores and cut flesh into ¼ inch slices.

Cover the bottom of a greased 8 inch springform pan with a quarter of the bread crumbs. Arrange one-third of the pears on top and sprinkle with a little sugar. Repeat the layers till all the ingredients have been used.

Dot with the butter and bake for about 45 minutes till the pears are tender and the top is crisp and golden. Remove from the pan and serve hot or cold with pouring cream or custard sauce.

Apple strudel

Overall timing 1¾ hours

Freezing Not suitable

To serve 8

2½ cups	Flour
1	Large egg
½ cup	Butter
	Pinch of salt
2½ lb	Tart apples
6 tbsp	Sugar
2 tsp	Ground cinnamon
⅔ cup	Raisins
1 tbsp	Grated lemon rind
1 cup	Ground almonds
1 cup	Soft bread crumbs

Sift flour onto a work surface. Add egg. Melt half butter in a pan, then add 6 tbsp water and salt. Add mixture to flour and mix to a soft, sticky dough. Knead till smooth. Leave in a warm place for 20 minutes.

Meanwhile, peel and core apples, then slice half very thinly. Coarsely grate rest into a bowl and mix in sugar, cinnamon, raisins, lemon rind, almonds and half bread crumbs.

Place a large patterned dishtowel on a flat surface and sprinkle it with flour. Roll out dough on top till it is same shape as towel. Slide your hands between dough and dishtowel. Lift and stretch dough till thin enough to see pattern of dishtowel through. The rectangle should eventually measure about 20 x 16 inches.

Preheat the oven to 400°.

Brush dough with half remaining melted butter. Sprinkle with remaining bread crumbs, leaving a 1 inch border all around. Spread almond mixture evenly over dough. Arrange apple slices on top. Fold border over filling, then roll up. Place on greased baking sheet, curving to fit.

Brush with remaining butter and bake for 10 minutes. Reduce heat to 375° and bake for a further 30 minutes. Sprinkle with confectioners' sugar and serve warm.

Apple soufflé omelette

Overall timing 50 minutes

Freezing Not suitable

To serve 2

Filling	
¾ lb	Tart apples
1 tbsp	Water
1 tbsp	Butter
3 tbsp	Sugar
	Vanilla

Omelette	
2	Eggs
2 tbsp	Sugar
¼ cup	Milk
¼ tsp	Vanilla
2 tbsp	Butter
	Confectioners' sugar
2 tbsp	Brandy

To make the filling, peel, core and roughly chop apples. Place in saucepan with water and butter, cover and cook for 15 minutes. Remove from heat and add sugar and a few drops of vanilla. Mix well, then cool.

To make omelette, separate one egg. Put the yolk in a bowl with the whole egg and the sugar and beat till light and frothy. Stir in milk and vanilla.

In another bowl, beat the egg white till very stiff. Stir 1 tbsp into yolk mixture to lighten it, then carefully fold in the rest with a metal spoon.

Preheat the broiler.

Melt the butter in an omelette pan. When it begins to turn a light brown, pour in the egg mixture. Cook over a low heat for 5-7 minutes. Place under the broiler until the top has set. Spread over the filling and fold over in half. Slide onto a warmed serving dish. Dredge with confectioners' sugar. Warm the brandy, pour over the omelette and set alight. Serve flaming.

Banana pudding with rum sauce

Overall timing 1 ¼ hours

Freezing Suitable: reheat in 350° oven

To serve 6

2lb	Bananas
7 tbsp	Sugar
¼ cup	Softened butter
¼ cup	Flour
	Grated nutmeg
2	Eggs
2 tbsp	Confectioners' sugar
1 tbsp	Rum or rum flavoring
½ cup	Light cream

Preheat the oven to 350°.

Reserve half a large or 1 medium-sized banana for decoration. Peel the rest. Mash them with a fork in a bowl with sugar, butter, flour and a pinch of nutmeg.

Separate the eggs. Add yolks to banana mixture and beat well with a wooden spoon until smooth and creamy. Beat the egg whites till very stiff, then gently fold into the banana mixture.

Lightly grease and flour a pudding basin or ovenproof mold. Fill with the banana mixture and bake for 1 hour.

Remove from oven. Leave to cool slightly then unmold onto a warmed serving plate. Sprinkle with confectioners' sugar and decorate with the reserved banana, sliced. Mix rum or few drops rum flavoring into cream and serve separately.

Blackberry and pear meringue

Overall timing 50 minutes

Freezing Not suitable

To serve 6-8

3 cups	Ripe blackberries
¼ cup	Sugar
3 tbsp	Ground almonds
4	Large ripe pears
3	Egg whites
1¾ cups	Confectioners' sugar

Preheat the oven to 350°.

Hull the berries and arrange over the bottom of a shallow ovenproof dish. Mix the sugar and 2 tbsp of the almonds together and sprinkle over the berries.

Peel and halve the pears lengthwise. Remove the cores. Arrange cut sides down in a single layer on the berries. Bake for 20 minutes.

Put the egg whites and sifted confectioners' sugar into a large heatproof bowl over a pan of simmering water. Beat till the meringue is stiff and glossy. Spoon or pipe the meringue over the pears and sprinkle with the reserved almonds.

Return to the oven and bake for a further 10 minutes till lightly browned. Serve immediately.

Cherry pudding with jam sauce

Overall timing 1¾ hours

Freezing Not suitable

To serve 4-6

½ cup	Butter
½ cup	Sugar
2	Eggs
1½ cups	Self-rising flour
⅔ cup	Glacé cherries
6 tbsp	Milk
½ tsp	Almond extract
Sauce	
¼ cup	Red jam
½ cup	Water
1 tsp	Arrowroot
1 tbsp	Lemon juice

Cream butter with sugar till pale and fluffy. Gradually beat in the eggs one at a time. Fold in the sifted flour and cherries, adding milk and almond extract to give a soft dropping consistency. Place in greased pudding basin or steaming mold and cover with greased foil.

Put basin into a pan and fill up to rim of basin with boiling water. Cover and steam for 1½ hours.

To make the sauce, melt the jam with the water in a small pan, then sieve. Blend arrowroot with lemon juice and stir into sauce. Bring to a boil, stirring.

Unmold pudding and serve immediately with the hot jam sauce.

Irish lemon pudding

Overall timing 1 hour

Freezing Not suitable

To serve 4-6

½ cup	Butter
¾ cup	Sugar
4	Eggs
1	Lemon
2 tbsp	Flour
1½ cups	Milk
1 tbsp	Confectioners' sugar

Preheat the oven to 400°.

Cream the butter and sugar in a bowl till light and fluffy. Separate the eggs and add the yolks to the creamed mixture. Beat well. Grate rind from lemon and squeeze out juice. Beat into the creamed mixture. Gradually stir in the flour, then the milk.

Beat egg whites till stiff, then carefully fold into mixture. Turn into a greased 7 inch soufflé dish and sift confectioners' sugar over. Place dish in roasting pan containing 1 inch hot water. Bake for 40-50 minutes till the pudding has risen and the top is golden. Serve hot or cold.

Caribbean crêpes

Overall timing 40 minutes

Freezing Not suitable

To serve 6

10 tbsp	Flour
	Pinch of salt
¼ tsp	Ground ginger
1	Egg
1 cup	Milk
¼ cup	Butter
Filling	
16oz	Can of pineapple rings
16oz	Can of creamed rice
¼ cup	Rum
6	Glacé cherries

Sift the flour, salt and ginger into a bowl. Add the egg and milk and beat till smooth. Melt butter and add one-quarter to batter.

Brush a little butter over an 8 inch pan and heat. Pour one-sixth of the batter into the pan, tilting it so that the bottom is covered. Cook till crêpe is golden brown underneath, then flip over and cook other side. Make five more crêpes in this way.

Preheat the oven to 375°.

Drain the pineapple rings, and reserve three. Finely chop the rest and put into a bowl. Add creamed rice and mix well. Divide the mixture between the crêpes. Roll up the crepes loosely and arrange in an ovenproof dish. Heat through in the oven for 10 minutes.

Meanwhile, cut the reserved pineapple rings in half. Warm the rum in a small saucepan. Remove crêpes from oven and decorate with the halved pineapple rings and cherries. Pour warm rum over, set alight and serve flaming, with scoops of vanilla ice cream.

Red currant pudding

Overall timing 1 ½ hours

Freezing Suitable: reheat from frozen in 350° oven for 1 hour

To serve 6-8

3 cups	Red currants
12	Slices of stale bread
¼ cup	Butter
2½ cups	Milk
1	Vanilla bean
2	Eggs
6 tbsp	Sugar

Wash and drain the red currants. Remove the stalks. Remove the crusts from the bread. Spread with butter and cut into triangles.

Sprinkle a few red currants over the bottom of a well-greased 2 quart ovenproof dish and arrange some of the bread on top. Cover with red currants, then a layer of bread. Repeat the layers.

Put the milk and vanilla bean into a saucepan and bring to a boil. Remove from the heat and lift out the vanilla bean. Beat the eggs with 5 tbsp of the sugar till frothy, then pour in the hot milk, beating continuously. Strain the custard over the red currants and bread. Leave to soak for 20 minutes.

Preheat the oven to 375°.

Sprinkle the remaining sugar over the pudding and bake for about 40 minutes till golden. Serve immediately.

Russian pudding

Overall timing 30 minutes

Freezing Not suitable

To serve 4-6

3½ cups	Milk
	Pinch of salt
	Grated rind of
	½ lemon
½ cup	Sugar
½ cup	Semolina or ground
	rice
1	Egg
1 lb	Can of cherries
2 tbsp	Currant jelly

In a saucepan, heat the milk, salt, lemon rind and ¼ cup of the sugar. Stir in the semolina or ground rice. Remove from the heat.

Separate the egg and add the beaten yolk to the saucepan.

In a bowl, beat the egg white till stiff and carefully fold into the semolina or ground rice mixture.

Drain cherries. Place cherries and 2 tbsp of the juice in a pan. Stir in the currant jelly and cook for 5 minutes.

Preheat the broiler. Grease a flameproof serving dish. Pour in half the semolina or rice mixture, then all the cherry mixture and finally the rest of the semolina or rice. Sprinkle with the remaining sugar and place under the broiler. Cook till the sugar caramelizes and turns golden but not brown — it should take about 3 minutes. Serve immediately.

Cherry bread pudding

Overall timing 1 hour

Freezing Not suitable

To serve 4-6

7	Slices of bread
16oz	Can of cherries
4	Eggs
½ cup	Sugar
2 cups	Milk
	Grated rind of
	½ lemon
1 tbsp	Confectioners' sugar

Preheat the oven to 350°.

Cut the slices of bread into quarters diagonally. Arrange eight of the bread triangles over the bottom of an ovenproof dish.

Drain the cherries; halve and remove pits. Spread half the cherries over bread and cover with eight more triangles. Sprinkle over the remaining cherries and cover with the remaining bread, arranged in overlapping rows.

Beat the eggs with the sugar and add the milk. Sprinkle lemon rind over the bread and strain the egg mixture over. Sprinkle the surface with confectioners' sugar and bake for 35 minutes. Serve hot.

Canadian cherry pie

Overall timing 1¼ hours

Freezing Not suitable

To serve 6

½lb	Pie pastry
2lb	Fresh cherries *or*
2 x 16oz	Cans of cherries
⅓ cup	Ground rice
¼ cup	Sugar
1	Lemon
1	Egg white
	Sugar for sprinkling

Preheat the oven to 450°.

Roll out two-thirds of dough and use to line a 7½ inch fluted pie pan.

Pit cherries (drain first if canned) and put into saucepan with rice and sugar. Grate rind from lemon and squeeze out juice. Add both to pan and bring to boil, stirring. Simmer for 2 minutes. Cool.

Spread cherry mixture in pastry case. Roll out remaining dough and lay over filling. Moisten edges and press together to seal. Brush with lightly beaten egg white and dredge with sugar.

Bake for 10 minutes, then reduce heat to 350°. Bake for a further 40-45 minutes till top is golden.

Custard tart

Overall timing 1 ½ hours plus cooling

Freezing Not suitable

To serve 4-6

2 cups	Flour
¼ cup	Shortening
¼ cup	Butter
4-6 tbsp	Water
Filling	
2½ cups	Milk
1	Vanilla bean
	Strip of lemon rind
4	Eggs
¼ cup	Sugar
	Grated nutmeg

Preheat the oven to 400°.

Put the flour into a bowl and rub in the fats till the mixture resembles fine bread crumbs. Gradually add the water and mix to a smooth dough.

Roll out the dough on a lightly floured surface and use to line a 9 inch pie pan. Bake blind for 10 minutes. Remove from oven and reduce temperature to 350°.

Put milk, vanilla bean and lemon rind into a pan and bring almost to a boil. Remove from heat and leave to infuse for 10 minutes. Remove vanilla bean and lemon rind.

Beat eggs and sugar in bowl. Pour in milk, stirring. Strain into pastry case and sprinkle with nutmeg. Bake for 35 minutes or till just set. Cool.

Nectarine almond tart

Overall timing 50 minutes plus chilling

Freezing Suitable

To serve 4

2 cups	Flour
	Pinch of salt
½ cup	Butter
¼ cup	Sugar
1	Egg
Filling	
1 tbsp	Semolina
1 tbsp	Ground almonds
½ cup	Sugar
1¾lb	Nectarines
1 tbsp	Split almonds

Sift the flour and salt into a bowl. Add butter, cut into flakes, sugar and egg and work into a dough. Add a little water if necessary. Chill for 30 minutes.

Preheat the oven to 425°.

Roll out dough on a floured surface and use to line a 9 inch fluted quiche pan. Mix together the semolina, ground almonds and half the sugar. Sprinkle over the pastry.

Halve the nectarines and remove the pits. Arrange the fruit in the pastry case, cut sides down, and sprinkle with the remaining sugar and split almonds. Bake for 35-40 minutes.

Allow to cool slightly, then serve warm or cold with pouring cream.

Lime tart

Overall timing 50 minutes plus chilling

Freezing Suitable

To serve 8

6oz	Pie pastry
4 tsp	Unflavored gelatin
¼ cup	Water
4	Eggs
½ cup	Sugar
3	Limes
¾ cup	Heavy cream

Preheat the oven to 400°.

Roll out dough on a lightly floured surface and use to line an 8 inch straight-sided pie pan. Bake blind for 20 minutes till golden. Allow to cool, then carefully remove from the pan.

To make the filling, dissolve the gelatin in the water. Separate eggs. Beat the yolks and sugar together till pale and creamy. Grate rind from limes and squeeze out the juice. Stir two-thirds of the rind and all the juice into the egg mixture. Stir in the gelatin.

Whip cream till stiff. In another bowl, beat the egg whites till stiff peaks form. Carefully fold cream, then beaten whites into lime mixture. Spoon into pastry case and fluff up the surface.

Sprinkle with the remaining grated lime rind and chill for at least 3 hours or overnight before serving.

Linzertorte

Overall timing 50 minutes

Freezing Suitable

To serve 12

2 cups	Flour
½ tsp	Ground cinnamon
10 tbsp	Butter
¾ cup	Ground almonds
6 tbsp	Sugar
½	Lemon
2	Egg yolks
⅔ cup	Raspberry jam

Sift flour and cinnamon into a large bowl. Rub in butter. Stir in almonds and sugar. Grate rind from lemon and squeeze out juice. Add both to bowl with egg yolks and mix to a soft dough. Add a little water if necessary. Knead lightly, then chill for 1 hour.

Preheat the oven to 375°.

Roll out two-thirds of the dough on a floured surface and use to line an 8 inch pie pan. Don't trim away excess dough.

Spread jam over the pastry case. Roll out remaining dough and cut into strips. Arrange in a lattice pattern across the jam. Fold dough edges in, crimping to make a decorative border.

Bake for 30-35 minutes. Leave to cool in pan. Serve with pouring cream.

Spicy rhubarb pie

Overall timing 1 ¾ hours

Freezing Not suitable

To serve 6-8

2¼ cups	Flour
	Pinch of salt
¼ tsp	Apple pie spice
½ tsp	Ground cinnamon
10 tbsp	Butter
¾ cup + 2 tbsp	Sugar
2lb	Rhubarb
1	Egg yolk

Sift flour, pinch of salt and spices into a bowl. Rub in the butter till the mixture resembles fine bread crumbs. Stir in 2 tbsp sugar and enough water to make a soft but not sticky dough. Add a little water if necessary. Knead lightly till smooth, then chill for 30 minutes.

Meanwhile, trim the rhubarb and cut into 1 inch lengths. Put into a bowl with all but 1 tbsp of the remaining sugar and mix well.

Preheat the oven to 400°. Place a baking sheet in the oven. Roll out half the dough on a floured surface and use to line a 9 inch pie pan. Brush the edge with water. Pile the rhubarb into the pie in a dome shape. Roll out remaining dough and cover the pie, sealing and crimping the edges.

Beat the egg yolk and brush over top of pie. Place pie on hot baking sheet and bake for 20 minutes. Reduce the temperature to 350° and bake for a further 25 minutes till crisp and golden.

Remove from the oven, sprinkle remaining sugar over and serve immediately with cream or custard sauce.

Banana tart

Overall timing 1 hour 50 minutes

Freezing Not suitable

To serve 8

1¾ cups	Flour
½ tsp	Baking powder
½ tsp	Salt
3 tbsp	Sugar
7 tbsp	Butter
1	Medium-size egg
Filling	
½ cup	Raisins or
	pitted dates
2 tbsp	Rum
4	Ripe bananas
2	Eggs
6 tbsp	Sugar
½ cup	Heavy cream
½ cup	Split almonds

Sift flour, baking powder, salt and sugar into a bowl. Rub in butter. Add egg with a little water if necessary to bind to a dough. Chill for 1 hour.

Put raisins, or chopped dates, to steep in rum.

Preheat the oven to 400°.

Roll out dough and use to line a 9 inch fluted French flan ring set on a baking sheet. Prick and bake blind for 15 minutes. Remove from oven.

Drain dried fruit, reserving rum. Peel bananas and cut in diagonal slices. Cover bottom of pastry case with the banana and most of the dried fruit.

Beat eggs and sugar together till pale and thick. Whip cream with reserved rum. Blend both mixtures together and pour over the fruit in pastry case. Scatter over almonds and reserved dried fruit.

Bake for 25 minutes until puffed, golden brown and set. Serve hot with cream.

Sunburst peach tart

Overall timing 1 hour

Freezing Not suitable

To serve 6

6 tbsp	Butter
½ cup	Sugar
3	Eggs
1 ¼ cups	Flour
	Grated rind of
	1 lemon
16 oz	Can of sliced
	peaches
½ cup	Hazelnuts

Preheat the oven to 350°.

Cream the butter and sugar together till pale and fluffy. Beat in the eggs one at a time, beating well between each addition. Fold in the sifted flour and lemon rind with a metal spoon. Pour the mixture into a greased and lined 8 inch springform pan and smooth the surface.

Drain the peaches thoroughly and arrange the slices in circles on the cake mixture. Sprinkle the finely chopped hazelnuts over. Bake for 45 minutes.

Remove from the pan, place on a warmed serving dish and serve immediately with custard sauce or cream.

Plum tart

Overall timing 1¾ hours

Freezing Not suitable

To serve 6-8

Filling

2½ cups	Milk
1 tsp	Vanilla
1½lb	Ripe yellow plums
4	Egg yolks
¾ cup	Sugar
6 tbsp	Flour

Pastry

3 cups	Self-rising four
1 cup	Butter
3 tbsp	Sugar
1	Egg
	Milk to mix

To make filling, put milk and vanilla into a saucepan and bring to a boil. Remove from heat, cover and leave to infuse for 10 minutes.

Meanwhile halve and pit plums. Beat egg yolks with sugar till pale and thick. Beat in sifted flour, then gradually stir in milk. Pour back into saucepan and cook gently, stirring, till thick. Leave to cool.

Preheat the oven to 400°.

Sift flour into a bowl and rub in ¾ cup of the butter. Stir in sugar, and add egg and enough milk to give a soft dough. Roll out and use to line a greased 8 inch square deep cake pan, molding it into the corners. Rest in refrigerator for 15 minutes.

Pour filling into pastry-lined tin and arrange plums on top, pressing them in lightly. Bake for 30 minutes.

Meanwhile, melt remaining butter in a saucepan. Remove tart from pan and place on a baking sheet. Brush sides and top edge of pastry with butter and bake for a further 10 minutes till pastry is crisp and golden. Serve hot or cold.

Tarte Tatin

Overall timing 1 ¼ hours

Freezing Not suitable

To serve 8-10

½ lb	Frozen puff pastry
6 tbsp	Unsalted butter
6 tbsp	Sugar
7	Large apples

Thaw the pastry. Preheat the oven to 425°.

Cut butter into pieces and put into a 9 inch round cake pan with the sugar. Peel and core the apples; cut six of them in half. Arrange the apple halves on end around the side of the pan and place the whole apple in the center.

Place the pan over a low heat and heat till the butter melts. Increase the heat and cook, shaking the pan occasionally, till the sugar caramelizes and is golden. Remove from the heat. Brush a little water around the edge of the pan.

Roll out dough on a floured surface to a 9 inch round and place over the apples. Press down lightly.

Bake for 25-30 minutes till the pastry is well risen and golden brown. Leave to cool in the pan for 5 minutes.

Run a knife around the edge of the tart and unmold onto a serving dish so that the caramelized apples are on top. Serve hot or cold with whipped cream or scoops of vanilla ice cream.

Almond marmalade tart

Overall timing 1 ¼ hours

Freezing Suitable

To serve 6-8

7 tbsp	Butter
7 tbsp	Sugar
1	Egg
1 cup	Ground almonds
1 ¼ cups	Self-rising flour
¼ tsp	Salt
Filling	
¾ lb	Tart apples
	Juice of ½ lemon
2 tbsp	Sugar
6 tbsp	Fine-cut marmalade
1 tbsp	Dried bread crumbs

Put butter, sugar and egg into a bowl and beat until light and fluffy. Add almonds, sifted flour and salt and mix to a soft, but not sticky dough. Add a little water if necessary. Chill for 30 minutes.

Meanwhile, peel and core apples. Slice thinly into a bowl and sprinkle with lemon juice. Stir in the sugar and marmalade and leave to stand till pastry is ready.

Preheat the oven to 400°.

Put half the dough into a greased 8 inch layer cake pan and spread out to cover the bottom. Prick and sprinkle bread crumbs over. Spread the apple mixture over and cover with small spoonfuls of remaining pastry.

Bake for about 35 minutes till golden. Remove from pan and serve hot or cold, cut into slices, with cream or custard sauce.

Walnut pear pie

Overall timing 1 hour plus chilling

Freezing Suitable: decorate with cream after thawing

To serve 6-8

1½ cups	Flour
½ cup	Butter
¼ cup	Sugar
½ cup	Finely chopped walnuts
2 tsp	Ground cinnamon
1	Egg
Filling	
4	Ripe pears
3 tbsp	Sugar
½ cup	Whipping cream

Sift flour into a large bowl and rub in butter. Stir in sugar, finely chopped walnuts and cinnamon. Add egg with enough water to bind to a firm dough. Chill for 1 hour.

Preheat the oven to 375°.

Roll out two-thirds of dough and use to line an 8 inch fluted quiche pan. Peel, core and quarter pears. Arrange over pastry in a circle, core-side downwards and with the stem ends pointing towards the center but not joining up. Sprinkle with 2 tbsp sugar.

Roll out remaining dough and place over pears. Trim edges and pinch together to seal. Using a 3 inch pastry cutter, cut a circle out of the centre of the pastry lid. Brush pastry with egg white (from egg shell) and dredge with remaining sugar. Bake for 15 minutes, then reduce oven temperature to 350° and bake for a further 25 minutes. Cool in pan.

Whip cream and spoon or pipe into center of pie before serving.

English apple pie

Overall timing 1 hour

Freezing Not suitable

To serve 4-6

2 cups	Flour
	Pinch of salt
½ cup	Butter
1½lb	Tart apples
¼ cup	Brown sugar
½ tsp	Ground cinnamon
¼ tsp	Grated nutmeg
¼ tsp	Ground cloves
⅓ cup	Golden raisins
	Milk
1 tbsp	Sugar

Preheat oven to 400°.

Sift flour and salt together into a bowl and rub in butter. Add enough water to mix to a firm dough.

Peel, core and slice apples into a bowl. Add brown sugar, spices and raisins. Put mixture in a buttered deep 1 quart pie dish. Sprinkle over 2 tbsp of water.

Roll out dough and cover pie. Decorate with dough trimmings. Brush with milk and sprinkle with sugar.

Bake for 20 minutes. Reduce heat to 350° and bake for a further 20 minutes.

Blueberry boats

Overall timing 1 hour 20 minutes

Freezing Not suitable

Makes 8

¾ cup	Flour
3 tbsp	Sugar
1	Egg
	Vanilla
3 tbsp	Butter
Filling	
3 cups	Blueberries
¼ cup	Sugar
¼ cup	Flaked almonds
½ cup	Heavy cream
1 tbsp	Confectioners' sugar

Preheat the oven to 425°.

Sift flour into a bowl, make a well in the center and add sugar, egg and a few drops of vanilla. Add the butter, cut into pieces, and knead to a dough. Add a little water if necessary. Chill for 30 minutes.

Roll out dough to ¼ inch thick and use to line eight boat-shaped tartlet molds. Prick and bake blind for 15-20 minutes till cooked and golden brown. Cool.

Rinse blueberries and place in bowl. Sprinkle over the sugar and leave for 1 hour.

Preheat the broiler. Spread flaked almonds on broiler pan and toast. Whip cream till stiff with confectioners' sugar. Spoon into pastry bag.

Drain blueberries and divide between pastry boats. Pipe on cream and decorate with toasted almonds.

Caraway seed bread

Overall timing 1 ½ hours plus rising

Freezing Suitable: refresh in hot oven for 10 minutes

Makes 2 small or 1 large loaf

4 cups	Flour
3 tbsp	Sugar
2 tsp	Active dry yeast
5 tbsp	Lukewarm water
¾ cup	Lukewarm milk
1 tsp	Salt
2 tbsp	Caraway seeds
½ cup	Softened butter
2	Eggs
1 tbsp	Milk

Mix together 1 cup flour, 1 tsp sugar, the yeast, water and milk in a large bowl. Cover and leave in a warm place for about 20 minutes till frothy.

Mix remaining flour with salt, remaining sugar and caraway seeds. Add to yeast mixture with butter and beaten eggs. Mix well to a soft dough. Turn onto a lightly floured surface and knead till smooth and elastic. Cover and leave to rise until doubled in size.

Turn dough onto a lightly floured surface and knead till dough is firm again. Shape into two rolls about 6 inches long. Place on greased and floured baking sheet. Make three cuts across top of each loaf. Brush with milk. Cover with oiled plastic wrap and leave to rise until loaves double in size.

Preheat the oven to 400°. Bake the loaves for 30-35 minutes. Cool on a wire rack.

Sesame bread

Overall timing 2 hours plus rising

Freezing Suitable

Makes 2 loaves

6	Saffron strands
1 cup	Lukewarm milk
½ cup	Lukewarm water
1 pkg	Active dry yeast
4 tsp	Sugar
4 cups	Flour
¼ cup	Butter
2	Eggs
½ tsp	Salt
2 tbsp	Sesame seeds

Mix together saffron, all but 2 tbsp milk, the water, yeast, 1 tsp sugar and 2 tbsp flour. Leave in a warm place till frothy.

Melt butter and cool, then beat into batter with one egg and the remaining milk and sugar. Sift remaining flour and the salt over batter and mix to a soft dough. Knead till smooth. Leave to rise till doubled in size.

Punch down the dough. Knead till smooth and divide into six pieces. Roll into sausages about 9 inches long. Moisten ends of sausages wth beaten egg. Braid three together, pinching together at both ends to seal. Repeat with remaining three sausages and arrange on greased baking sheet. Leave to rise till doubled in size.

Preheat the oven to 375°. Brush braids carefully with beaten egg, then sprinkle with sesame seeds. Bake for about 35 minutes. Cool on wire rack.

Spicy fruit bread

Overall timing 1 ½ hours plus rising

Freezing Suitable: reheat in 350° oven
for 20 minutes

To serve 8

½ cup	Light brown
	sugar
1 cup	Milk
4 tsp	Active dry yeast
3 cups	Flour
½ tsp	Salt
1 tsp	Ground cinnamon
	Ground cloves
6 tbsp	Softened butter
1	Egg
1 cup	Golden raisins
⅓ cup	Currants

Dissolve ½ tsp sugar in all but 2 tbsp of the
milk and sprinkle yeast on top. Leave in warm
place till frothy.

Sift the flour, salt, cinnamon and a pinch of
cloves into a large bowl. Add the yeast
mixture, butter, egg, remaining sugar, the
raisins and currants. Mix to a soft dough.
Knead the dough on a floured surface till
glossy. Wrap in oiled plastic wrap and leave to
rise till doubled in size.

Turn the dough onto a floured surface and
knead till smooth. Shape into a thick sausage
and place on a greased baking sheet. Cover
with oiled plastic wrap and leave to rise till
doubled in size.

Preheat the oven to 400°. Brush the dough
with the reserved milk and bake for about
40 minutes. Cool on a wire rack.

Danish pastries

Overall timing 2 hours including chilling

Freezing Suitable

Makes 15

3 tbsp	Sugar
⅔ cup	Lukewarm milk
1 tsp	Active dry yeast
2¼ cups	Flour
½ tsp	Salt
¾ cup	Butter
	Marzipan
1	Egg
1 cup	Confectioners' sugar

Dissolve 1 tsp sugar in milk and sprinkle yeast on top. Leave till frothy. Sift flour and salt into bowl, rub in 1 tbsp butter and add rest of sugar and yeast mixture. Mix to a dough. Shape remaining butter into an oblong. Roll out dough into an oblong twice size of butter. Place butter in center and wrap dough around.

Turn dough so folds are at sides. Roll into an oblong three times longer than it is wide. Fold bottom third up, top third down. Chill for 10 minutes. Repeat turning, rolling and chilling twice.

Roll out dough into oblong, 15 x 9 inches, cut into 15 squares and shape as below:

Cockscombs: put marzipan in center of each and fold in half, sealing with beaten egg. Make cuts in folded edge, almost to cut edges; spread out in a fan shape. Envelopes: put marzipan in center of each and fold opposite corners to center, securing tips with beaten egg. Windmills: make diagonal cuts from each corner almost to center. Place marzipan in center and fold one corner of each triangle to it. Press firmly to secure. Arrange shapes on baking sheets and rise for 20 minutes.

Preheat the oven to 425°. Brush with beaten egg and bake for 18 minutes. Mix confectioners' sugar with 2 tbsp water and trickle over hot pastries.

Bagels

Overall timing 1 ¼ hours plus rising and cooling

Freezing Suitable: refresh from frozen in 400° oven for 10 minutes

Makes 10

1 tsp	Sugar
⅔ cup	Lukewarm water
1 tsp	Active dry yeast
2¼ cups	Flour
1 tsp	Salt
1	Egg
1 tbsp	Oil
1	Egg yolk
1 tsp	Caraway seeds
1 tsp	Poppy seeds
1 tsp	Coarse salt

Dissolve sugar in water and sprinkle yeast on top. Leave till frothy.

Sift flour and salt into a large bowl. Add egg, oil and yeast mixture. Mix to a soft dough. Knead till smooth and glossy. Leave to rise till doubled in size.

Punch down dough and knead till smooth. Divide into 10 equal portions and roll into sausage shapes about 7 inches long. Wrap sausage shapes around to make rings and pinch ends together to seal. Smooth joins by rocking dough on floured surface. Arrange on a baking sheet, cover with oiled plastic wrap and leave to rise till almost doubled in bulk.

Preheat oven to 425°.

Poach bagels, in batches, in boiling water for 2 minutes, turning them once. Remove from the pan with a slotted spoon and arrange on a floured baking sheet.

When all the bagels are ready, brush them with egg yolk. Sprinkle some with caraway seeds, some with poppy seeds and some with coarse salt. Bake for about 15 minutes till crisp and golden brown. Cool on a wire rack.

Wholewheat bread

Overall timing 3 hours minimum

Freezing Suitable

Makes 2-4 loaves

1 tbsp	Brown sugar
3¾ cups	Lukewarm water
3 pkg	Active dry yeast
12 cups	Wholewheat flour
1 tbsp	Salt
2 tbsp	Lard

Dissolve 1 tsp of the sugar in 1 cup of the warm water in a bowl. Sprinkle the dried yeast on top. Leave for about 10 minutes till frothy.

Mix flour, salt and the remaining sugar in a bowl. Rub in the lard, then add the yeast liquid and the rest of the water. Mix to a dough. Knead the dough thoroughly till it feels firm and elastic and no longer sticky. This should take 5-10 minutes. Shape the dough into a ball and place in an oiled plastic bag. Leave to rise till doubled in size.

Turn the dough onto a board and knead again till firm. Divide into two or four and flatten each piece firmly with the knuckles to knock out air. Shape and place in loaf pans.

Brush the tops with a little salted water and put each pan into an oiled plastic bag. Leave to rise till the dough comes to just over the top of the pan and springs back when pressed with a floured finger — about 1 hour at room temperature.

Preheat the oven to 450°. Bake the loaves for 30-40 minutes. Unmold to cool on a wire rack.

Brioche

Overall timing 1 ¼ hours plus rising

Freezing Suitable: shape dough and bake after thawing

Makes 1 large or 12 small

2 tsp	sugar
⅓ cup	Lukewarm water
2 tsp	Active dry yeast
2 cups	Flour
	Salt
¼ cup	Butter
2	Eggs
	Milk for glazing

Dissolve ½ tsp sugar in water and sprinkle yeast on top. Leave till frothy.

Sift flour, a pinch of salt and remaining sugar into a large bowl. Add yeast mixture, melted butter and eggs and mix to a soft dough. Knead till smooth and glossy. Leave to rise in a warm place till doubled in size.

Punch down dough and knead for 3-4 minutes till smooth. To make one large brioche, cut off one-quarter of the dough and shape both pieces into balls. Place large one in lightly greased 8 inch brioche mold and push a finger down through center to base. Place smaller ball in indentation and press down lightly.

To make 12 small brioches, divide dough into 12 pieces and remove one-quarter from each. Shape all pieces into balls. Place each large ball in a 3 inch brioche mold, push a finger down through center, then top with small balls, pressing down lightly. Leave to rise till doubled in size.

Preheat the oven to 450°. Brush each brioche with milk and bake for 8-10 minutes (small) or 15-20 minutes (large) till well risen and golden. Serve warm.

Italian fruit bread

Overall timing 1 ½ hours plus rising

Freezing Suitable: reheat in 350° oven for 10 minutes

To serve 6

3 cups	Flour
4 tsp	Active dry yeast
¼ cup	Sugar
1 cup	Lukewarm milk
¼ tsp	Salt
½ cup	Pine nuts
⅓ cup	Chopped candied peel
⅓ cup	Raisins
¼ cup	Butter
1	Egg
1 tbsp	Marsala

Mix together 1 cup flour, the yeast, 1 tsp sugar and the milk to a smooth batter. Leave till frothy.

Sift remaining flour and the salt into a large bowl. Add remaining sugar, the pine nuts, candied peel and raisins. Stir melted butter, beaten egg and Marsala into frothy batter, then add to fruit mixture. Mix to a soft dough. Turn onto a lightly floured surface and knead till smooth and glossy. Cover with oiled plastic wrap and leave to rise till doubled in size.

Punch down dough and knead till smooth. Shape into a smooth ball and place on greased baking sheet. Leave to rise till doubled in size.

Preheat the oven to 400°. Score a cross on top of the ball and bake for 10 minutes. Reduce the heat to 350° and bake for a further 25 minutes. Cool on a wire rack.

Moist date and ginger cake

Overall timing 1¼ hours

Freezing Suitable

To serve 12

½lb (1½ cups)	Pitted dates
1 tsp	Baking soda
¾ cup	Boiling water
½ cup	Butter
⅔ cup	Dark brown sugar
2 tbsp	Molasses
1 tbsp	Light corn syrup
2	Eggs
2 cups	Self-rising flour
2 tsp	Ground ginger
2 tbsp	Confectioners' sugar

Preheat the oven to 350°.

Chop the dates and place in a small bowl. Sprinkle with baking soda, then pour on the boiling water. Leave to cool.

Cream the butter with the sugar till light and fluffy. Beat in the molasses and corn syrup, then the eggs, one at a time, beating well. Sift in the flour and ginger, and add the dates and soaking liquid. Stir till well blended.

Pour into a greased and lined 9 inch round cake pan. Bake for 50-60 minutes till the center of the cake springs back when lightly pressed. Cool on a wire rack. Dredge with confectioners' sugar before serving.

Marble ring cake

Overall timing 1 ½ hours

Freezing Suitable

To serve 10

½ cup	Butter
10 tbsp	Sugar
3	Eggs
1¾ cups	Self-rising flour
½ cup	Milk
¼ cup	Cocoa powder

Preheat the oven to 350°.

Cream the butter with the sugar till mixture is pale and fluffy. Beat in the eggs, one at a time. Divide the mixture into two. Sift 1 cup of the flour into one-half and fold in with half of the milk. Sift the rest of the flour and the cocoa into the other half of the mixture and fold in with the remaining milk. Add more milk to both mixtures if necessary.

Spread a little of the plain mixture over the bottom and sides of a greased and floured 7½ inch ring mold. Carefully spread a thin layer of the chocolate mixture over the layer. Repeat the careful layering until both mixtures are used up.

Bake for 1 hour till well risen and firm to the touch. Cool cake slightly in the mold before unmolding onto a wire rack to cool completely.

Jelly roll

Overall timing 30 minutes plus cooling

Freezing Suitable: fill after thawing

To serve 8

3	Large eggs
6 tbsp	Sugar
¼ tsp	Vanilla
¾ cup	Flour
	Pinch of salt
3 tbsp	Warm water
¼ cup	Jam

Preheat the oven to 400°.

Separate the eggs. Beat yolks with the sugar and vanilla till mixture forms trails when beaters are lifted. Sift flour and fold into mixture.

Beat the whites with salt till mixture forms soft peaks that curl downwards. Fold into yolk mixture with metal spoon, then fold in warm water. Place mixture in greased and lined jelly roll pan, spreading to sides. Bake for 12-15 minutes till sides of sponge shrink a little.

Unmold sponge onto sheet of wax paper sprinkled with sugar. Carefully peel away paper from sponge. Trim edges of sponge with a sharp knife.

Working quickly, spread jam over sponge. With the help of the paper, roll up sponge away from you. Place seam-side down on wire rack to cool.

Caramel ring cake

Overall timing 1 ¼ hours

Freezing Suitable: ice cake after thawing

To serve 12

½ cup	Butter
1 cup	Brown sugar
1 tbsp	Light corn syrup
2	Eggs
1 ½ cups	Self-rising flour
1 tsp	Ground cinnamon
	Pinch of salt
¼ tsp	Baking soda
½ cup	Milk
	Vanilla
Icing	
2 tbsp	Butter
2 tbsp	Light corn syrup
1 tbsp	Milk
1 tsp	Vanilla
2 cups	Confectioners' sugar
1 tsp	Ground cinnamon

Preheat oven to 350°.

Cream butter with sugar; beat in eggs and corn syrup. Sift in flour, cinnamon and salt and beat well. Mix soda with milk and a few drops of vanilla and add to mixture. Place in a greased and floured 9½ inch ring mold and bake for 45-50 minutes. Cool on wire rack.

For the icing heat butter and corn syrup in saucepan. Stir in milk and vanilla and remove from heat. Sift half of confectioners' sugar and the cinnamon into saucepan and stir well. Stir in rest of sifted sugar.

Pour icing over cake and smooth with spatula dipped in hot water.

Cocoa Madeira cake

Overall timing 1 hour 20 minutes

Freezing Suitable

To serve 10

¾ cup	Butter
¾ cup	Sugar
3	Eggs
1 cup	Self-rising flour
½ cup	Cocoa powder
	Pinch of salt
3 tbsp	Madeira
¼ cup	Milk
½ cup	Chopped walnuts

Preheat the oven to 350°.

Cream the butter with the sugar till light and fluffy. Beat the eggs and add to creamed mixture a little at a time, beating well after each addition. Sift together the flour, cocoa and salt. Add to creamed mixture a little at a time, alternating with the Madeira and milk. When the mixture is smooth and will flick easily from the spoon, fold in half the chopped walnuts.

Put mixture into greased and lined 7 inch round deep cake pan and smooth top. Bake for 45 minutes. Sprinkle with remaining walnuts and bake for further 15-20 minutes till skewer inserted into cake comes out clean. Cool on a wire rack.

Lemon and cardamom cake

Overall timing 1 ½ hours

Freezing Suitable

To serve 8

2 cups	Self-rising flour
1 tsp	Ground cardamom
½ cup	Butter
½ cup	Sugar
1	Lemon
1	Egg
¼ cup	Milk
¼ cup	Flaked almonds
½ tsp	Ground cinnamon

Preheat the oven to 350°.

Sift flour and cardamom into a large bowl. Rub in the butter till mixture resembles fine bread crumbs. Stir in all but 1 tsp of the sugar. Grate the lemon rind and squeeze out the juice. Add both to bowl with the egg. Gradually mix ingredients, adding enough milk to give a soft consistency that won't drop unless flicked from the spoon.

Put mixture into a greased and lined 7 inch round deep cake pan and smooth the surface. Mix together almonds, cinnamon and reserved sugar and sprinkle over cake. Bake for 1¼ − 1½ hours till cake comes away from the sides. Cool in pan for a few minutes, then unmold onto a wire rack and cool completely.

Gingerbread

Overall timing 1 ¼ hours

Freezing Suitable

To serve 9

2 cups	Flour
1 tsp	Baking soda
1 ½ tsp	Ground ginger
3 tbsp	Molasses
⅓ cup	Light corn syrup
6 tbsp	Butter
⅓ cup	Brown sugar
2	Eggs
¼ cup	Milk

Preheat the oven to 325°.

Sift flour, soda and ginger into a bowl. Place molasses and corn syrup in a saucepan with butter and brown sugar. Heat till melted.

Beat eggs and milk. Add with melted ingredients to dry ingredients. Mix to a thick batter. Pour into a greased and lined 7 inch square cake pan. Bake for 1 hour.

Hazelnut and honey cake

Overall timing 1 ¼ hours

Freezing Suitable

To serve 8

¾ cup	Butter
⅔ cup	Light brown sugar
¼ cup	Clear honey
2	Whole eggs
2	Egg yolks
2 cups	Wholewheat self-rising flour
	Pinch of salt
1 cup	Toasted hazelnuts
½ cup	Milk

Preheat the oven to 350°.

Cream the butter with the sugar and honey, then beat in the whole eggs and yolks. Fold in flour, salt and chopped hazelnuts alternately with the milk.

Put mixture into a greased and lined 7 inch round deep cake pan. Bake for 1 hour until springy to the touch. Cool on wire rack. Coat with a fudgy frosting if a more elaborate cake is desired.

Orange and almond sponge

Overall timing 1 hour plus cooling

Freezing Suitable: ice after thawing

To serve 10

1	Large orange
5	Eggs
10 tbsp	Sugar
¾ cup + 2 tbsp	Self-rising flour
	Pinch of salt
¼ tsp	Ground ginger
½ tsp	Ground cinnamon
1¼ cups	Ground almonds
	Almond extract
1¼ cups	Confectioners' sugar
1 tbsp	Curaçao

Preheat the oven to 400°.

Grate the rind from the orange and squeeze out the juice. Separate the eggs. Beat egg yolks with the sugar till the mixture is pale and thick. Sift the flour, salt and spices over the mixture and add the ground almonds, three drops of extract, orange rind and 3 tbsp of the orange juice. Add more orange juice if necessary. Fold in gently.

Beat the egg whites till stiff and fold into the mixture with a metal spoon. Carefully pour mixture into a greased and lined 9 inch cake pan and smooth the surface. Bake for about 35 minutes till springy to the touch. Cool on a wire rack.

Sift the confectioners' sugar into a bowl and add the Curaçao and 1 tbsp of the remaining orange juice to make an icing that will coat the back of the spoon. Pour the icing onto the top of the cake. Lift the wire rack and tap it several times on the working surface so that the icing flows over the cake and trickles down the sides. Leave to set.

Praline-topped lemon cake

Overall timing 1 ½ hours

Freezing Suitable

To serve 8

½ cup	Butter
10 tbsp	Sugar
4	Eggs
1 ¼ cups	Flour
¾ cup	Cornstarch
2 tsp	Baking powder
2 tbsp	Grated lemon rind
½ cup	Chopped almonds
Buttercream	
10 tbsp	Butter
1 ¼ cups	Confectioners' sugar
1	Egg yolk
2 tbsp	Lemon juice

Preheat the oven to 350°.

Cream butter with ½ cup sugar till light and fluffy. Separate eggs and beat egg yolks into creamed mixture. Sift flour, cornstarch and baking powder together and fold into creamed mixture with lemon rind. Beat egg whites till stiff and fold in.

Pour into greased and lined 8 inch round deep cake pan and smooth surface. Bake for 50-60 minutes till top springs back when lightly pressed. Cool on wire rack.

Melt remaining sugar with 1 tsp water in a heavy-based saucepan. Boil until caramelized to a pale golden color. Add chopped almonds and mix well. Spread onto a greased baking sheet. Allow to cool and set hard, then break praline into tiny pieces with a rolling pin.

To make buttercream, cream butter with sifted confectioners' sugar till soft, then beat in egg yolk and lemon juice.

Cut cake into three layers and put back together with most of buttercream. Spread remainder on top and lightly press in praline.

Fresh cherry cake

Overall timing 1 ½ hours

Freezing Suitable

To serve 8

6	Graham crackers
2lb	Fresh cherries
¾lb	Ground almonds
1 cup + 2 tbsp	Sugar
½ tsp	Ground cinnamon
5	Eggs
2 tbsp	Kirsch
1	Lemon
1 cup	Flour

Preheat the oven to 350°.

Crush the crackers and sprinkle over the bottom and sides of an oiled 10 inch cake pan.

Pit cherries. Arrange over the bottom of the coated cake pan.

Mix together the almonds, ¼ cup of the sugar and the cinnamon. Separate the eggs. Beat together the egg yolks, remaining sugar, Kirsch and grated rind and juice of the lemon. Stir in the almond mixture, then fold in the flour lightly. Beat the egg whites till stiff and fold into the cake mixture using a metal spoon.

Spread the cake mixture over the cherries. Bake for 1 hour 10 minutes. Cool on a wire rack. Dredge with confectioners' sugar before serving.

Whiskey cake

Overall timing 2 hours plus cooling

Freezing Suitable

To serve 12

⅔ cup	Raisins
¼ cup	Whiskey
⅔ cup	Chopped candied peel
	Grated rind of
	1 orange
¾ cup	Butter
¾ cup	Sugar
3	Eggs
1 cup	Flour
1 cup	Self-rising flour
¼ tsp	Ground cinnamon

Preheat the oven to 350°.

Soak the raisins in the whiskey. Add the candied peel to the raisins with the orange rind. Mix well and leave to soak for 10 minutes.

Cream the butter with the sugar till pale and fluffy. Beat the eggs and add, a little at a time, to the creamed mixture, beating well between each addition. Sift the flours and cinnamon over, add the fruit and soaking liquid and fold into the mixture with a metal spoon.

Spread the mixture in a greased and lined 8 inch round deep cake pan, smooth the surface and make a slight hollow in the center. Bake for 1¼ − 1½ hours till a skewer inserted in the cake comes out clean. Allow to cool slightly in the pan, then transfer to a wire rack and leave to cool completely.

Coffee ring cake

Overall timing 1½ hours

Freezing Suitable

To serve 16

10 tbsp	Butter
10 tbsp	Sugar
	Salt
2	Large eggs
1	Orange
1 tbsp	Instant coffee powder
1¼ cups	Self-rising flour
¼ tsp	Ground cinnamon
2 x 1oz	Squares semisweet chocolate
Icing	
1½ cups	Confectioners' sugar
2 tsp	Instant coffee powder
1 tsp	Cocoa
2 tbsp	Hot water
	Vanilla

Preheat the oven to 325°.

Cream butter with sugar and a pinch of salt till light and fluffy. Add eggs one at a time and beat well. Grate orange and add rind to bowl. Squeeze orange and mix ¼ cup juice with the instant coffee. Sift flour and cinnamon and mix into the creamed mixture alternately with the orange/coffee mixture. Grate chocolate and fold in. Add more orange juice or water if necessary.

Spoon mixture into a greased 8½ inch ring mold. Bake for 40-50 minutes. Cool on a wire rack.

To make the icing, sift confectioners' sugar into bowl. Dissolve coffee and cocoa in hot water, then add to confectioners' sugar with a few drops of vanilla and mix well. Pour over cooled cake and smooth surface with a knife.

Cherry and lemon loaf

Overall timing 1 ½ hours

Freezing Suitable

To serve 16

2 cups	Self-rising flour
	Pinch of salt
½ cup	Butter
½ cup	Sugar
	Grated rind of
	1 lemon
1	Egg
¾ cup	Milk
⅔ cup	Glacé cherries

Preheat the oven to 350°.

Sift all but 1 tbsp of flour and the salt into a bowl. Rub in butter until mixture resembles fine bread crumbs. Stir in sugar and lemon rind. Make a well in center and break in egg. Mix together, adding enough milk to give a soft consistency that won't drop unless flicked from the spoon. Coat cherries into reserved flour and fold into mixture.

Pour into greased and lined 9 x 5 x 3 inch loaf pan and smooth surface. Bake for 45 minutes. Cover with parchment paper and bake for further 30 minutes. Cool on a wire rack.

Mocha cake

Overall timing 1 ¼ hours

Freezing Suitable

To serve 12

2 tsp	Instant coffee powder
4	Large eggs
½ cup	Sugar
1 cup	Flour
¼ cup	Butter
Filling and topping	
1 tbsp	Cornstarch
½ cup	Milk
3 tbsp	Sugar
1 tbsp	Instant coffee powder
1	Egg yolk
¾ cup	Butter
¾ cup	Confectioners' sugar

Chocolate shavings
Candy coffee beans

Preheat the oven to 375°.

Dissolve coffee in 1 tbsp water in large bowl over pan of hot water. Add eggs, sugar and pinch of salt and beat till very thick. Remove bowl from pan. Sift flour and fold in alternately with melted butter. Pour into greased and lined 8 inch round deep cake pan. Bake for 40 minutes. Cool on wire rack.

To make filling, place cornstarch in small saucepan and blend in milk. Add sugar and coffee and bring to a boil, stirring. Simmer for 2-3 minutes, stirring constantly. Remove from heat and cool slightly, then add egg yolk and beat well. Cook over gentle heat for 2 minutes, then remove from heat and leave to cool.

Beat butter with sifted confectioners' sugar. Add cooled custard and beat to a smooth creamy consistency.

Cut cake into two layers and put back back together with one-third of filling. Coat and decorate cake with remainder and top with chocolate shavings and candy coffee beans.

Banana and walnut layer cake

Overall timing 1 hour plus cooling

Freezing Not suitable

To serve 8-10

4	Large eggs
¾ cup	Sugar
2 tbsp	Warm water
1 cup	Flour
1 tsp	Baking powder
⅓ cup	Milk
¼ cup	Butter
1 cup	Heavy cream
5	Large bananas
	Chopped walnuts
	Walnut halves

Preheat the oven to 375°.

Separate eggs. Beat yolks with sugar and water till light and fluffy. Sift flour with baking powder and add to yolk mixture alternately with milk. Melt butter and add.

Beat egg whites till stiff and fold into mixture. Spoon into a greased and lined 8 inch round deep cake pan. Bake for 30-35 minutes. Cool on a wire rack.

Whip the cream till thick. Peel and slice the bananas.

Cut the cake into three layers. Put back together with most of the cream and banana slices and the chopped walnuts. Decorate the top with the rest of the cream and bananas and walnut halves. Serve immediately.

Chocolate log

Overall timing 40 minutes plus chilling

Freezing Not suitable

To serve 10-12

2	Eggs
3 tbsp	Sugar
¼ cup	Flour
¼ cup	Cornstarch
¼ cup	Chopped pistachio nuts or candied angelica
Filling and icing	
7 tbsp	Softened butter
1¾ cups	Confectioners' sugar
7 x 1 oz	Squares semisweet chocolate
2 tbsp	Rum or brandy (optional)

Preheat the oven to 400°.

Separate the eggs. Beat whites in a bowl with sugar till stiff peaks form. Beat yolks till pale, then fold into whites. Sift flour and cornstarch into mixture and fold in gently. Spread mixture evenly in greased and lined 13½ x 9½ inch jelly roll pan and bake for 10 minutes till lightly golden. Unmold cake onto dish-towel. Carefully peel off paper and roll up cake enclosing towel. Cool.

Cream butter with sugar. Melt chocolate and beat into creamed mixture with rum or brandy, if using.

Unroll cake and spread with half chocolate mixture. Roll up and place on a serving plate, seam underneath. Cover cake with remaining chocolate mixture. Make marks in chocolate icing with a fork so that it looks like bark. Sprinkle log with chopped pistachio nuts or angelica and chill before serving.

Christmas fruit cake

Overall timing Cake: 2-2½ hours.
Icing: 30 minutes plus 24 hours
standing

Freezing Not suitable

3½ cups	Mixed dried fruit
⅓ cup	Chopped candied peel
1 cup	Dark brown sugar
3 tbsp	Light corn syrup
½ cup	Butter
1½ cups	Self-rising flour
1½ cups	All-purpose flour
2 tsp	Baking soda
2 tsp	Apple pie spice
2	Large eggs
3 tbsp	Apricot jam
¾ lb	Marzipan
2	Egg whites
4 cups	Confectioners' sugar
2 tsp	Lemon juice
1 tsp	Glycerine

Put fruit in saucepan with peel, sugar, syrup, butter and 1 cup water. Bring to a boil, then simmer for 3 minutes. Turn into a bowl and cool.

Preheat the oven to 325°.

Sift flours, soda and spice three times, then add to fruit mixture. Beat in eggs. Place in greased and lined 8 inch round deep cake pan, making a slight depression in center. Bake for about 1½-2 hours or till skewer inserted in center comes out clean. Cool in pan.

To decorate cake, brush top and sides with warmed apricot jam. Roll out marzipan and use to cover top and sides. Smooth all seams.

Beat egg whites to a fairly stiff foam. Gradually beat in sifted confectioners' sugar and lemon juice. When icing forms little peaks when lifted up with a knife blade, mix in glycerine. Cover bowl and leave for 24 hours.

Beat icing gently. Spread over cake, flicking up into peaks with a knife blade. Add decorations. Leave to set for a week before cutting.

Frosted walnut cake

Overall timing 1 ¼ hours plus cooling

Freezing Suitable: fill and ice after thawing

To serve 10

¾ cup	Shortening
1 ½ cups	Sugar
½ tsp	Vanilla
2 cups	Flour
1 tbsp	Baking powder
1 cup	Milk
4	Egg whites
Frosting	
1 lb	Cube sugar
¼ tsp	Cream of tartar
2	Egg whites
½ tsp	Vanilla
½ cup	Chopped walnuts
10	Walnut halves

Preheat the oven to 350°.

Cream shortening with sugar and vanilla till fluffy. Sift flour, baking powder and a pinch of salt together and fold into creamed mixture alternately with milk. Beat egg whites till stiff and fold in. Divide between three greased and lined 8 inch layer cake pans. Bake for 30-35 minutes. Cool on a wire rack.

To make frosting, put sugar, cream of tartar and ¾ cup water in a saucepan and stir over a low heat till sugar dissolves. Stop stirring and bring to a boil. Boil to a temperature of 240°.

Meanwhile, beat egg whites till stiff. Pour syrup in a thin stream onto whites, beating constantly till frosting stands in soft peaks. Beat in vanilla. Fold chopped walnuts into one-quarter of frosting and use to put cakes together. Spread remaining frosting over cake and decorate with walnut halves.

Pistachio cake

Overall timing 1 hour plus chilling

Freezing Not suitable

To serve 10

3 cups	Flour
	Pinch of salt
1 cup	Butter
10 tbsp	Sugar
2	Egg yolks
Filling	
1 cup	Shelled pistachios
4	Egg whites
1 cup	Sugar
1 cup	Ground almonds
	Grated rind of
	½ lemon
1 tbsp	Rum
2 x 1oz	Squares sweet
	chocolate

Sift the flour and salt into a bowl and rub in the fat till the mixture resembles fine bread crumbs. Stir in the sugar and egg yolks and mix to a soft dough. Chill for 30 minutes.

Preheat the oven to 400°.

Divide the dough in half. Roll out and use to line two 9 inch layer cake pans. Prick bottoms and bake blind for 15 minutes. Cool on a wire rack.

Reserve a few pistachios for decoration; finely chop the rest. Beat the egg whites till soft peaks form. Gradually beat in the sugar till the mixture is stiff and glossy. Fold the chopped nuts into the meringue with the ground almonds, grated lemon rind and rum. Spoon into the pastry cases. Place one pastry case on a baking sheet and invert the other on top. Return to the oven and bake for a further 15 minutes. Cool on a wire rack.

Melt the chocolate in the top of a double boiler over hot water. Spread over the top of the cake with a palette knife. Cut the reserved pistachios in half and arrange in a circle around the edge of the cake.

Sachertorte

Overall timing 1 ½ hours plus cooling

Freezing Not suitable

To serve 8

4 x 1oz	Squares semisweet chocolate
½ cup	Unsalted butter
¾ cup	Sugar
5	Eggs
¾ cup	Ground almonds
¼ cup	Self-rising flour
1 cup	Heavy or whipping cream
	Hazelnuts
Icing	
8 x 1oz	Squares semisweet chocolate
4oz	Butter

Preheat the oven to 400°.

Melt chocolate with butter till smooth. Beat in the sugar. Separate eggs and gradually add yolks to chocolate mixture, beating well. Beat egg whites till stiff. Gently fold whites into chocolate mixture, followed by ground almonds and flour. Divide mixture between two greased 8 inch layer cake pans and smooth top. Bake for 20-25 minutes. Cool on a wire rack.

Whip half cream till thick and use to sandwich together the cooled cakes.

To make icing, melt chocolate with butter in the top of a double boiler over hot water. Leave to cool for 20-30 minutes until of a coating consistency, then spread over top and sides of cake. Whip remaining cream and pipe large swirls around the edge of the cake. Decorate each swirl with a hazelnut.

Special honey sponge

Overall timing 35 minutes plus cooling

Freezing Suitable: fill and decorate after thawing

To serve 8

1¾ cups	Self-rising flour
¼ cup	Cornstarch
½ tsp	Baking powder
¾ cup	Confectioners' sugar
½ cup	Butter
½ cup	Sugar
1 tbsp	Clear honey
2	Large eggs
⅔ cup	Milk
¾ cup	Chopped nuts
Filling and decoration	
¼ cup	Butter
1 cup	Confectioners' sugar
1 tbsp	Clear honey
1 tbsp	Warm water
½ cup	Chopped almonds and walnuts
½ cup	Heavy cream

Preheat the oven to 350°.

Sift flour, cornstarch, baking powder and confectioners' sugar together. Cream butter with sugar and honey. Beat in eggs, then fold in flour mixture alternately with milk. Stir in chopped nuts. Divide between two greased 7 inch layer cake pans. Bake for 20 minutes. Cool on wire rack.

To make the filling, cream butter with confectioners' sugar, honey and water. Spread on one cake, sprinkle with most of the chopped nuts, then place second cake on top. Whip cream until stiff. Spoon into pastry bag fitted with large star tube and pipe decorative swirls around top of cake. Decorate with rest of nuts.

Queen of Sheba cake

Overall timing 2 hours plus cooling

Freezing Suitable

To serve 8

9 x 1oz	Squares semisweet chocolate
6	Eggs
1 cup	Butter
⅔ cup	Honey
1¼ cups	Flour
1 tbsp	Oil
1 cup	Hazelnuts
1 cup	Split almonds
1 tbsp	Chocolate hundreds-and-thousands
3 tbsp	Confectioners' sugar

Preheat the oven to 350°.

Gently melt 8 squares of the chocolate. Separate the eggs. Cream the butter with the honey, then beat in the chocolate and egg yolks. Add sifted flour, oil and chopped nuts and beat well. Beat the egg whites till stiff and fold into the mixture.

Turn into a greased and lined 9 inch round deep cake pan. Bake for 1½ hours.

Meanwhile, make curls from remaining chocolate; melt chocolate in saucepan and pour onto oiled marble slab or hard, cold surface. When chocolate has almost set but is not hard, scrape off thin slivers or curls with a knife. Chill.

Cool cake on a wire rack.

Sprinkle chocolate hundreds-and-thousands over cake, then sift confectioners' sugar around edge. Arrange the chocolate curls in the center.

Duchesses

Overall timing 2 hours

Freezing Not suitable

Makes 12

2	Egg whites
½ cup	Sugar
½ cup	Ground hazelnuts
¼ cup	Toasted hazelnuts
2 x 1oz	Squares semisweet chocolate

Preheat the oven to 250°.

Beat the egg whites with half the sugar till stiff. Carefully fold in the ground nuts, then the remaining sugar. Spoon the mixture into a pastry bag fitted with a plain wide tube. Pipe 1 inch wide fingers about 3 inches long onto a baking sheet lined with rice paper. Sprinkle with chopped toasted hazelnuts and bake for 1½ hours.

Cut paper around fingers with a sharp knife, then remove from baking sheet.

Melt the chocolate. Spread rice-papered sides of half the fingers with chocolate and join to remaining fingers. Leave to set.

Honey galettes

Overall timing 40 minutes plus chilling

Freezing Suitable: refresh in 375° oven for 5 minutes

Makes 8

1½ cups	Self-rising flour
½ cup	Butter
3 tbsp	Thick honey
1 tbsp	Sugar
1	Lemon
1	Egg
	Sugar for sprinkling

Preheat the oven to 375°.

Sift the flour into a mixing bowl. Make a well in the center and add the softened butter, honey and sugar. Grate the rind from the lemon and add to the bowl with 1 tbsp of the juice. Separate the egg and add the yolk to the bowl. Mix well together with a wooden spoon until the mixture forms a ball and leaves the sides of the bowl clean. Add a little water if necessary. Chill for 30 minutes.

Divide mixture into eight and roll out each piece on a lightly floured surface to a round about ½ inch thick. Place on baking sheets.

Beat egg white lightly and brush over cookies. Sprinkle each cookie with 1-2 tsp sugar. Bake for about 15 minutes, then remove from sheets and cool on wire rack.

Lemon refrigerator cookies

Overall timing 20 minutes plus
overnight chilling

Freezing Suitable: bake after thawing

Makes 48

2 cups	Flour
1 tsp	Baking powder
½ cup	Butter
6 tbsp	Sugar
	Grated rind of
	2 lemons
½ tsp	Ground cinnamon
1	Egg

Sift flour and baking powder into a bowl. Rub in butter till mixture resembles fine bread crumbs. Add sugar, lemon rind and cinnamon, then beat the egg and mix well into the dough.

Shape the mixture into one or two sausage shapes about 1½ inches in diameter. Wrap in foil, twisting the ends to seal. Chill overnight.

Preheat the oven to 375°.

Remove dough from foil wrapper and thinly slice. Place slices on greased baking sheets. Bake for 10-12 minutes, till golden. Cool on wire rack.

Shortbread fingers

Overall timing 1 ½ hours plus cooling

Freezing Not suitable

Makes 6

1 ½ cups	Butter
½ cup	Sugar
2 cups	All-purpose flour
2 cups	Self-rising flour
¼ tsp	Salt

Preheat the oven to 275°.

Cream the butter with the sugar till pale and fluffy. Sift the two flours and salt together and work into the creamed mixture to make a dough. Add a little water if necessary.

Turn dough onto a floured surface and press out to a thick rectangle. Make decorative notches down the long sides by pinching with the fingers. Place on a baking sheet and prick all over with a fork. Mark lines for the fingers.

Bake for 1 hour. Cool, then break into fingers on the marked lines. Dredge with extra sugar.

Scones

Overall timing 20 minutes

Freezing Not suitable

Makes 8

2 cups	Flour
1 tbsp	Baking powder
	Pinch of salt
¼ cup	Butter
2 tbsp	Sugar
¾ cup	Milk
	Milk or egg for
	glazing

Preheat the oven to 450°.

Sift flour, baking powder and salt into a mixing bowl. Rub in butter. Add sugar and milk and mix to a soft dough. Add more milk if necessary.

Roll out quickly to ½ inch thickness on a lightly floured board. Lightly flour a round cutter and cut out scones. Place on lightly floured baking sheet and glaze tops with milk or lightly beaten egg. Bake for 10 minutes. Wrap in dish-towel till ready to serve.

Variation

Peel, core and grate 1 apple and scatter over rolled-out dough. Fold in half and press firmly together. Cut and bake as above.

Madeleines with cinnamon

Overall timing 50 minutes plus chilling

Freezing Suitable: bake after thawing

Makes 16

1½ cups	Flour
6 tbsp	Butter
1 tbsp	Sugar
1	Egg yolk
Filling	
½ cup	Butter
½ cup	Sugar
2	Eggs
½ cup	Ground almonds
¼ tsp	Almond extract
1 cup	Self-rising flour
1 tsp	Ground cinnamon
	Milk to mix
	Apricot jam
1 tbsp	Confectioners' sugar

Sift flour into a bowl and rub in butter. Stir in sugar, egg yolk and enough water to bind to a soft dough. Roll out to ¼ inch thickness and use to line two madeleine sheets. Trim the edges and chill for 30 minutes.

Preheat the oven to 375°.

To make filling, cream butter with all but 1 tbsp sugar. Gradually beat in eggs, then mix in almonds and almond extract. Sift in flour and cinnamon and fold in with enough milk to give a soft dropping consistency.

Put ½ tsp jam into each pastry case, then spoon filling into each case. Bake for 15-20 minutes till the filling is golden and springs back when lightly pressed. Cool on a wire rack.

Mix confectioners' sugar and remaining sugar together and sift over tartlets before serving.

Almond crescents

Overall timing 30 minutes plus cooling

Freezing Suitable; bake from frozen,
allowing 20-25 minutes

Makes 20

1½ cups	Ground almonds
¼ cup	Sugar
	A few drops of
	vanilla
1	Egg white
¼ cup	Flour
1	Egg
¼ cup	Flaked almonds
2 tbsp	Milk sweetened with
	confectioners' sugar

Preheat the oven to 400°.

Mix ground almonds with sugar and
vanilla. Moisten with egg white until evenly
combined. Add flour and gather mixture
together with fingertips. Divide into "nut-sized"
pieces. With lightly floured hands, roll into
small cigar shapes with pointed ends. Brush
each one with beaten egg and sprinkle with
flaked almonds. Bend into a crescent shape.

Place on a greased baking sheet and brush
lightly with any remaining egg. Bake for about
10-15 minutes till evenly colored. Remove
from oven and brush immediately with
sweetened milk. Using a palette knife or
spatula, carefully loosen crescents and
transfer to wire rack to cool.

Macaroons

Overall timing 2½ hours

Freezing Not suitable

Makes 55

4	Egg whites
1½ cups	Sugar
2¾ cups	Ground almonds
	Grated rind of 1
	orange
	Grated rind of 1
	lemon
	Pinch of salt
1 tsp	Ground cinnamon
½ tsp	Ground cardamom

Preheat the oven to 275°.

Beat the egg whites till stiff. Gradually beat in the sugar, a spoonful at a time. Fold in the almonds, orange and lemon rind, salt and spices.

Place heaped teaspoonfuls of mixture on baking sheets lined with rice paper. Put on the middle and lower shelves of the oven and leave to dry for 1½-2 hours. Halfway through, swap sheets around.

Cool on baking sheets. Break paper from around each macaroon.

Orange liqueur cookies

Overall timing 45 minutes plus chilling

Freezing Suitable; cut out and bake after thawing

Makes 36

2	Hard-cooked egg yolks
2 cups	Flour
½ cup	Sugar
	Salt
	Ground cinnamon
½ cup	Butter
2 tbsp	Orange liqueur

Push egg yolks through a sieve into a mixing bowl. Sift in the flour and mix well. Make a well in the center and add sugar and a pinch each of salt and cinnamon.

Cut the butter into pieces and work into the mixture, a little at a time. Work in the liqueur and roll paste into a ball. (Add a little more liqueur or water if necessary.) Lightly dust with flour and leave in a cool place, not the refrigerator, for a least 1 hour.

Preheat the oven to 375°.

Roll out the paste thinly and stamp out shapes with fancy cookie cutters. Place cookies on a greased and lined baking sheet and bake for 10-15 minutes, till light golden. Remove cookies carefully from paper and cool on a wire rack.

Brownies

Overall timing 45 minutes plus cooling

Freezing Suitable

Makes 30

4 x 1oz	Squares semisweet chocolate
½ cup	Unsalted butter
1 tsp	Vanilla
4	Eggs
½ tsp	Salt
1¾ cups	Sugar
1 cup	Flour
1 cup	Chopped walnuts

Preheat the oven to 350°.

Put chocolate into the top of a double boiler with the butter and vanilla and place over simmering water. Stir till melted, then remove bowl from heat and cool.

Beat eggs and salt till pale and fluffy. Sprinkle the sugar on top and continue beating till evenly mixed. Fold in the chocolate mixture with a metal spoon, then fold in the sifted flour and coarsely chopped nuts.

Pour into a greased and lined 9 x 13 inch pan and smooth the top. Bake for about 25 minutes till firm. Cool in the pan, then cut into squares.

Iced marzipan cookies

Overall timing 1½ hours plus cooling

Freezing Not suitable

Makes 30

3½ cups	Flour
1 cup	Sugar
	Pinch of salt
1	Large egg
1 cup	Butter
Filling and icing	
½lb	Marzipan
1¼ cups	Confectioners' sugar
1 tbsp	Rum
	Lemon or almond
	extract
⅓ cup	Apricot jam
2 tbsp	Water

Sift flour, sugar and salt into a bowl. Add egg and butter, cut into small pieces. Quickly knead together to form a smooth dough. Add a little water if necessary. Chill for 30 minutes.

Preheat the oven to 350°.

Roll out dough to ¼ inch thickness. Cut out small shapes with a cookie cutter and place on a greased baking sheet. Bake for 15 minutes.

Meanwhile, knead marzipan, ½ cup confectioners' sugar, rum and a few drops of extract together. Roll out to ⅛ inch thickness on a board dusted with confectioners' sugar. Cut out shapes using the same cutter as for the pastry.

Remove pastry shapes from oven and immediately spread thickly with jam. Sandwich a piece of marzipan between two hot cookies. Work quickly — the hot cookies and jam need to adhere to the marzipan. Lift off baking sheets and place on wire rack.

To make icing, mix together remaining confectioners' sugar, a little almond extract and water and use to coat the warm cookies. Leave to dry and cool.

Index